Ghost of an Idea

Hauntology, Folk Horror and the Spectre of Nostalgia

William Burns

HEADPRESS

A HEADPRESS BOOK
First published by Headpress in 2024, Oxford, UK
headoffice@headpress.com

GHOST OF AN IDEA
Hauntology, Folk Horror, and the Spectre of Nostalgia

Book layout: G. FOLEY
Cover design: MARK CRITCHELL mark.critchell@gmail.com
With thanks to Gareth Wilson and Jennifer Wallis

10 9 8 7 6 5 4 3 2 1

A CIP catalogue record for this book is available from the British Library

ISBN 978-1-915316-31-8 paperback
ISBN 978-1-915316-32-5 ebook
ISBN NO-ISBN hardback

Exclusive NO-ISBN special editions and other items of interest are available at
HEADPRESS.COM

HEADPRESS. We publish the books you love.

For Mark Fisher

'Oh whistle, and I'll come to you, my lad'

Contents

"Alas, for poor human nature! How we are cursed in the realization of our own wishes! How we struggle and sin to attain what we are never to enjoy!"

—Catherine Crowe, *Ghosts and Family Legends*

Introduction

The Seductive Liar, or Are We What We Used to Be?

ALBERT CAMUS' MEMOIR 'Return to Tipasa' is probably best known for providing the quote 'A man's work is nothing but this slow trek to discover through the detours of art, those TWO or three great and simple images in whose presence his heart first opened'. Immortalized on the back cover of Scott Engels' (née Walker née Engels) art-pop classic *Scott 4*, it is probably more commonly encountered here than in Camus' original essay. In 'Return to Tipasa', Camus describes two visits he made to Tipasa, the capital of the Tipasa Province in Algeria, where he spent much of his youth. Since he was last there, Camus had suffered through the horrors of WWII, joining the French resistance in Paris. Camus left Tipasa as an intellectually brilliant but emotionally naïve young man and came back an older, jaded cynic, traumatized by unprecedented brutality and inhumanity expressed on a massive scale. Camus returns to the scenes of his childhood happiness, searching for a pre-absurd existence, a time before his philosophical perspective was justified through his wartime experiences. The first return to Tipasa is a disappointment to Camus; much of the town is in ruins and he can't seem to connect to places in the same ways he did as a child. Nothing lasts forever, not even forever. But with his second journey to the locale, he realizes that not only has the geography changed but he has also; he realizes that it's not so much Tipasa that he longs for, rather it is the past feelings, emotions, and states of being that he is looking to recapture. The 'invincible summer' of his youth in Tipasa may only exist as a memory, but it's still alive within him, an inner cartography that can be returned to at any time and in any place where Camus may find himself (truly an example of psychogeography). He doesn't need to go back to the actuality of Tipasa because his Tipasa has always been his own creation. This understanding of reminiscence, the power of longing for past joy, affection, and comfort, provides Camus with the foundation from which to rebuild his confidence and restore his hope for the postwar world. Through the internal reality of nostalgia, Camus has come home again: 'I found exactly what I had come seeking.'[1]

While nostalgia recharges Camus' seriously drained existential batteries, other thinkers are not as enthusiastic. In the introduction to his book *Brain Droppings*, comedian and misanthropic prophet George Carlin skewered the concept that nostalgic thinking could ever lead to liberatory creativity:

> Listening to comedians who comment on political, social, and cultural issues I notice most of their material reflects an undying belief that somehow things were better once and that with just a little effort we could set them right again. They're looking for solutions and rooting for particular results, and I think that necessarily limits the tone and substance of what they say. They're talented and funny people, but they're nothing more than cheerleaders attached to a specific, wished for outcome. I don't feel so confined.[2] [And he wasn't]

To Frankfurt School critics Max Horkheimer and Theodor Adorno, nostalgia was even worse than one of the seven words you can never say on TV. The authors of *Dialectic of Enlightenment* expressed a fear

1 Albert Camus, *The Myth of Sisyphus and Other Essays* (New York: Vintage, 1991).
2 George Carlin, *Brain Droppings* (New York: Hyperion, 1998).

norance particularly, as a lack of awareness and failure to confront these serious societal problems will continue the cycle of suffering that is embodied in Tiny Tim and the bleak future the innocent child must face without assistance from men like Scrooge who exploit their fellow humans rather than helping them. The potential for Tiny Tim's ghost to haunt not only Scrooge but the reader as well is a powerful indictment of a society that creates the ghosts that haunt it.

Scrooge's final spectral confrontation is with The Ghost of Christmas Yet to Come. As this ghost represents the unknown future, Scrooge comments that he fears this manifestation more than the others. This ghost's appearance is the most wraith-like and inhuman, with none of the compassion or connection that the previous ghosts offer to Scrooge. The future brings both trepidation and fascination, expectation and retribution, as Scrooge is faced with his own mortality and reminded of Marley's ghostly spiritual punishment, fated to return over and over again without the ability to intercede and change the future. Scrooge's death is juxtaposed with Tiny Tim's, as no one mourns Scrooge, but there is a tremendous outpouring of grief and emotion for Tim. Indeed, Scrooge's demise only feeds into the cycle of economic exploitation of predatory capitalism he benefited from as the only people who show any emotion over Scrooge's end are the charwoman, laundress, and undertaker who steal some of his possessions and sell them to a trafficker in stolen goods. Scrooge's human worth has been reduced to commodities that are mercilessly haggled over and deceptively exchanged, just as he practised business and monetized the lives of those in debt to him. Scrooge's misplaced faith in finance rather than humanity, and his pitiless greed, come back to haunt him as this future offers no hope for redemption. This view into his icy impending destiny ends appropriately at Scrooge's neglected grave as not only is his body interred but also the lost opportunities that Scrooge wasted throughout his life.

Scrooge's hauntings end with the miser begging for a second chance and claiming that these spectral visions of past, present, and future have transformed him, and he will embrace the hope, kindness, and selflessness that the Christmas holiday is supposed to reflect. Scrooge wakes up a changed man and follows through on the vows he made to the ghosts to become the embodiment of the Christmas season all year round, thereby creating a 'lost future', escaping the fate in which he dies alone, miserable, and forgotten. The traumas he suffered as a youth and the traumas he inflicted on his fellow human beings have been exorcized through ghostly intervention with the opportunity to regain a future that is not devastatingly bleak, but rather, a chance to change others' futures for the better through the actions that Scrooge does in the present. The future can be altered just as the self can be. It's never too late.

By confronting the ghosts of past, present, and future, Dickens suggests that our lives are not preordained; the individual human being can make a difference on personal and societal levels by heeding the ghosts of one's one past, present, and future. 'A Christmas Carol' emerged from Dickens' own deep personal and social outrage over the inhumanity of systems, institutions, and ideologies that ignore the crucial experiences of benevolence, empathy, and understanding in exchange for power, avarice, and cruelty. Dickens's own past saw his family broken by heartless economic policies, and these practices still had not dealt with the economic and social ghosts created during Dickens' lifetime. If anything, this laissez faire capitalism had created even more ghosts that haunted Victorian England and continue to haunt the western world today. 'A Christmas Carol' is a hauntological warning of lost opportunities and yet retains faith in individual agency, the quest for personal resistance and justice in the face of oppressive social and economic systems of authority, the human capacity to rise above the traumas that create the very ghosts that caution and advise us.

While Dickens had hope that the repetitious cycle of exploitation and suffering could be broken through the intervention and acceptance of ghosts, another proto-hauntological author did not share his optimism. H P Lovecraft's work embodies many of the themes that

Derrida would later categorize as hauntological. Lovecraft even fashioned himself as a hauntological figure, not belonging to his own contemporary times, but, rather, a Classical refugee from America's colonial and Georgian past, born too late for togas and powdered wigs, but also too soon for the scientific innovations he expected from the future. Lovecraft's works have a trepidation and fascination with time, endless cycles of repetition, disjointed experiences of how time upsets human beings' notions of who we are, what we are, and why we are.

Lovecraft's spectres are not the traditional ghosts found in folklore and fiction; his ghosts are biological imperatives that we can't escape, destinies that grind us down to nothing, beings from other worlds and other species that we can't understand, forms of cosmic indifference that disturb us until madness seems like the only sane option. These ghosts emerge from endless gulfs of time and space, way before and after human beings can even begin to comprehend how haunted we really are. Lovecraft's ghosts are existential in both personal and temporal manifestations, so far beyond the realm of human agency and understanding that past, present, and future are merely illusions, delusions we use to keep a fragile hold on our own teetering significance. The warnings that Lovecraft's ghosts have for humanity are in the end futile because there is no way for us to intervene: the traumas that caused the hauntings go so far back and so far beyond our notions of time that we are better off ignoring them rather than admitting our own insignificance. For Lovecraft, human beings don't just experience the hauntological notion of lost futures, but also forgotten pasts and indifferent todays too.

Perhaps Lovecraft's most hauntological story is 1936's 'The Shadow Out of Time.' Although Lovecraft had a few literary inspirations for 'The Shadow Out of Time', the key inspiration was Frank Lloyd's film *Berkeley Square* (1931), a proto hauntological movie about a contemporary man so obsessed with an eighteenth-century ancestor (and discovering that "Real time is all one in the mind of God") simply walks through a door to live as his predecessor in Georgian

England. Lovecraft would explore this same spectral, recurring nature of time, history, and reality, and the inherent traps that come with trying to establish an objective, materialistic grounding in any of these subjective experiences, in other works such as his novels *At the Mountains of Madness* (1931) and *The Case of Charles Dexter Ward* (1927), which went unpublished in his lifetime.

The narrative of 'The Shadow Out of Time' focuses on Nathaniel Wingate Peaslee, a Miskatonic University economics professor living in the first decade of the twentieth century. During a class lecture, Peaslee's personality mysteriously changes. He acts completely differently than his usual self, abandoning his wife and children to engage in travel and research for five years. His wife divorces him and all but one of his children reject him. Then, as mysteriously as it came upon him, Peaslee's original personality reasserts itself. Peaslee is shocked to find out what has happened to him and tries to figure out why he suffered from this five year 'amnesia'. Following the re-establishment of his old self, Peaslee is haunted by strange dreams of other worlds and beings that seem more like memories than nightmares. Initially believing he suffers from mental illness, Peaslee's investigations uncover similar cases and experiences to his own over large spans of history, so close that they can't just be coincidence, but are somehow connected. Peaslee's increasingly vivid dreams cause him to become obsessed with ancient history and he delves deeper and deeper into the past in order to find the source for his present amnesia and personality transformation.

This quest to find the reason for his change and his dreams/memories leads him to excavate a prehistoric structure in Australia, a city that he remembers living in millions of years ago. Peaslee discovers that his personality shift was the result of exchanging bodies with a member of the Great Race of Yith, an alien species that is able to manipulate time and space. During the five years of Peaslee's transformation, a Yithian was controlling his body, gathering information about the twentieth century for their vast library. While the Yithian was in possession of Peaslee's body, Peaslee was trapped in the Yithian's body, experiencing life as a Yithian in the Yithian city in Australia millennia ago.

Peaslee's amnesiac fugue was actually an alternate life, a ghost-like existence that not only disrupted and destroyed his personal relationships, but also his notions of linear time and space. The Yithians 'possess' humans from the past and the future in order to gather information for their immense library, effectively making a mockery of not only the sanctity of one's consciousness through the forceful exchange of minds with the unknowing victim, but also the connections humans have with their era and surroundings, displacing the centrality of humanity from temporal and spatial understanding. Unmoored from absolute notions of time and space, the transported human subjects drift both back and forward in space, ghost-like in their in-between states. The frame of reference for experiencing time and space has been upset, the idea that time flows one way and space obeys the laws of science are forever destroyed for Peaslee. Peaslee is not only haunted by his upsetting dreams and memories that he cannot escape, but, in effect, he has become a living ghost: he has lost all his connections to the present by having 'lived' millions of years ago. His time in the past and his presence in the present have caused time to go out of joint for him. Nostalgia has become a state of paranoia and horror for Peaslee. He has attained the hauntological both/and 'in-between' status through his displaced consciousness that has violated the known rules of time and space. Peaslee's traumas are personal (losing his family), nostalgic (losing his ability to escape into his own past), scientific (time/space desecration), and metaphysical (the manipulation of his consciousness).

The Great Race have erased themselves from linear time, as the Yithians, on the brink of being wiped out by another alien race in the prehistoric Earth time period, mass project their minds into the future to inhabit the bodies of the species that will replace human beings as the dominant lifeform on this planet. On a personal level,

Peaslee can no longer see himself as being whole; his attempts to exorcize the ghostly memories and dreams that haunt him have actually confirmed his status as a man haunted by time itself. On a larger, existential scale, Peaslee is haunted by the realization that humanity's understanding of time and space, the very beliefs and perceptions that have given human beings a notion of their primacy and importance in the universe, are ghostly illusions; not only are we not the masters of our own minds, bodies, and fates, but humanity is also totally at the whim of a superior civilization that can easily manipulate and disrupt everything we have taken as absolute and foundational.

The ghost of 'The Shadow Out of Time' effectively haunts himself by coming to this realization; Peaslee's very existence confirms the traumatic transgressions that the Great Race has wrought on a helpless victim. The abyss of deep time is scarier than deep space; humanity's trauma of temporal haunting goes beyond the material and the physical as deep time extends both back and forward endlessly, with the only sanctuary being the present placid island of ignorance that the majority of us live in and cling to. Peaslee is a human out of time who has lost the luxury of blissful ignorance: past, present, and future are all devasting mockeries to him. Peaslee experiences what Schopenhauer called the 'ghost of our own nothingness', the terrifying existential and metaphysical consequences of coming face to face with spatial and temporal magnitude:

> If we lose ourselves in contemplation of the infinite greatness of the universe in space and time, meditate on the past millennia and on those to come; or if the heavens at night actually bring innumerable worlds before our eyes, and so impress on our consciousness the immensity of the universe, we feel ourselves reduced to nothing: we feel ourselves as individuals, as living bodies, as transient phenomena of will, like drops in the ocean, dwindling and dissolving into nothing.[10]

10 Arthur Schopenhauer, *The Essential Schopenhauer: Key Selections from The World As Will and Representation and Other Writings* (New York: Harper, 2010).

'The Shadow Out of Time' suggests that our own flawed beliefs in humanity's ultimate meaning, value, and centrality amongst the titanic sweep of space and the deep gulfs of time are false, sardonic spectres whose hauntings are actually necessary to propagate comfortable notions of humanity's past, present, and future. The theories of Darwin and Einstein (two thinkers who had profound influences on Lovecraft) helped create the idea of deep time for both Earth and the cosmos, the almost inconceivable billions of years that went into the creation of our planet, the beginnings of life, natural selection, and transmutation, as well as the destabilizing effects of space/time distortions that suggest the universe does not abide by mechanistic, objective, clearly understandable rules. The theory of evolution and the theory of relativity are the real shadows out of time: contemptuous jeers at the notions of intelligent design and human beings' ability to grasp and come to terms with all the chronological implications of a chaotic universe, infinite spans of time and space which can only appear as fleeting ghosts, millions of years already dead and millions of years to come, to insignificant humanity.

Although his 1973 novel *Red Shift* lacks Lovecraft's galactic sprawl, Alan Garner also utilizes the notion of a consciousness that reaches across time to suggest that we are haunted by emotions and relationships that can repeat through obsession and trauma, infused through our identities as well as our environments. *Red Shift* focuses on the same geographical area (Cheshire, England) across three different historical periods: the Roman occupation of Britain, the English Civil War, and the early 1970s. *Red Shift* traces recurring notions of despair, passion, anger, pain, and hope and how these emotions can transcend time and space; reoccurring traumas that remain unhealed and disturbing, refusing to be easily exorcized.

The novel explores three interrelated love stories, narratives that trace the effects of jealousy, alienation, violence, and the lack of communication on three couples. The novel opens with the story of Macy, a Roman soldier whose battalion pillage the village of

Mow Cop, massacring all the inhabitants except for a girl who they keep as a slave. The girl exacts a fearsome revenge for the slaughter of her community and her own violation by poisoning the soldiers' food, sparing Macy because he was the only soldier that did not participate in her gang rape. Stunned by the brutality of his comrades and their murderous comeuppance, Mason deserts his regiment, joining the girl to try to heal their wounds and encounter the world together. As an act of contrition for his participation in the destruction of Mow Cop, Macy places his stone axe in a burial mound, seeking forgiveness from the land he has helped to soil with the blood of the innocent, turning from violence to compassion as he begins an uncertain future with the girl in the nearby village of Barthomley.

The novel then jumps to the English Civil War, as Macy's consciousness echoes in the mind of Thomas Rowly, an epileptic who resides with his wife Margery in Barthomley. Thomas has seizures, which produce hallucinations that may be visions of his past self (Macy) and his future self (Tom). Thomas and Margery are rummaging through the surrounding hills when they discover Macy's long buried stone axe. The couple take the axe to use as a stone in their chimney. Their plans are interrupted with the arrival of Royalist troops who are ruthlessly searching for "traitors" accused of betraying the King and siding with Cromwell's Roundheads. When the Royalists suggest that the entire town is a Roundhead stronghold and deserves to be liquidated for their complicity with the rebels, Thomas and Margery flee the escalating tensions and journey to Mow Cop, using Macy's stone axe as the corner stone in the chimney of their new home, facing an uncertain future together.

In the final section of the novel, we are introduced to Tom, a teenager living in the early 1970s. Tom is in a relationship with Jan, who is preparing to leave their small town to study nursing in London. Exploring the ruins of Mow Cop, they unearth Macy's stone axe in the crumbling remnants of a chimney. As they physically and emotionally prepare for the inevitable separation, Tom discovers that Jan has not been faithful to him, having an affair even though they had both pledged to be abstinent in a symbol of their pure love. This news devastates Tom as his notions of self and trust are shattered, leading to increasingly unstable and self-destructive behaviors. Tom sells the axe to a local museum, symbolically letting go of his connection to Jan. The novel ends with Jan departing for London as Tom is left to deal with bitter disappointment, estrangement from his parents, detachment from his environment, and self-alienation as he faces an uncertain future. One wonders if the future of which Tom has been robbed has also affected his ability to feel nostalgia because of this devastating event at such a pivotal point in his maturation.

Red Shift's major theme is how trauma haunts not only human beings, but time and space themselves. Garner suggests that it is the repetition of personal trauma, not political, social, cultural ideas, or even historical figures, institutions, or events, that leave lasting impressions; it is unresolved pain and traumas that are the spectres that haunt places, eras, and people (Garner called these lingering subconscious ordeals 'engrams' that affect our 'inner time'[11]). This notion is personified in the characters of Macy, Thomas Rowley, and Tom: three different men living in three different historical periods haunted by the same ghosts, who through their suffering reach out to each other across space and time, experiencing the same visions and memories, feeling the same time slippages and disjunctions, sharing the same tortured soul as rage, despair, passion, longing, and loss are repeated over and over again through their collective pasts, presents, and futures. Emotional, historical, and geographical ghosts haunt these men as they all attempt to deal with and heal from a variety of traumas that cannot be easily faced or exorcized. All these men are searching for a place and identity of their own, some stability and hope in a world that offers very little no matter what time period they live in. Psychologically and existentially, they (Tom in particular) are looking for the 'red shift', a

11 Andrew Tate, 'Mind Out of Time: Interview with Alan Garner', *High Profiles* (August 10, 2021), https://highprofiles.info/interview/alan-garner/ [Last accessed June 13, 2024]

cosmological movement that signals change, escape, and freedom, and yet their traumas keep them grounded physically in the landscape and emotionally in cycles of endless repetition. *Red Shift* suggests these painful spectres that haunt the three protagonists are actually a self-haunting phenomenon and may be necessary to mature and be able to deal with the shocks and uncertainties of the future.

Geography, landscape, and place have increasingly become an important part of hauntology. In particular, the Situationist International's notion of 'psychogeography', or the psychological, subjective experiences of space and place being just as, if not more, important, as the scientific, academic study of geography and cartography, has become central to understanding how ghosts and hauntings are materialized, encountered, and felt by those who are affected. These ghostly 'dérives' (unplanned drifting through settings or, as Guy Debord defined it, 'a mode of experimental behaviour linked to the conditions of urban society: a technique of rapid passage through varied ambiances'[12]) have their antecedents in Walter Benjamin's *Arcades* project (1927–1940), vagabond philosopher Stephen Graham's 'zig-zag walking', and the Dadaist/Surrealists' 'déambulations' in which Paris was experimentally mapped through a rhetoric of walking, guided by chance, feeling, and nostalgia. André Breton once remarked 'No *walk*, as far as I am concerned, is ever wasted.'[13] This aimless strolling, walking against the imposed structures and strictures of urban movement, encourages new perspectives for the walker as the secret meanings embedded in the city reveal themselves. These 'déambulations' are also political statements against oppressive commercial zoning and urban planning, rebelling against the 'proper' and 'expected' ways people are forced to experience space, habitat, and geography as part of economic and social indoctrination through material conditions. Moving, dwelling, alternative mapping, and alternate

12 Guy Debord, *Theory of the Dérive and Other Situationist Writings on the City* (Barcelona: Museu d'Art Contemporani de Barcelona, 1996).
13 Andre Breton, *The Lost Steps* (Lincoln: University of Nebraska, 2010).

place histories can be acts of resistance, 'haunting' modern and postmodern progress that seeks to control and erase in the name of the new, the profitable, the homogeneous.

Psychogeography is both a personal and collective bonding with our settings that goes beyond the dominant material, topographical, and social discourses that prescribe what geography is and how we are expected to interact with it. Psychogeography can be an act of resistance that rejects authoritarian geographical concepts and practices that restrict on the basis of politics, class, and culture, offering more liberating, accumulated, and multiple experiences with our surroundings. These emotions, moods, traumas, events, and usages can 'haunt' a place, its environmental features, its dwellings, and its people for a long time, manifesting in natural and human-made 'ghosts'. Psychogeography is particularly interested in the urban: how cities and their layering upon layering of innumerable people, structures, stories, events, and emotions can create a fertile environment for hauntological experiences. These explorations have also been dubbed the 'urban wyrd': a relationship between the vast, densely populated artificial environments of a metropolis and the feelings of isolation, fear, and uncertainty of its inhabitants, both living and spectral: 'I have spoken of systems of thoroughfare, and I assure you that walking alone through these silent places I felt fantasy growing on me, and some glamour of the infinite.'[14] The city's 'protoplasmic streets', as Arthur Machen saw them, incubate dark atmospheres that are conjured by the crumbling, abandoned, and hidden aspects of municipal architecture and civic planning as well as in the urban legends and lore that uncover smoke ghosts, wolfen, and city hobgoblins that lurk in subway stations, underpasses, roofs, alleys, and high rises.

UK hauntologists seem to have nostalgia for the Brutalist architecture of postwar Britain: the utilitarian, authoritative style that created the fortress-like, imposing tower blocks and housing estates, a mod-

14 Arthur Machen, *The Three Impostors and Other Stories* (Hayward: Chaosium Inc., 2007).

ernist scheme to address the damage of the Battle of Britain that uprooted thousands of citizens, and to deal with the crumbling infrastructure of many UK cities. (Postwar reconstruction and utopian civic engineering projects are also the muses for musician Gordon Chapman-Fox's sonic preservation enterprise Warrington-Runcorn New Town Development Plan, which not only electronically explores Brutalist architectural designs but also the angst, hopes, and dreams of their inhabitants.) And yet many of these massive construction projects that created affordable housing would later deteriorate into depressing, crime-ridden tenements. Perhaps the digging up and demolition of the former buildings and roads of the old cities uprooted and unleashed the trauma, longing, and sadness repressed under layers of living, now able to haunt the modern world as they did the ancient. The older the city, the more ghosts it can produce and contain; therefore, a city such as London offers many hauntological possibilities.

Peter Ackroyd's 1985 novel *Hawksmoor* revolves around the parallel narratives of its two protagonists: Nicholas Dyer, the architect of seven London churches during the early 1700s, churches imbued with sacred geometry, black magic, and murderous ritual sacrifices, and Nicholas Hawksmoor, a police officer in the 1980s investigating a series of murders that are occurring in the shadows of Dyer's churches. (To further blend fact and fiction, Dyer is based on the real historical figure of Nicholas Hawksmoor, who lends his name to the fictional detective in the novel). It's revealed that Dyer's churches represent an immense occult working that has allowed the eighteenth-century architect to step through time and space, haunting twentieth-century London through the repeated ritual murders that feed Dyer's satanic power. The supernatural aspects of the murders confound the rationalist detective Hawksmoor, who seeks local, objective evidence and motives to solve cases that are irrational, mystical, and esoteric. Hawksmoor must trust his intuition and instinctive impressions in order to truly grasp the enormity of occult patterns that have been recurring from the eighteenth to the twentieth centuries.

The clues to solve the crimes are embedded not only in history, but also in place: the churches themselves, haunted sites that were baptized in sacrificial blood and which radiate misery and despair. Characters, dialogue, events, issues, songs, sayings, nursery rhymes, poems, and imagery echo across both narratives, repeating like magical incantations. Ackroyd weaves real people, places, and events throughout the fictional structure of coincidences, occurrences, ambiguities, and horrors. The ghosts that manifest in *Hawksmoor* are irrationality and nihilism as represented by Dyer's worldview that sees only contagion, affliction, filth, corruption, scatology, and darkness as real. He debates with his mentor, real historical architect Christopher Wren, over whether the dawning Enlightenment's innate trust in science, reason, and truth will ever fully conquer the evil in the human psyche and the blackness that surrounds human existence. Dyer's churches, especially the imposingly austere Christ Church in Spitalfields, are testaments to the primacy of the irrational hidden behind a façade of sanity and sanctity, as the patterns and design of his churches reflect the pain, suffering, and tragedy of humanity, the physical and emotional suffering of the workers who built them, and the poor cowed worshippers who seek hope and mercy from a silent God. Built in appalling slums and over burial pits of plague victims, Dyer's churches absorbed and now demand more of the blood shed on their grounds through the sacrificial murders committed to demonically consecrate their erection, a blasphemous reversal of the Holy Communion that bonds Christian believers to their God, their savior, and their church.

Dyer embodies these black magic rites, becoming the irrational spirit that haunts the illusion of rational progress and the enlightened evolution of humanity. Dyer transubstantiates into a murderous shadowy spectre, a literal negative darkness, the other side of the light of rationalism, the negation of logic and reason, the necessary correlative to the radiance of the Enlightenment. Dyer's churches are not only haunted by his occult obsessions, but also by the very real tragedies of urbanity such as the homeless and mentally disturbed who are drawn to the churches, loitering in their shadows, seeking refuge and solace but entrapped by their hypnotic power. As his investigation delves deeper and deeper into Dyer's abyss, Hawksmoor's slips into the irrational and the absurd; there is even the suggestion that the paragon of deduction and logic will participate in the perpetual series of sacrifices, continuing, and in thrall to, the horrors unleashed by Dyer, fracturing Hawksmoor's sense of stability and order. Hawksmoor resigns himself to his role in the ritualistic cycle that permeates London: he is the hanged man of the Tarot, suspended in time, unable to stop or solve Dyer's bloody incantations that will seemingly go on forever, fortified by the dark energies radiating from the city itself.

Ackroyd's use of repeating motifs, parallel storylines that intertwine, and simultaneous experiences that transcend time and space, suggest that our own understanding of time and geography are fabrications marred by flawed perception and perspectives, what Ackroyd calls 'the perpetual present of the past'. History doesn't unfold in a progressive straight line towards a finite point in the future; in *Hawksmoor*, time and space are endlessly cyclical, powered by traumas and horrors that devour themselves like the Ouroboros snake. Time and space are not as stable as we believe or hope they are. The future is not lost; it's already happened again and again; nothing ever really progresses, caught in a wheel of pain, obsession, trepidation, and the unknowable, trapped in an eternally recurring loop like ghosts that must recreate the moment of their murders. London and its inhabitants are haunted by the endless layers of suffering, brutality, instability, and the hidden evil of history and humanity, essences that have seeped into the very streets, buildings, and spaces that create the material, spectral, and psychic geography of that teeming metropolis. (The perfect soundtrack to Ackroyd's novel is *Hawksmoor* by James McKeown, a crepuscular aural tour of the, in actuality, six sinister churches designed by the real Hawksmoor.)

A major influence on Ackroyd's *Hawksmoor* is the hauntological work of Welsh poet, writer, and filmmaker Iain Sinclair. The subject/theme/muse of all of Sinclair's works is London, which he imagines as a poem always in the state of revision, a material text that is constantly being written and rewritten, with additions and deletions, demanding analysis, interpretation, and participation in its writing by all its inhabitants. Combining poetry, prose, essay, creative nonfiction, historical research, and oracular conjurings in multiple mixed media, Sinclair's writing are séances calling up ghosts of the past to tell their often-forgotten tales as well as opening portals into London's chaotically hybridized future through rhetorical divination and lyrical cut-up associations. Sinclair's idiosyncratic views of time and geography would inspire many key psychogeographical and hauntological works. It is Sinclair who conjectured that Nicholas Hawksmoor built his churches in accordance with a magickal geometry of opposites, creating a system of gnostic energies that connected the past and the present. These gnomic structures melded Christian and pre-Christian archetypes, calling ghosts out of the collective unconscious that resonated deeply in the hidden recesses of Londoner's minds.

1975's *Lud Heat* is Sinclair's first great achievement in the hauntological and psychogeographical genres. *Lud Heat* is a prose poem that excavates the historic, geographic, and cabalistic ley lines that connect the six churches designed by Nicholas Hawksmoor, identifying the hermetic mixture of Dionysian, Masonic, and Egyptian iconography embedded in the façades and design of the churches. This arcane geometry creates a preternatural power grid that draws from surrounding locations of death and suffering (graveyards, slums, plague burial pits) that resonates through the hidden alignments of the churches. Sinclair's novel *Scarlet Trappings White Chappell* (1987) suggests that the infamous Jack the Ripper murders stained not only the streets of Victorian London but penetrated into the very psyche of London itself, haunting the metropolis ever since the autumn of 1888. This notion of a crime so monstrous that it could traumatize not only the immediate era of its commission, but also reach across time to haunt the future, is portrayed brilliantly in the graphic novel *From Hell.*

Writer Alan Moore and artist Eddie Campbell's *From Hell* was a limited comic book series that ran from 1989–1996, originally serialized in the graphic illustrated anthology *Taboo* before moving into its own independent series. The focus of the narrative is the Jack the Ripper murders that occurred in 1888 in the Whitechapel area of London, proposing that the motive for the murders was a conspiracy to protect the royal family from a scandal involving Prince Albert Victor, the Duke of Clarence's illegitimate child and secret marriage to a Catholic commoner. This potentially empire-shattering information is used in a blackmail plot by a group of Whitechapel prostitutes to extort money from the royals, which necessitates the extermination of the blackmailers by Sir William Gull, real-life royal surgeon, on orders from Queen Victoria herself. Based on a now discredited theory expounded in Stephen Knight's *Jack the Ripper: The Final Solution* (1976), Moore utilizes this clash of the highest and lowest in British society to examine how this exact point in history marked the end of the nineteenth and the beginning of the twentieth century, as the murders not only look back to the ancient struggle between patriarchal and matriarchal power, but also look forward to the coming social, economic, and political forms of male domination that will become the foundations for institutional and ideological systems of control for the next 150 years.

In *From Hell*, the Ripper murders and the society that spawned them are presented as a midpoint between pre-civilized ritualistic sacrifices and the misogynistic lust killings of twentieth-century serial killers as witnessed in the very constitution of London itself. In one of the most vivid chapters of *From Hell*, William Gull takes his accomplice/carriage man John Netley on a tour of London's most famous landmarks, revealing the esoteric, occult significance of each site in London's hidden, secret geography, suggesting that London's savage pagan past still haunts the metropolis. One of Gull's brooding points of interest is Nicholas Hawksmoor's Christ Church in Spitalfields, the church that all the Ripper victims would stroll by on their way to The Ten Bells Pub. In this one haunting locale, Ackroyd, Sinclair, and Moore converge.

Amongst these ancient, unholy landmarks sprawls the squalor of modern industrialization and urbanism, the rising buildings of the financial district tributes to the birth of global capitalism, while in the shadows of these paeans to 'speculation', and the ghostly movement of capital and interest, the poor must turn themselves into commodities and sell their bodies just to survive. The ascendancy of liberalism intertwines with dispossession, dehumanization, and social trauma. Moore suggests that to understand historical events like the Ripper murders and the beginnings of the twentieth century one must look before the event and after the event, peer through multiple timelines and geographies in order to truly understand what and why it happened. Moore and Campbell perform both an autopsy and a séance for the Victorian age through the prism of these horrible crimes, tracing the various causes and effects as they intersect and double back on one another. The need to see the Ripper crimes holistically challenges linear portrayals of time as *From Hell* portrays past, present, and future as co-existing, parallel streams that ebb and flow into and out of one another.

This hauntological concept of time as the vessel through which a both/and consciousness can be achieved is best seen in the fictional William Gull's mystical visions and ghostly experiences throughout his life, viewing the ancient Egyptian gods that inspired his Masonic beliefs in congruence with his deathbed journey through the twentieth century as he witnesses the lineage of serial killers that he helped to inspire. Following Gull's most violent murder where he slaughters and dismembers his final victim Mary Kelly, he is transported to 1990s London and, while he is relieved to see that the masculine hegemony that inspired his crimes has been thoroughly established, he is frightened by the 'degeneracy' of the future, disgusted by his perception of the denizens of modern London as being apathetic, conformist, and lacking decorum and propriety. William Gull delivered the twentieth century when he ripped open the womb of the first Ripper victim Polly Nichols, but the future he midwifed has spawned even worse monsters, monsters that the Victorian madman is actually horrified by.

From Hell is an exorcism of not only the female victims of Jack the Ripper (whomever they might have been), but for all victims of misogyny and sexual violence throughout history and into the future: traumas that can never heal and will continue to occur until women are no longer exploited, objectified, and terrorized. The ghosts of the Ripper victims join the ancient ghosts of Queen Boadicea and her daughters humiliated and raped by the Roman legions, as well as the future ghosts of women who will be enslaved and abused by predators, sex traffickers, husbands, boyfriends, fathers, and other authority figures in twenty-first-century London. The nostalgic history of London has its façade ripped off to reveal the layers of tormented souls crying out in their anguish, yet unheard by the teeming millions of the metropolis. Although Moore would use hauntological aspects of psychogeography masterfully in his novels *Voice of the Fire* (1996) and *Jerusalem* (2016), it is *From Hell* that represents his most powerful spectral call for justice, mourning, protest, and resistance, especially for those women whose traumas are forgotten, ghosts that still haunt London, looking for voices to tell their stories.

v. Television

'The television picture is a man-made ghost.'
—T C Lethbridge, *Ghost and Ghoul*

ALTHOUGH TELEVISION HAS not produced a significant amount of hauntological texts, one of the most important hauntological writers found his home in the medium. Author and television screenwriter Nigel Kneale produced several key hauntological programs that continue to inspire other hauntological artists in a variety of media. Kneale was one of the first staff writers for the British Broadcasting Corporation (BBC) and the majority of his work for television focuses on the uncanny intersection of ancient folklore and superstitions coming into contact with ultramodern science and technology. One of his first teleplays, 1952's *You Must Listen*, concerns a telephone repairman who realizes that a telephone line has preserved the last communication between a woman and her lover before her suicide, a modern convenience memorializing the haunting end to a tragic affair.

Kneale became a household name in England with his character Professor Bernard Quatermass in the sci-fi/horror *Quatermass* serials broadcast on television. In particular, 1958's *Quatermass and the Pit* (Hammer Films version, 1967) brought together past, present, and future in a hauntological manner. The series starts with the discovery of a metallic object as workers are excavating a new subway tunnel. Quatermass discovers that the object is an ancient alien spacecraft from Mars, and though its occupants have been dead for hundreds of thousands of years, they still exert a cerebral power that has been resonating in the district of 'haunted' Hobb's End for centuries. Ghostly images and spectral hauntings ('Badly observed and wrongly explained') have been experienced in the area since it's been inhabited by humans and are subsequently revealed to be emanations from a cosmic psychic databank that is replayed over and over in the minds of the Hobb's End inhabitants. The Martians used primitive humans in experiments, manipulating DNA and the development of the primeval mind; alien science has made humans susceptible to these mind projections that are recalled from deep in our foundational genetic material. Quatermass is able to temporarily exorcize these instinctual ghosts and the psychological and physical damage they have wrought, and yet the future is not as secure as we'd like to believe, as the realization of Martian engineering of our evolutionary progress and the consequences of the chromosomal manipulation have created a trauma that all human beings must come to terms with, a ticking psychic time bomb that can detonate at any time in the future without any control over it. The contemporary digging in the London Underground is really the unearthing of the primal ghosts in our collective unconscious, a Jungian haunted house we have all inherited. The hope of a post-WWII utopian future of science, reason, peace, and human ascension has been short circuited by the wiring we received in our prehistoric beginnings.

Kneale's 1963 teleplay *The Road* is even more hauntologically terrifying. Though the program is lost from the BBC's archives[15] (how hauntological), Kneale's existent script and a 2018 radio drama adaptation detail the strange ghostly visitations that are haunting an eighteenth-century English village. Along a long-feared road, strange sounds and bloodcurdling screams terrify wayfarers. Two intrepid explorers, one a believer in natural philosophy, seek answers to these supernatural occurrences, believing them to be phantom echoes of the doomed final battle between Queen Boadicea and the Roman legions that has somehow become trapped in a repeating time loop, a phantasmagorical repetition of the past event. The end of *The Road* reveals that it is not the past intruding into the present, but, rather, a future nuclear Armageddon that has opened an aural portal to the past as sirens, car horns, and dying howls keep reoccurring along the 'haunted' road. Unfortunately (or fortunately) the naïve inhabitants of the 1700s cannot understand this dire warning of what is to come, and yet it is the pragmatic yet hubristic curiosity of these two Enlightenment men (one the prototype of the self-deluded scientist, the other the prototype for the self-interested capitalist) investigating the unnatural sounds along the road which will set the paradigm for future scientists and industrialists whose egotistical curiosity will result in the building of the atomic bomb. The ghosts of an apocalyptic future cry out in vain to the past: the traumas of the nuclear age are so horrible that they cannot stay contained in their own time, cycling

15 Not only have we lost the program, but also BBC Radiophonic pioneer Brian Hodges' sound effects/score.

back to actually inspire the very beginning of a long chain that will ensure humanity's destruction. Kneale reverses the contemporary world's usual notions of past and future by making the past a time of naïve, hopeful potential and the future a time of forlorn, hopeless dead ends.

Perhaps Kneale's greatest hauntological work is 1973's *The Stone Tape*, which alludes to the theory of residual hauntings as explained in paraphysical researcher/archeologist T C Lethbridge's 1961 book *Ghost and Ghoul*. (Who actually thought up this paranormal concept depends on who you ask. Nineteenth-century mathematician Charles Babbage and late twentieth-century chemist Don Robbins have also been suggested as the theory's originator.) The 'stone tape theory' asserts that traumatic events can be imprinted on natural objects and geographical sites, stored and played back when another traumatic field of energy triggers the supernatural apparatus. (For the record, Kneale claimed to have never heard of this theory of enduring place/object hauntings.) The teleplay focuses on a group of audio technicians who are experimenting with different recording techniques and materials in a nineteenth-century mansion. As they test out their equipment, the engineers discover that the very stones in the walls of the basement (another delve into the subterranean Jungian collective unconscious) act as recording devices and amplifiers for violent, emotionally traumatic experiences that have transpired in the past, storing the ghostly traces of victims and events that can be replayed under certain psychic and acoustical circumstances as a haunting. The researchers discover that the past can be imprinted, stockpiled, unlocked, and replayed through the supernatural science of elemental technology.

At first, they are thrilled by their discovery and all the financial and industrial implications for their corporation, but the hubristic technicians[16] soon learn that the ancient energies the stones record

16 The male scientists' arrogance goes beyond just the intellectual but also into gender relations, as female character Jill is the target of sexist comments and harassment. Interestingly, she and

and broadcast are far more powerful and uncontrollable then they ever could imagine. These 'recordings' are not nostalgic reminders of the quaint Victorian inhabitants of the house, but something far more sinister. Events that happened in the past and will keep happening throughout the present into the future don't obey the orders of the engineers and their machines, resulting in the death of one of the technicians, the psychically sensitive Jill Greeley. Her horrible demise is now another addition to the stone tape. Director Peter Sasdy presents these spectral phenomena as fuzzy, staticky, wavering images (like a television signal going in and out of transmission) and reverberating screams: a 'mass of data' broadcast through 'dead mechanisms' that reach back to the Saxon age, yet still have resonance in the modern era. Adding to the eerie atmosphere of the teleplay is the ingenious sound design/soundtrack by BBC Radiophonic sound wizard Desmond Briscoe, utilizing bleeping electronic echoes, oscillations, and buzzing drones to amplify the repeating patterns of both the hauntings and the technicians' computer programs. As Kneale has shown throughout his career, tomorrow's science is sometimes indistinguishable from yesterday's magic.

Although there is no American television writer who is the hauntological equivalent to Nigel Kneale, writer/producer Rod Serling incorporated hauntological themes into the scripts he wrote for his acclaimed series *The Twilight Zone* and *Night Gallery*. Many of Serling's works are concerned with ghostly themes and the feelings of nostalgia that can provide an escape from a cruel present and an uncertain future. Serling's nostalgic reverie is short lived though, as one cannot stay in the past forever, and so Serling's protagonists become anachronisms unable to adapt to a competitive, harsh present yet cannot move forward into an ambiguous future. For Serling, nostalgia is both the cause and cure for existential loneliness, a desperate cycle

a Victorian household servant are both the only residual victims recorded on the stone tape that the viewer sees, suggesting that the same kind of chauvinistic behaviors that drove Jill to hysteria and death could have also played a part in the trauma of the ghostly maid.

of murdering to dissect. Serling even put his own spin on that foundational hauntological holiday chestnut 'A Christmas Carol' in his political teleplay *A Carol for Another Christmas* (1964), in which he used the spirit of Dickens' tale to critique self-interest, xenophobia, and an anticipated Cold War annihilation through the ghosts of past, present, and future. We are given a peek into the future of a world in which arrogant jingoism, isolationism, and fear have led to the destruction of civilization, now a blasted heath lorded over by an ubu roi (played with madcap barbarity by Peter Sellers). Serling sees the only way to a better, more progressive imminent world is through participation in the global United Nations rather than through American exceptionalism.

The Twilight Zone episode 'A Stop at Willoughby' (1960) is a particularly poignant example of Serling's brand of hauntology. Williams, a middle-aged Madison Avenue advertising executive, is burnt out from the win-at-all-costs corporate culture that values youth, ambition, and ruthlessness and ridicules, age, wisdom, and experience. His boss is furious at him for losing an important account, his wife is selfishly materialistic and cold, and he must suffer a grinding daily commute from manic New York City to a soulless suburbia. Falling asleep on the train, he awakens to find he has traveled back in time to a tranquil nineteenth-century small town called Willoughby. As Williams gazes out the train window, he sees sunshine, smiling neighbors laughing and singing, a bright wholesome caring community of parades, marching bands, and ice cream socials, a slower, friendlier and more understanding way of life. The conductor asks if Williams is getting off at this stop but Williams, unsure of what he's seeing, turns him down. Back in his regular anxiety-ridden, empty present life, the run-down executive faces more humiliation and degradation as he suffers a breakdown at work, and his wife leaves him. He pines for the lost opportunity of going back to Willoughby. On his next train ride home, Williams gets another chance to step off the train into the welcoming arms of Willoughby, and he does not hesitate, leaving behind the horrible present for a serene past, joining the phantoms of a bygone era. The episode ends with the revelation that Williams has died, killed by leaping off the speeding train into a blizzard. As his body is put in the hearse, we see the name of the funeral home he will be interred with: Willoughby & Sons. Williams chooses to be haunted by nostalgia and a carefree, idyllic step back into the world of his childhood,[17] escaping the demeaning present and bleak, purposeless future, becoming a ghost himself.

Serling echoed this theme of ghostly hope, haunting memories, and escaping present traumas with spectral reverie in his 1971 *Night Gallery* teleplay 'They're Tearing Down Tim Riley's Bar.' Randolph Cane is a salesman at a plastics factory who is on the downside of a twenty-five-year career with the company. A young, striving co-worker is gunning to push Cane out of the top salesman spot and force him into retirement. To escape his inevitable future, Lane haunts an abandoned watering hole called Tim Riley's, a bar that had been the scene of celebrations for many of the milestones in Lane's life: his homecoming from WWII, his initial hiring at the plastics company, his promotions and awards for sales, and moments with his late wife. The bar is scheduled to be demolished and so Lane goes back to reminisce in the dusty, empty space, interacting with ghosts from his past, people who are no longer here and yet he is able to talk to them, laugh, and drink with them in the condemned tavern. He spends more and more time there, missing business meetings and work commitments. In the end, Lane decides to sojourn in Tim Riley's forever, staying there even as the wrecking ball swings, destroying place and man, joining all the ghosts of the past that haunt both the bar and Lane. The trauma of obsolescence and the yearning for his lost youth have caused Lane to retreat to the safety of the past even though it costs him his life, a life he is willing to sacrifice. A condemned bar and

17 For an incredibly queasy Oedipal spin on this theme of retreating into childhood to evade the pressures of current adulthood, check out Richard Matheson's teleplay 'Young Man's Fancy' in the third season of *The Twilight Zone*.

a condemned man share the same soul and so when one is destroyed, so is the other.

The plight of Lane, like Williams, begs the question of what happens when people get left behind. Is the past, nostalgia, and memory the only respite for outdated people? For Serling, the ghosts of the past are the only balm for those who no longer fit into a fast-paced world, people who are seen as valueless and unnecessary with nothing to contribute to a hollow, materialistic society that worships youth and the new. The escape into a ghostly past is not really an escape, though, as death provides the only way to fully leave the soul-crushing present and a non-existent future. In order to join the spectres of the past, one needs to become a spectre in the present, giving up a future that was pointless anyway.[18]

In all hauntological works, confronting the past is a crucial component of the experience. In some works, the past is a happy refuge, while in others, the past is a place of pain and suffering, a reckoning with spectres that can no longer lie buried or repressed, but, rather, erupt into the present, destabilizing the future, but also offering some hope of deliverance through a true accounting with the ghostly. Written by Bryan Elsley and directed by David Hayman, the 1980 BBC *Play on One* 'Govan Ghost Story' combines both personal and social histories coming to a head during an economic recession in Edinburgh, Scotland. Set in the working-class Iona Count tower blocks, Joe McGinn is a retired shipyard worker and former union activist who encounters a ghostly little girl in the uninhabited flat next to his. Joe is haunted by this spectral figure, forcing him to face his past failures not only as a father but also as a union activist. Joe, like many other denizens of the council estate where he lives, confronts the reality of unemployment, obsolescence, and powerlessness. McGinn is tor-

18 Serling's unproduced *Night Gallery* script 'The View of Whatever' also contains familiar hauntological themes. The story focuses on a man who has not only lost his son in the Vietnam War but has also lost the will to live. The present reminds him of his deceased son so much that he starts to see scenes from his own childhood playing out through his bedroom window. Stepping through the window, the man is ten-years-old again, enjoying a glorious summer and the youth he had left behind.

mented by his memories of neglecting the relationship with his daughter in order to devote his life to his activism, a choice that, with the collapse of worker solidarity in the face of Thatcherite economic policies of the late seventies and early eighties, has resulted in the loss of everything that was once dear to him.

McGinn's failures are intertwined with the crushing disappointments of leftist politics in the UK during this time period. The haunting of Joe McGinn reflects the personal sacrifices he has made as well as the death of working-class collective power and unity through the breaking of unions, robbing McGinn and his fellow wage earners of a stable, fruitful future. Joe's familial failures and the larger social/political/economic failures of Great Britain are manifested in the ghostly little girl, forever trapped in a state of childhood with no hope of maturing: her potential arrested and stunted by forces beyond her control. The nostalgia, fears, and hopes conjured up by working-class dreams and camaraderie have created ghosts of resistance, protest, and lost promise not only for a whole social class, but also for the individual.

'Govan Ghost Story's use of ghosts to reflect on the past, connect to the present, and question the future as both a communal and singular experience is also seen in 1974's *Play for Today*: 'Penda's Fen' written by David Rudkin and directed by Alan Clarke. 'Penda's Fen' focuses on Stephen Franken, the seventeen-year-old son of a reverend who is going through an identity crisis that is sexual, spiritual, and psychological, a rite of passage moving from naïve innocence to self-aware experience. Stephen's intense growing pains are materialized through his encounters with ghosts, angels, and demons representing England's symbolic and literal past. The conflicting forces within Stephen are also spirits that England has had to confront and work through in order for its national identity to mature: political authority, religious tradition, social strife, and historical trauma. In order for Stephen and England to move forward and continue developing into the future, they must both face their ancestral past as manifested in the pagan and metaphysical visions and apparitions that still reverberate in contemporary England.

For Stephen, these supernatural revelations represent a vision quest that encompasses the personal, social, psychic, sexual, and metaphysical. Stephen is searching for his true self as opposed to what his parents, teachers, peers, and community want him to be; he must discover himself by facing both private and public traumas. Stephen's religious, political, familial, and sexual convictions are all overturned through his encounters with the ghosts of the past and prophecies of the yet to come, leading the young man to discover that multiple identities, beliefs, and emotions can co-exist in a healthy paradox of both/and consciousness. Stephen confronts himself through accepting the simultaneity of the past, present, and future, just as England must come to terms with its many social and national identities, its successes and failures. Personal dreams and historical visions cut across past, present, and future: phantasms, spectres, angels, and devils reflect the triumphs and tragedies that befall the individual as well as a country. In the teleplay's final scene, Stephen meets King Penda, the last pagan king of England, who teaches Stephen that obeying is not living, and that he (and by extension, England) must follow his own path not influenced by nostalgic, conservative, parochial, or exceptionalist beliefs. Stephen must invent himself for himself if he is to have a fully realized future. 'Penda's Fen' is perhaps the most complex expression of hauntology's focus on the trepidation and fascination with time, how ghosts can disrupt absolutes, and how hauntings can bring to light both personal and collective traumas, obsessions, and truths in order to offer future resistance, justice, and redemption. Rudkin's hopeful hauntings would be countered in Derek Jarman's punk-influenced satire *Jubilee* (1978), in which Queen Elizabeth I, her lady in waiting, her orphic advisor John Dee, and Ariel from *The Tempest* time travel to late 1970s London to experience just how far England has fallen politically, culturally, socially, and aesthetically.

The vast majority of hauntological television works are either self-contained entities or episodes from an anthology. Sustained hauntological narrative arcs in a series, or even a full-blown hauntological series, are rarer to find as the necessarily disjointed timelines and blurring of boundaries for a true hauntological work would make for challenging primetime viewing. The Gothic soap opera *Dark Shadows* employed hauntological themes in its wondrously convoluted multiple story lines (called 'parallel time'), reaching its apex in a story arc where Byronic vampire anti-hero Barnabas Collins and Dr Julia Hoffman are accidently transported to the future (1995) and discover that both the Collins family line and their ancestral home of Collinwood have been destroyed. Revenants and degraded remnants of the Collins family literally haunt the derelict ruins of a Collinwood yet to come, and Barnabas must return to a distant era (1840) to restore the present timeline (1970), saving the Collins from supernatural revenge in the past in order to ensure the continuation of his familial brood into the future. The perpetually ghost-infested Collinwood manor seemed to host séances weekly as its inhabitants could never escape the sins of their fathers or the repercussions of their own proclivities that always ended up punishing another member of their enclave today, tomorrow, or yesterday. The storylines of *Dark Shadows* interconnect the trials and tribulations of the evolution of the Collins familial line with the tumultuous maturation of the US, from the colonial era to the late twentieth century, echoing the precarious, protean fortunes of both kin and country. The eternally tormented House of Collins is the ultimate American dynasty: unbroken repetitions and reiterations across time that the anguished Collins family are doomed to replay generation after generation against the backdrop of a haunted history of affluence, privilege, betrayal, tragedy, and death.

Perhaps the BBC's greatest institution and export, *Doctor Who*, would seem a natural place for hauntological storylines, and yet over its forty-plus years, the ghosts encountered by the Doctor in his travels across time, space, and relative dimensions have not been of the hauntological kind, but, rather, reflect extraterrestrial subterfuges or scientific anomalies. The closest the Time Lord got to a truly hauntological experience (not counting his companion Sarah Jane Smith's *Stone Tape*-like experience with spectral nuns and the Gorgon) was in the serial 'The Awakening' (broadcast in 1984) as the Fifth Doctor confronts the Malus, an alien who feeds off psychic energy produced by anger, hatred, violence, and brutality. The Doctor and his companions arrive in the village of Little Hodcombe, which is celebrating its place in English history by recreating a battle from the English Civil War that occurred there in 1643. The nostalgic celebrants seem to be taking the re-enactment a bit too seriously, fueled by ghostly apparitions of Roundheads and Cavaliers that actually fought in the original clash. While most re-enactments downplay the historical traumas in exchange for pomp and circumstance, the pain and upheaval for those who originally experienced these events have come back with a vengeance. It seems that these spectres are actually psychic projections created by the Malus, hoping to engender disturbing emotions and vicious tendencies in the current inhabitants of Little Hodcombe. By repeating the traumatic, bloody warfare from the past in the present, the alien entity can become energized and fully awaken in 1984. The Malus can not only generate psychic projections, but can also pull actual bodies from the past into the present through a passageway between two points in time that would allow travel from the past into the future. Poor Will Chandler becomes a living ghost, a seventeenth-century peasant wrenched into the twentieth century due to the Malus's hauntological scheme. Luckily, the Doctor is able to defeat the Malus, restore composure to the traumatized denizens of the village, and return Will to his own era. Although he can exorcize the fake ghosts conjured by the evil alien, the affable Time Lord is unable to quiet the countless restless spirits always ready to emerge in Albion, reminders of layered historical pain and suffering.

The BBC mini-series *The Living and the Dead* (2016) also incorporates similar hauntological elements into its mythos, culminating in its final episode. *The Living and the Dead* chronicles the lives of Nathan Appleby, a pioneer Victorian psychologist, and his wife Charlotte, who take up residence on the Appleby family estate in the village of Summerset. Over the six episodes, the Appleby family encounter young girls possessed by the spirits of vindictive men, the haunting of workers in a mine where orphan child workers suffocated, the spectre of a local wise woman killed as a suspected witch, and the revenants of Roundhead soldiers on the anniversary of a brutal battle of the English Civil War. The final episode moves into hauntological territory when it is revealed that Nathan's increasing psychological problems are being caused by his great great granddaughter, a twenty-first-century paranormal investigator who is trying to contact the restless ghost of Appleby's drowned son. Instead of the past reaching out to the present, the future is flowing back into the past, causing mental, physical, and spiritual disruption. The future is haunted by the past, which, in turn, causes the past to be haunted by the future, a hauntological cycle. (This ability for the past and future to gaze at each other and not interact in helpful ways, to see and acknowledge each other but have no agency to break the Möbius strip of fate, is also a characteristic of the films of cinematic master Nicolas Roeg.) *The Living and the Dead* suggests that the boundaries between life and death, science and the supernatural, and the past, present, and future are permeable, unstable, and highly subjective, but, in the end, meaningless.

The only sustained hauntological television series is *Sapphire and Steel*, which ran from 1979–1982. Created by television writer Peter Hammond (who also contributed to the weird children's fantasy *Ace of Wands* as well as to Richie Richard and Eddie Hitler's favorite show *Emmerdale Farm*), this enigmatic series focused on two extraterrestrial (perhaps) interdimensional (maybe) time travelers (the series never really makes it clear what they are) who are agents protecting the universe from the evils of chronology. Time itself is the antagonist of *Sapphire and Steel*, a malignant force that attempts to disrupt the flow of history, destabilizing the linear structure of reality. Time opens rifts through space and eons, allowing ghosts, creatures, and otherworldly/othertimely beings to break through and destroy the borders and boundaries of reality. Sapphire (Joanna Lumley) and Steel (David McCallum) are sent to address these dangerous situations and intervene in combating these disruptive entities, not to assist humanity (if anything their attitude towards Earthlings is ambiguous at best) but, rather, to repair these fissures and contain the chaos of time. In the series, the presence of the past in the present, something antique or anachronistic in modern times, of the contemporary holding onto the historical, is in opposition to a healthy sense of progress, allowing time to fragment and displace the present. The settings of *Sapphire and Steel* (an eighteenth-century house, an abandoned railway station) suggest that the more fixated we become on the past, the more we allow the ghosts of memory and history to manifest themselves; the more we obsess about what happened rather than what's happening or will happen, the easier it is for time to destabilize the present and erase any hope for the future. The hauntings of *Sapphire and Steel* are traps laid out by Time to ensnare us in yesterdays and rob us of our tomorrows. In the series, ghosts are dangerous and should be left behind because they keep humans static and repetitious; it is progress and evolution that protect us from the prison of Time, not fixating on the past.

Sapphire and Steel encourages its viewers to look forward and outward, not backward and inward, to anticipate and move towards the wonders of the future rather than fixate on a morbidly confining past, inculcating nostalgia as one of the weapons Time utilizes against humans. *Sapphire and Steel*'s stories are cryptic and paradoxical, often raising many more questions than they provide answers. This is particularly true of the absurd (in the existential way) final episode of the series in which Time's agents set a trap for the titular characters in a motorway café where Sapphire and Steel end up detached from space and time, trapped in a Beckettian repeating loop for eternity. In the end, Time will always triumph, and Sapphire and Steel will never die, nor will they ever really live again, forever haunting themselves. *Sapphire and Steel* offers an almost inverse hauntological perspective: the past and nostalgia offer no refuge from the present, offering only the ghostly bait of nostalgia, escape, and safety, drawing victims into a dead end, until the future is stripped away from them: "This is the trap. This place, you see… this place is nowhere. And it's forever."

vi. Film

> 'Cinema is the art of ghosts, a battle of phantoms.'
> —Jacques Derrida, 'Cinema and Its Ghosts: An Interview with Jacques Derrida'

THE PERFECT GENRE for hauntological works would appear to be film, with its ability to edit and create jumps in time, space, and continuity, not bound by linear narratives or perspectives. Movies are also nostalgic talismans that reverberate in the hearts and minds of viewers, whether they are cineastes or not. Although there have been plenty of ghost movies, the hauntological film is harder to identify; perhaps, again, like television, viewers are not accustomed to nonlinear works and the culture industry would rather entertain and make money on a safe investment rather than challenge viewers and gamble on an experimental work, producing low box office receipts. Just because a film has a ghost in it doesn't necessarily mean it is hauntological. (Some hauntological films don't even have traditional ghosts in them.) Ghosts and hauntings need to be metaphoric and indefinite, not just fodder for jump scares; spectres in hauntological films can be both literal and figurative representations of personal and collective traumas. These hauntings must remain ambiguous, problematizing notions of past, present, and future, taking the forms of memories, longings, and obsessions that are conjured, fetishized, and exorcized through personal, historical, spatial, and temporal dislocations and experiences.

Perhaps the greatest hauntological film is Stanley Kubrick's 1980 adaptation of Stephen King's *The Shining*. This film has become such a pop culture touchstone that a synopsis seems redundant, but it is important to note that the vast majority of the hauntological aspects of the film were added by Kubrick (and Kubrick's collaborator Diane Johnson) to King's family melodrama. While King's novel uses ghosts to illustrate the dysfunction in the Torrance family as well as the insecurities and failures of head of the family Jack Torrance, Kubrick elevates King's premise to the hauntological by making the haunting of the Torrances a microcosm for the spectres of colonialism, racism, and patriarchy that possess both the Overlook Hotel and the United States itself. The family, the hotel, and the country are all haunted by personal, social, economic, and historical traumas that feed into each other, repeated, validated, and imprinted on cycles of violence, terror, and exploitation. The same forms of imperialism, sexism, and class hierarchy are evident in how the US westward expansion treated indigenous peoples, how the Overlook treats its workers, and how Jack treats his wife and son.

The spectral temptations that the Overlook uses on Jack (alcohol, sex, power, status, promises of access to the elite class) to lure him into doing their murderous bidding are the same lies that have been used to keep the political, social, and economic status quo in the United States, starting with the genocide of Native Americans and the enslavement of Africans, through to the racist and sexist policies of the last 400 years. Just as the Overlook has a history of violent hauntings, the American family and the United States of America must identify, accept, and exorcize these ghosts, breaking an endlessly repeating chain of cruelty, dominance, and repression. The myths of the Old West, frontier spirit, and American exceptionalism are revealed to be cancerous phantoms that have infected Americans across time and space. The ability to 'shine' originates as a defense from and warning of trauma, whether it is located in Danny's dislocated shoulder or Dick Halloran's life as a black man in a racist society. The notion and practice of 'Manifest Destiny' manifests not only the God-given right to dominate and oppress but also manifests its self-generated traumas as ghosts. The sexism, racism, brutality, humiliation, and selfishness that Jack exhibits towards his family are all spectres that echo in our national consciousness as much as life, liberty, and the pursuit of happiness.

Jack Torrance is the working-class pawn of the ruling elite as represented by the glamorous and elegant phantasmagorical roaring twenties cocktail parties into which Jack finds himself magically transported: a gold ballroom, tuxedoed gentlemen, tipsy flappers, servile bartenders, and helpful butlers. These anachronistic nostalgic clichés are the carrot on the stick, leading Jack to kill by appealing to his basest desires. Marx himself stated that 'capital is dead labor' that parasitically sucks the life out of workers, and that's exactly what the Overlook's ruling class revenants do to the lumpen custodian. The chilling end of the film shows that Jack (or a look-a-like factotum) has always been the caretaker and ends up a class traitor, a dupe who is rewarded for his acceptance of the sexist, racist, and classist ideologies which help to consolidate power for the plutocrats: we are shown a close-up of a photo from 1921 (the beginning of the roaring twenties, a nostalgic time of unprecedented economic growth, massive wealth, social change, and the dawn of consumerist culture in the US) of a smiling Jack amongst a crowd of revelers. The date on the picture: July 4, the birthdate of the United States of America, the nostalgic rich and powerful celebrating the founding of a country created by the rich and powerful for the rich and powerful.

The hauntological question raised by *The Shining* is how does the American family, and, by extension, America itself, go forward from the tyrannical, colonizing patriarchal relationships that often structure households? How do we put to rest the ghosts of both the perpetrators and victims of these beliefs and actions? Who can break the chains of oppression, sexism, racism, and classism? Kubrick's cautious hope for tomorrow is young Danny Torrance, Jack's psychic son gifted with the ability to see the future. The Overlook's need to possess Danny is its attempt to gain control over the future; it already has total domination over the past. Danny is a victim and a witness to his father's brutality. Perhaps Danny will not follow in his father's footsteps, and he will be able to participate in a more equitable form of family and citizenship as he gets older and matures, and yet there is also the potential for the abused to become the abuser. (Some of these questions are addressed in Mike Flanagan's 2019 adaptation of Stephen King's sequel to *The Shining*, *Doctor Sleep*, but the novel/film are extensions of King's work, not necessarily Kubrick's.) Jack, literally and figuratively, is frozen in the past. Danny escapes to find a new way into the future, a future that holds both the promise of healing, but also the threat of repeated violence, trauma, and cycles of abuse wrought on another generation if the ghosts of the past are not confronted and exorcized.

Artistic works concerned with the African diaspora/slavery and the consequences of these historical/cultural/personal traumas on generations of displaced peoples have utilized ghosts and hauntings to represent and explore the way an oppressive past can conjure spirits of both horror and hope in the search for a present identity and a future direction. Films such as Bill Gunn's *Ganja and Hess* (1973), Ray Marsh's *Lord Shango* (1975), Julie Dash's *Daughters of the Dust* (1991), Bernard Rose's *Candyman* (1992), Nia DaCosta's updated and expanded *Candyman* (2021), and Jonathan Demme's mediumistic adaptation of Toni Morrison's *Beloved* (1998), brilliantly utilize the supernatural and spirituality to conjure the spectres of an exploited and suffering, yet proud and resilient, people. These films use the spectral and spiritual to protest the subjugation of individuals, cultures, and histories, to recognize the crimes perpetrated, to protest treatment and erasures, but also to exorcize the suffering and move forward into a more inclusive, self-aware, and healing future. The metaphors of folk beliefs, legends, music, Creole religions, and a repressed African culture enhance these feelings of being simultaneously blessed and cursed by the spirits of the past, as well as suggesting an animistic struggle for a future. The historical traumas of slavery and colonialism, the unfulfilled promise of Reconstruction, and the ongoing spectres of racism, haunted by the ghost of Jim Crow, offer up America as the (unfortunately) perfect atmosphere for the hauntological, as it seems that the country was built on suffering, ordeal, and hopes that never came to fruition for (nearly) anyone.

The potential for younger generations to finally put the ghosts of the past to rest is at the core of Charles Burnett's 1990 film *To Sleep with Anger*. In the film, the revenants are not literal manifestations, but, rather, are expressed through the beliefs, expectations, and reminders of a past way of life that won't stay exorcized even as new ways of life are being proposed. Gideon, his wife Susan, and his extended family have moved from the rustic South to the urban sprawl of South-Central Los Angeles. Though they believe they have left their country beliefs and behaviors behind them, when the family is faced with new tensions and apprehensions, their past returns to haunt them even in the bright lights of LA. As both the older and younger generations struggle to acclimatize themselves to urban customs and behaviors, an old friend from the past unexpectedly arrives to stay with Gideon and his family. Harry Mention is a traveling salesman who hasn't seen Gideon in thirty years. Harry's down-home charms and folksy ways are nostalgic reminders of Gideon's rural, Cotton Belt past, but Harry's charismatic presence also re-awakens pre-existing tensions in Gideon's family. Harry pokes and prods the family, questioning Gideon's decisions, his Christian faith, and the stability of his marriage and the family itself. Gideon's children are caught between the past and the future as Harry unleashes the power of old traditions, cultural superstitions, social repressions, and racial traumas that Gideon's family sought to leave behind for the promised land of California. Harry and Gideon struggle not only over patriarchal authority (Harry usurps Gideon's role when Gideon mysteriously falls ill) but also who will decide what the family's guiding principles and values will be moving into tomorrow. Harry's use of Southern dialect, anachronistic idioms, and vernacular folk expressions act as ghostly signifiers of historical, cultural, and personal memories and past ordeals that still haunt Gideon as he tries to change not only his surroundings but also his lexicon in a new environment filled with the expectation of social change.

The hope and trepidation of their new urban life and the worry and fear over whether they have made the right choice to leave their ancestral roots conjure up emotional ghosts to which Gideon's family are particularly susceptible. Are the portents and omens that Harry seems to bring with him authentic supernatural warnings or irrational fears with no basis in reality? Harry is the tempting trickster serpent in the Garden, undermining their security, testing their solidarity, sowing doubt, conducting a metaphoric séance that calls up these cultural and spiritual spectres to test Gideon and his family. Is Gideon's family strong enough to accept and face the ghosts they ran from? Can they ever fully escape these spirits? In the end, the social and personal anger, frustrations, and fears are purged with Harry's death; the ghosts of the past haven't exactly been banished, but Gideon, his wife, their children, and grandchildren can learn to live with these anxieties in their new home. The next generation of Gideon's family can cautiously look to the future, a future that will be informed but not overwhelmed by the nostalgic ghosts of the family's past as well as the spectres of historical and social traumas. Gideon and his family must choose between the devil they know (the poor, rural, explicitly racist Deep South) and the devil they don't (lower middle-class suburbia, implicitly racist California). Burnett's film brilliantly attempts to unearth and exorcize the personal and collective traumas of living with different kinds of oppressive conditions, of leaving behind one type of haunting to acclimatize to new ghosts, shifting the haunting from one temporal and geographical site to a new one.

David Lowery's 2017 *A Ghost Story* operates in the tradition of romantic ghost stories/films for much of its running time, but becomes hauntological in its final half hour. 'C' is a musician living with his new bride 'M' in a suburban home. One night C awakens to hear someone strike a note on his piano but can find no one causing the sound. Soon after this strange occurrence, C is killed in a car accident and returns as the conventional ghost covered in a white sheet with two eye holes cut out. He returns to haunt his own home and watches over his grieving wife. Days and weeks go by and eventually M brings home another man. C reacts by making the lights flicker and books fly off the shelves. M moves out but leaves behind a note she has written and secreted in a small hole in a wall. Other families move in and out and occasionally C makes his presence known.

The house is later abandoned and left derelict, yet C still inhabitants the sad remnants of a once happy home. Time passes through the growth of a massive futuristic cityscape that replaces the house and quiet suburban neighborhood. C finally steps out of the space he has haunted and is transported to a nineteenth-century prairie where settlers are camping. A girl writes something on a piece of paper and hides it under a rock. The settlers are massacred by Native Americans as C watches. C's house is built again, and he witnesses the moment when he and M move in. That night, the ghost of C strikes the note on the piano that awakens his former/future self. As events repeat themselves, the ghost of C reads the note that M hid in the wall and is finally able to disappear and move on, breaking his connection to the material world and leaving the cycle of time and space he was either trapped in or clinging to.

A Ghost Story takes an innovative approach by giving viewers the ghost's perspective of the unfolding cyclical events. C's nostalgic attachment to M and to his home prevents him from moving on, and it is only when he can let go emotionally that he can leave the hauntological circle. In a sense, C must exorcize himself, finally accepting the passing of his life, his relationship, and time and space itself. C's haunting violates the natural progression of grief as well as human beings' relationships with time, space, and other humans. By finally accepting that nothing lasts and that everything changes, C is allowed to fade away into the past so that the future can progress. With the chronological turn from a personal to a historical narrative, *A Ghost Story* suggests that hope, loss, sadness, and mourning transcend any individual, couple, or community relationship, that these emotions and traumas saturate any and all times and places where humans interact in meaningful ways, hauntings that echo and repeat with the persistence of memory until the chain is broken and both the haunter and haunted can move on.

Nicolas Roeg's stunning 1973 adaptation of Daphne du Maurier's short story 'Don't Look Now' utilizes the spectral accoutrements of séances, auguries, and apparitions to summon an atmosphere of loss, trauma, and mourning. After the accidental death of their young daughter Christine, Laura (Julie Christie) and John Baxter (Donald Sutherland) attempt to leave their tragic memories behind, immersing themselves in a new place (Venice), work (restoring a medieval church), and sex. Their grief follows them and seems to saturate the dank canals and shadowy, labyrinthine alleyways that are also concealing a murderer. Laura's serendipitous (or is it?) meeting with a blind psychic who claims to be in contact with the Baxter's dead daughter is the catalyst that brings to the surface all the repressed anguish and confusion that a child's death brings to parents. The inability to deal with the past, to let go and exorcize the sorrow of yesterday, negates the present so much so that the future winds up as only the devastating inevitability of fate. John Baxter is especially haunted by the guilt of not being able to save Christine; it is his denial of these nagging feelings that blinds him to the 'hauntings' and precognitions that are right in front of him. John's insistence on the absolute exactitude of his way of seeing as the only possible reality for what is happening to him and his wife results in his inescapable downfall (falling is one of many leitmotifs in the film). The recurring clues are all around him: flashes of red consistently warn him to stop and pay attention yet he refuses to see the eerie forebodings. Roeg's elliptical, synchronistic editing compounds the hauntological aspects of the film as the viewer experiences flashbacks, flashforwards, and flash-sidereels as we try to piece together the uncanny events of that shocking red December in the City of Masks.

With its focus on different, alternate experiences and conceptions of time as well as its conjectural depictions of the future, the genre of science fiction seems especially attuned to the tenets of hauntology. Though ghosts may seem antiquated and superstitious to the more objective, progressive focus of sci-fi, no matter how far into the future one goes or how far away into space one ventures, the spectres of the past aren't easily left behind. One of the most iconic science fiction films contains several hauntological themes as well as incorporating them into the look of the movie. Ridley Scott's *Blade Runner* (1982) features characters striving to discover what makes a human a human, and it is revealed that the essence of humanity is our ability to conjure up, interact with, and finally exorcize ghosts of our pasts, presents, and futures. Scott's film asks the key question: are we born human or must we earn that appellation through the development of empathy and care for all living things?

A loose adaptation of Philip K Dick's *Do Androids Dream of Electric Sheep?*, the film is set in a futuristic Los Angeles, where Rick Deckard is a Blade Runner, a police officer whose job is to hunt down and 'retire' rogue replicants, artificially created beings who are used as slave labor in off-world colonies. Replicants are programmed with a four-year life span in order to keep them at the level of alienated, commodified drones. When five replicants reject their subservient place in this dystopian society and journey back to Earth to meet their creator and demand extended life, Deckard is charged with stalking and ruthlessly exterminating them. As he gets deeper into the case, Deckard starts to question what real differences there are between humans and replicants, questioning his own humanity in the process.

The ghosts in *Blade Runner* are the memories, nostalgic spectres from the past that are believed to be evidence of what makes a human genuine. Replicants are implanted with memories to make them more 'human' than human, but the question becomes what makes an authentic memory? Are memories objective or subjective? Are all memories (and, by implication, nostalgia) externally 'implanted' in some way? Memories are like ghosts, real and ephemeral, past and present at the same time. The replicants are especially attached to photographs that are visual reminders of their 'pasts'. It is revealed that the replicants are unaware that their memories are fabricated, a particularly cruel way for their creators to control and manipulate them. In *Blade Runner*, memories and photographs are phantasms, spectres of a lost past, a past that never was but is longed for by the replicants, desperately clinging to anything that validates them as authentic, 'real' human beings, thus the irony of using non-existent nostalgia to prove reality. Even Deckard, a 'real' human, is fixated on photographs as we see that his apartment is filled with them, some looking surprisingly anachronistic and fake. Memory is rhetorical rather than an objective, absolute, exact recollection of past events and experiences. *Blade Runner* suggests that all our memories are 'implanted' as our relationships and interactions with other people and their perspectives influence how we remember the past and how we integrate the past into the present and future.

All the characters in *Blade Runner* are haunted by memories, experiences that we can never fully live again not only due to the passage of time but due to the constructed nature of memories themselves. The replicants have no future; their life spans are programmed into them, and so it is in the ghosts of the past, not even their own pasts, that they search for solace. Memories haunt us in positive and negative ways: ghosts of traumas and triumphs fill us with hope and dread, much as they do the doomed replicants in *Blade Runner*. This nostalgic yearning for a recognizable past in order to understand the present and move into the future is also reflected in the aesthetic of *Blade Runner*. The set design, architecture, and costumes blend trends, designs, and fashions from multiple eras into a postmodern future, an aesthetic that Scott calls 'retrofitting': blending 1940s film noir, 1950s futurism, 1960s pop art, 1970s punk rock, 1980s corporate chic, even looking forward to twenty-first-century globalization to create a polyglot world of future Los Angeles. Past, present, and future are mixed together in the look of the film as the denizens of this world are haunted by the ghosts of past cultures, social movements, and urban designs, all returning to manifest themselves in new combinations and permutations. Even the soundtrack to *Blade Runner* by Vangelis combines futuristic synthesized soundscapes with sultry 1950s jazz saxophones and a song by 1930s vocal group the Ink Spots.

Chris Marker's 1962 short film *La Jetée* also reverses the usual hauntological focus on lost futures by suggesting we are haunted by lost pasts and the opportunities now lost to the passage of time. *La Jetée*, told in a series of haunting still photographs, relates the story of a time travel experiment in post-apocalyptic Paris. Forced to live underground, the survivors of WWIII research time travel and attempt to send test subjects to either the past or the future in order to prevent the war that has devastated their world or to receive aid from future civilizations to rectify the global devastation that has been wrought. Scientists discover that those subjects (actually political prisoners forced into the experiments) who have particularly strong memories have the best chance of traveling through time. The most successful subject has a vague but obsessive vision from before the war of a woman standing on a pier at an airport and the death of a man, shot on the pier. Fixating on these phantasms of the past, the subject is able to go back and meet the woman from his memory. They fall in love and he is able to return to her more frequently. Receiving no help from the past, the scientists send the subject into the future, where he is given an unlimited power supply unit that can rejuvenate his destroyed society. His usefulness over, his captors plan to execute him, but the people of the future offer the subject an escape to the past to be with the woman he loves. He materializes on the pier at the airport from his memory. As he runs to meet his lover, an executioner from his own time shoots him, and he dies on the pier as his younger self looks on, creating the very memory which will pull him back in time over and over again: "Half of him is here, the other half is in the past."[19]

Marker's existentially oblique film suggests that there is no escape from the present, that both the past and the future are ghostly emanations that are like the grapes offered to Tantalus, tempting and alluring but forever out of reach. Echoing Hitchcock's elliptical masterpiece and most hauntological film, 1958's spiraling *Vertigo* (both Hitchcock and Proust initiated desperate searches into the past spurred on by the memory of a Madeleine), *La Jetée* rejects linear concepts of time, seeing lifespans as concentric circles, cycles of life and death, rings which no human can control; everything repeats over and over, trapped on the wheel of fate with no respite. No matter how much we nostalgically pine for the past or hope for the future, we will always be dragged back to the eternal now. It is the subject's obsession with memory and the ghosts of the past that end up being his downfall, as his own death creates the very ghost that will forever be his fate. Time and memory are locked in a recursive war of attrition, and, in the end, human beings, battered by the consequences of that war — distortion, fragmentation, erosion, loss — are only left with ephemeral ghosts. (Marker's most in-depth exploration of time, place, memory, and death is in his docu-travelogue-collage-reflection/projection, 1983's *Sans Soleil*.) The use of still photographs to express the narrative suggests that we are just as trapped in time and place as the stuffed animal exhibits that the two doomed lovers look at in a museum. The haunting meaning of the subject's murder is a warning against trying to escape the temporal and the spatial, and yet his need for love, security, and escape will cause him to push against these barriers forever, a Sisyphean time traveler endlessly repeating his useless quest. The past belongs in the past, behind glass cases in the museum that the subject and his lover visit on their dates.

19 Director Terry Gilliam would use *La Jetée* as the foundation for his own expansion on these themes in his 1995 film *12 Monkeys*.

And yet Marker makes the past look so romantic, so inviting, so beautiful, and so fulfilling, especially in contrast to the radioactive ruined hell of post-WWIII Paris. Is it any wonder that the subject would choose to live in the past, love a ghost, and risk becoming a ghost himself? The subject was barely living in his present, and so his self-willed 'future amnesia' and the attraction to even a ghostly life in the past cannot be easily dismissed. This feeling of nostalgic longing and love across time, a longing and love that cannot last and will eventually result in death and despair, would later be echoed in James Cameron's *The Terminator*, where a soldier from the future sacrifices himself to protect a woman he is in love with from the past, fully knowing he is doomed to die, but willing to do it anyway if only to have a fleeting, tender moment with a ghost, before he himself becomes a ghost as well.

Peter Weir's *The Last Wave* (1978) follows a similar thematic hauntological approach to Kubrick's *The Shining*, as Weir combines both personal and collective hauntings to comment on European colonialism and the continued erasure of the indigenous peoples of Australia. *The Last Wave* is the story of David Burton, a white lawyer who defends a group of Aboriginal people who are accused of murder. His clients' hesitancy to explain what happened, or even to defend themselves from the charges, baffles Burton as he tries to build their defense. As Burton investigates the crime, the victim, and those who are on trial for the murder, strange meteorological and environmental phenomena have been erupting in Sydney as torrential downpours, black rain, frogs falling from the sky, and weird solar effects cannot be explained. These apocalyptic omens are paralleled in Burton's dreams and visions of Aboriginal shamans, owls, and a colossal wave which will cover the city. (Why are the best apocalyptic/post-apocalyptic films based in Terra Australis?)

Burton is forced to confront his own European heritage as well as the collective consequences of the colonization of Australia and the subjugation of its indigenous peoples. Both Burton's personal and

Australia's historical ghosts are conjured up when Burton and the Australian justice system are faced with the tribal beliefs of the Aboriginal people, two very different views of not only justice but the world itself. As he delves further into the folk customs and mysteries of his clients' beliefs, Burton questions his own religious, social, and familial influences, how he himself has also been colonized by traditions, ideologies, and authority figures/systems, all ghosts of the past that he is forced to confront and exorcize in order to not only understand the motives of his clients but also to understand himself. In the courtroom, European colonialism faces its own ghosts when it shows no interest and gives no credibility to the artifacts and mythological perspectives that Burton tries to introduce as evidence to explain that the death of the victim was caused not by his clients but through 'magical thinking' that caused the demise of a man who believed so strongly in the spiritualism of his tribe. It was animistic folk faith rather than physical violence that caused the heart attack that killed him.

The personal and collective ghosts of the past collide in a sequence where Burton chases an indigenous Australian under the city of Sydney, finding a secret subterranean Aboriginal sacred site, a cavern filled with artifacts, wall paintings, and a ghostly guardian. Existing underneath a sewage treatment plant (Weir's commentary on how Europeans treated Aboriginal peoples like scatological waste?), Burton delves into an alternate notion of temporality and spatiality called Dreamtime, an experience outside of logical, linear space and time, which is more authentic and genuine to the Aboriginal characters than objective, scientific material reality. 'Regular' time ceases to exist in Dreamtime, as past, present, and future flow simultaneously and all living things achieve a collective totality, interconnected in a transcendent oneness. Burton comes to not only a universal/metaphysical insight by confronting the ancient ghosts that have been almost but not quite banished by European colonialism, but he also comes to vital self-knowledge, recognizing himself as a reincarnated soul, a continued existence that searches backwards and forwards throughout time.

Given two tunnels to choose from in order to get back to the surface, Burton chooses the path that leads to intuitive supernaturalism, rejecting western logic, reason, and linearity, phantasms that encouraged and justified the colonialist perspective and their actions in exterminating a people. Emerging from the womb-like tunnel, Burton collapses on the beach, staring out to the horizon as a towering tidal wave begins to break on the shore to engulf Sydney and Burton himself. This ending is both apocalyptic and hopeful at the same time, offering a cleansing of the past to bring about a better future. Is this a global or personal apocalypse? Is the wave destroying western civilization altogether or only western ideas that have created the traumatic ghosts that haunt Australia and all other places that have been exploited and victimized by colonialization? Will this wave sweep out not only collective historical and political ideas, but also the personal notions that have imprisoned all of our minds, bodies, and souls?

The ghosts of *The Last Wave* suggest that apocalypses and exorcisms are not only destructive but also constructive, that the world and our own identities go through a series of beginnings and endings rather than the singularities of western notions of time, history, and selfhood. Water, like ghosts, can represent both life and death, a both /and proposition, and we must understand both aspects in order to truly experience the totality. There is an enormous gulf between how westernized Australia and its indigenous peoples perceive, conceive, and live time, life, death, and reality. The haunting of David Burton is a metaphor for the haunting of the west: in order to move into the future or, at least, move past the traumas of the past, we must give voice and justice to those who were sacrificed in the name of progress and civilization.

The most hauntological director must be Andrei Tarkovsky, one of the most renowned artists in the history of cinema. Almost all of Tarkovsky's films focus on the twin themes of time and memory, applied through the lenses of the personal, the artistic, the historical, and the metaphysical. His utilization of dreams, visions, childhood, nature, reflections, miracles, and soaring above are cinematic séances (enhanced by his use of bells and candles), trance states that lure the viewer into hypnagogic, languid viewing experiences. Tarkovsky's slow, long takes create the sense of a hovering unseen presence watching events transpire over a lengthy period, haunted and haunting simultaneously. Tarkovsky called his aesthetics and approach to film 'sculpting in time', through which he can manipulate the viewer's sense of place and duration, encouraging them to reflect on those moments lost and forgotten as his characters struggle with connecting those fading memories with their identities, relationships, and places in the world around them. Points of pain, suffering, loss, and doubt haunt his characters, and yet the majesty and beauty of nature acts as a solace to them, spaces and periods of time outside the rational, objective, scientific understanding of the third and fourth dimensions where one can, momentarily, escape.

Although these hauntological themes appear in many of his films, two in particular are especially noteworthy: *Solaris* (1972) and *Mirror* (1975). (Tarkovsky made a movie entitled *Nostalgia* [1983], but, surprisingly, it's one of his least innovative hauntological films, although still a deeply personal, private work that displays the contradictory impulses of longing and disillusionment intrinsic to reminiscing and yearning for home.) *Solaris* is an adaptation of Stanislaw Lem's 1961 science fiction novel. The film focuses on the character of Kris Kelvin, a psychologist sent to a space station that is orbiting the planet of Solaris, trying to figure out why the crew of the space station have suddenly become emotionally unstable and withdrawn and if research on the mysterious planet should continue. Before he leaves for space, Kris talks with his father about his mission, as his father had been a part of the crew that discovered Solaris and had witnessed bizarre phenomena on the surface of the planet. These observations had affected the crew, but the images had been dismissed as hallucinations.

Kris arrives on the space station and discovers the crew acting strangely in connection with the weather patterns of the ocean planet. He is stumped as to whether there is a causal relationship between the planet and the psyches of the scientists. Kris awakens one morning to find his wife Hari in bed with him. Hari committed suicide ten years ago, and she can offer no reason why she has appeared. Horrified by this apparently living ghost, Kris jettisons his 'wife' into space and learns that similar 'ghosts' have been appearing to the crew after they projected radiation at the surface of Solaris. Hari reappears and has no knowledge of her suicide on Earth. After a birthday party in which she is accused of being artificial, Hari kills herself but comes back to life almost immediately afterward. Shaken by these events, Kris dreams of his mother, caring for her by washing her arms. Kris awakens to find Hari gone and wonders whether he should return to Earth or venture to the surface of Solaris. The end scene is of Kris at his family home on Earth, hugging his father. As the camera pulls back it is revealed that Kris is actually on Solaris.

The hauntings of *Solaris* are directly connected with past traumas, repressed nostalgia, and unresolved issues. Kris is haunted by his relationships with his parents, but, more poignantly, his unsettled guilt over the suicide of his wife. The Haris that keep reappearing and can't be 'killed' will keep manifesting themselves until Kris faces his emotions over his loss and lets go of his grief. His breakthrough is shown by his ability to not only embrace his father but to actually live on Solaris, a place of dreams, memories, and happiness that exists outside of science, psychology, and objectivity. The subjective, emotional reality of Kris's inner conflict is more real than the scientific posturing and hypotheses that lead nowhere on the space station. Hari's resurrections go beyond logic and reason into the magical and spiritual as science, psychology, and medicine can offer no hope of exorcizing these ghostly projections from Kris's soul. Hari's spectral manifestations end when Kris decides to confront his deep feelings of loss by not forgetting his wife, not dismissing her presence, and not repressing his feelings for her, but, rather, by accepting her ghost and making peace with her and, by proxy, his father and mother. By doing this, Kris is able to step outside the constraints of past, present, and future, and live without the anger, bitterness, and guilt that have haunted and grounded him in the material world. Tarkvosky's movies always end with a 'miracle', which suggests that the future is hopeful and can be achieved and actualized: expect great revelations.

Mirror is an autobiographical film that not only has a hauntological theme but which also takes on the visual aesthetics of the hauntological genre. *Mirror* visualizes the inner workings of a dying poet's mind as we see his dreams, recollections, fantasies, feelings, hallucinations, and observations in a collage-like stream-of-consciousness symphony that actually resembles hauntological musical compositions more than cinematic ones. Much of the material in the film is drawn from Tarkovsky's life, with his wife and mother appearing in the film, and yet it is the ghost of his father Arseny Tarkovsky that haunts the film, with the incorporation of sound recordings of Arseny reading his poems (his father's spiritual presence hovers over almost all of Tarkovsky's films). Tarkovsky uses a patchwork of both modern and anachronistic styles and media in the film, as color, B&W, and sepia film stock in various states negotiate both personal and social remembrances, suggested the disintegration and degradation of private and collective memory over time. The ghosts of the protagonist's life flash before our eyes: we see his childhood, his wartime experiences, his marriage, and his relationships as a series of both celebratory and traumatic events.

Tarkovsky's sense of time is one of overlapping, simultaneously layered recursive moments that go beyond the expected binaries of reality and fantasy, consciousness and unconsciousness, fiction and nonfiction, the mundane and the poetic. The film jumps from time period to time period based not on a linear narrative or progression, but, rather, on emotional and symbolic leitmotifs. By using this structural device and nostalgic blurring, some critics have connected

Mirror with Proust's modernist masterpiece *Remembrance of Things Past* (and, perhaps, both can be linked to their future hauntological progeny, Sebald's *Austerlitz*?) as random, involuntary sights, smells, and sounds call up incredibly detailed reminiscences for the novel's narrator. In these works, memory is shown to be imperfect, brittle, and unreliable; it is only in artistic recollection that structure, validity, and meaning become evident. Both Proust and Tarkovsky are fighting a losing battle against the slow fading away of the past, trying to use art to rescue these nostalgic moments from 'progress' and the inevitable deterioration of the mind and media that attempt to record these memories, 'like tears in rain'.

vii. Music

> 'The 'futuristic' in music has long since ceased to refer to any future that we expect to be different; it has become an established style. Invited to think of the futuristic, we will still come up with something like the music of Kraftwerk, even though this is now as antique as Glenn Miller's big band jazz…' —Mark Fisher, *Ghosts of My Life: Writings on Depression, Hauntology and Lost Futures*

CURRENTLY, THE MOST prolific area of hauntological art is the field of music. Ironically, hauntological music seems to be the vaguest in terms of how exactly these forms of art relate to Derrida's original conceptions. It seems as if many hauntological musical artists integrate the themes of hauntology into the conception and explanation of their approaches to music, and so some of their music itself seems only to have a tenuous link to the philosophical framework, transforming and extending the tenets first explored in Derrida's lecture and essay. Musician Elvis Costello (supposedly) once remarked that writing about music is like 'dancing about architecture', as written descriptions and analyses of music are missing a vital aspect of the experiences of hearing and feeling the medium of music, and so perhaps the absence of definitive textual connections between a philosophical theory and an aural phenomenon are to be expected. Most hauntological music contains no lyrics at all, as sound, album art, and liner notes provide the ghostly connections to hauntology. Hauntological music, then, cannot be reduced to its lyrical content or message; it's more of a sensibility, a feeling, a mood, and an approach to not only creating music but listening to and experiencing music as well.

Hauntological music is often suffused with an existential sadness and longing nostalgia, a painful yearning to preserve memories, feelings, fleeting images, half-heard sounds, even types of recordings and recording technologies that have disappeared or perhaps never truly existed. This music's ethos seeks to invoke the emotional world between anticipation and disappointment. In this manner, hauntological music expresses Schopenhauer's own view of the futile quest for contentment and joy through time, nostalgia, and future expectations:

> Happiness lies always in the future or else in the past, and the present may be compared to a small dark cloud driven by the wind over the sunny plain; in front of and behind the cloud everything is bright, only it itself always casts a shadow. Consequently, the present is always inadequate, but the future is uncertain and the past irrecoverable.[20]

Often hauntological music calls attention to how fragile and ethereal recording anything really is; the inevitable breakdown and decay of all recordings and recording materials and recorders themselves; the imperfect nature of recording and playback is pushed to the forefront of much hauntological music as pops, crackles, skips, static, distortion, surface noise, and tape degradation are not muted or erased but rather enhanced to make the listener feel the loss and slipping away within that moment of listening. Like memory, hauntological

20 Arthur Schopenhauer, *The Essential Schopenhauer: Key Selections from The World As Will and Representation and Other Writings* (New York: Harper, 2010).

music starts to break down, warp, and dissipate even at the moment of its creation.

Hauntological musicians utilize their recording media and technology much as human mediums were conductors and conduits for spiritualist contact, plucking voices and sounds from the ether. Hauntological music exhibits an uncanny (in a Freudian sense) nostalgia for the forgotten, the discarded, opportunities lost or squandered that will never come back again, the abandoned and neglected. Childhood and adolescence are popular subjects for hauntological music as time, memory, and wistfulness conjure up could-have-beens, should-have-beens, and never-weres. This kind of longing for unrequited teenage love or the safety and unconditional happiness of childhood has its predecessors in pre-hauntological musical works such as The Beach Boys' Caroline, No (indeed the whole *Pet Sounds* album), The Beatles' Strawberry Fields Forever, The Kinks' *The Kinks Are the Village Green Preservation Society*, and even in less acclaimed pop songs like The Dream Academy's Life in a Northern Town, and R.E.M.'s Nightswimming. While past sentiments and reflective memories can be lauded in songs, there is also the potential trap of a nostalgic miasma that discourages and paralyzes personal growth as reflected in tracks such as Japan's plaintive electro-minimalist Ghosts: "Just when I thought I could not be stopped/When my chance came to be king/The ghosts of my life/Blew wilder than the wind."

Critics Simon Reynolds and Mark Fisher loosely define hauntological music as music reflecting temporal disruption, retrofuturism, Cold War paranoia, and nostalgic childhood memories, often using anachronistic or obsolete instruments and recording media, drawing upon esoteric cultural references, library music, soundtracks, field recordings, analogue electronic music, psychedelia, musique concrete, and media sound sources like public service messages and educational film narratives. The aesthetic is one of futurism, utopianism, and ultramodern progressivism meeting the failed, the forgotten, the discarded, the decommissioned, and the abandoned. Hauntological music foregrounds the eerie, the odd, the out of sync, the disjointed, the unsettling, reclaiming cultural 'debris', neglected history, and deteriorating memory. At once functional, official, institutional, and scientific, and yet doomed, broken, failed, occult, and supernatural, hauntological music is intentionally anachronistic, especially in its invocation of promised futures through the triumph of technology and scientific technocracy, a yearning for a future that was imagined, guaranteed, and idealized in post-WWII England and World's Fair USA. British hauntological music artists have created an alternate utopia, a time and place where all the promise, hope, and optimism of the fifties, sixties, and seventies have come to fruition in a celebration of a perfect world of stylish leisure, technological marvels, and personal freedom. This retrofuturism was integrated into popular music with early Roxy Music's mix of 1940s Hollywood glamour and the wild hedonism of freak-out postmodern synthesized sound, as well as with Kraftwerk's romanticized 1920s Weimar/Teutonic/Bauhaus aura recreated by precisely syncopated Futura robots, but can ostensibly be traced back to Sun Ra's Afro-Futurist jazz, stage appearance, and philosophy. Psychedelia's first hauntological casualty Syd Barrett, the Edwardian psychonaut, had one foot on an interstellar spacecraft and the other on a penny farthing bicycle, haunting his own acid-addled mind, becoming rock's premier living ghost.

Time is not the only obsession of hauntological music as place, setting, and environment are all crucially invoked through sound compositions. Like the Situationist psychogeographers, hauntological music seeks to recreate the emotional, ethereal, and psychological aspects of space and place. Hauntological geography, much like psychogeography, is not concerned with the mapped, the measured, the official, the surveilled, or the known. Hauntological music conveys the feelings of stepping into the hidden, the obscure, the unknown, the transitory, areas that cannot be mapped objectively, the just out of reach either temporally or geographically. Landscapes are more than just boundaries and borders; they are haunted by all the events that have seeped into the ground. Precedents for this kind of sonic mapping can be found in former Roxy Music provocateur/Renaissance man Brian Eno's *On Land* (1982), a subjective sound recreation of the brooding Suffolk coastline in eastern England, half remembered from Eno's childhood trips there. Sound invokes remembrance when it becomes a virtual place, even if the listener has never been there physically, only in the mind. Just as the music genre Exotica conjured up spaces and places that were half-real and half-desired, hauntological music indulges both nostalgic reminiscence and projected imagination, as the lines between these psychological and emotional states blur into a third space beyond the perceived and imagined. Personal and collective memories along with long promised but never realized dreams are the ghosts that are both conjured and exorcized through hauntological music, transforming the hopes, fears, pain, trepidations, and fascination for what was, what might have been, and what never can be again into sound.

Often identified as the first purely hauntological musician, John Foxx is a performer, artist, photographer, and graphic designer who pioneered the use of sound and music to recreate past, present, and future moments in sonic time. His work creates emotions of contemplative, disintegrating loss as well as futuristic disorientation. Foxx's career in music began as the singer in the punk/electronic group Ultravox! Foxx's tenure with Ultravox! resulted in a few proto-hauntological pieces such as Just For A Moment and Hiroshima Mon Amour ("Walk through Polaroids of the past/Futures fused like shattered glass, the sun's so low/Turns our silhouettes to gold/Hiroshima mon amour"), but it wasn't until he pursued a solo career that Foxx started to express his unique vision of the ghosts of the future pure and unfettered. His first solo album *Metamatic* (1980) grappled with the effects of both future shock and future longing, the gulf between human evolution and technological liberation, haunted by a future we crave but are frightened of, not being able to fully comprehend the consequences of a mechanized world and a mechanized humanity.

After recording four solo albums, Foxx would take a break from recording, but returned in 1997 with two key hauntological works: the ambient *Cathedral Oceans* and *Shifting City*, a collaboration with Louis Gordon. In these works, space and geography become the central focus of Foxx's oeuvre: our relationship with place and how the ghosts of our lives are trapped in decaying environments that will eventually crumble and be overtaken by entropy and nature, forever silencing the human narrative as the sounds of slow collapse continue on. Our alternating connections and alienation from time and place haunt our lives and how we interact with our environments and each other. Foxx's prolific output has included such eerie solo releases as *My Lost City* (2009) and *London Overgrown* (2015) as well as works with his group Ghost Harmonic, and alliances with his spectral aesthetic progeny: Ghost Box Records' Belbury Poly and The Advisory Circle. Foxx cemented his status as hauntological music's elder statesman when he collaborated with sand artist Justin Barton and philosopher Mark Fisher on the 2013 audio-visual-walking essay/art project *On Vanishing Land*, which documented a tour along the Suffolk coastline (invoking Eno's seminal *On Land*) from Felixstowe to an Anglo-Saxon burial ground at Sutton Hoo, a psychogeographical 'mapping' of ghosts and haunted areas, both historic and folkloric. Foxx's album *The Arcades Project* (2023) connects spectral piano ambling with the wanderings of proto-hauntologist Walter Benjamin and his Angel of History, turning its back to the hereafter and only able to gaze on the ruins of the bygone, searching in vain for the Paris that once was and has never been; the city's future lies in its past.

Perhaps the only composer in residence in academic geography and astrophysics departments, Drew Mulholland, recording under the names Mount Vernon Arts Lab and Mount Vernon Astral Temple, was called the 'godfather of psychogeographical rock' by Ghost Box Records, the standard bearers of hauntological music. Mulholland's work is inspired by excavations of forgotten places, people, events, and rituals that have fallen between the cracks and layers of 'official' history. Using a wide range of electronic, acoustic, and found sounds as well as recording in non-traditional 'magickal' locations, Mulholland's music calls forth and celebrates the ghosts of the UK's past, present, and future. *One Minute Blasts Running to Three and Then Diminishing* (2000), recorded in Kelvedon Hatch at the decommissioned Kelvedon Hatch Secret Nuclear Bunker, reconstructs the aural tensions of Cold War Armageddon while 1991's *The Séance at Hobb's Lane* (alluding to Nigel Kneale's hauntological connection of the science of Quatermass with the occult) takes the listener on a guided tour of British supernatural sites both real and imagined. Mulholland's sound artistry raises the ghosts that remain subterranean and secret, coaxing them out of the shadows to disrupt the known, the accepted, the mapped, the recorded. Just as history and memory become convoluted and chimerical, Mulholland's music is necessarily warped and oblique, changing, repeating, familiar and then unfamiliar, recreating the discrepancy between what we nostalgically remember, what we want the experience to be, and what we find on returning.

The artist who has taken the hauntological aesthetic most to heart is Antony Hardy, who records in collaboration with Benjamin Holton and Robert Glover as July Skies. (Holton and Glover also have their own long-running expansive hauntological project, the shimmering driftscapes of epic45.) Mixing melancholic indie pop, shoegaze miasma, and playful ambient, July Skies is an effort to reach the past, to reconstruct memories, to address the nostalgic longing for an escape from contemporary society to an imagined simpler time. July Skies, named after the feeling of unending summer days as a child, invokes the ghosts of an idyllic remembered past, not necessarily the actual historical past, but the nostalgia of distant youth and forgotten moments in life, like love lost in time's game of chance. July Skies recreates the mood and atmosphere of abandoned WWII airfields, ruined churches, lonely outposts by the sea, bucolic countryside neglected in the rush to the urban. July Skies' music is haunted by faded reveries and the onset of adulthood and maturity not only for the individual but for societies, communities, and nations: having to leave innocence and youth behind in the name of progress and 'growing up'.

July Skies' dreamy, hazy remembering is recreated by the use of echo, reverb, drones, delay, and gentle guitar effects, which add texture to these sonic memories, aided by the occasional soft, floating vocals that speak to all our yesterdays. *The Weather Clock* (2008) is a hauntological masterpiece that recreates the carefree days of 1950s and sixties Britain, the beauty of new towns in the country, futuristic designs, modernist architecture, traveling by train to seaside resorts and, yet, summer must fade, vacations inevitably end, and the days of garden parties celebrating quaint England are gone. Much like Rod Serling's 'A Stop at Willoughby', the hauntings of July Skies are filled with ghosts of a past that can never come back and a future never completely achieved.

One of the most critically lauded electronic artists of the last twenty years, Boards of Canada use anachronistic technology and unusual sound sources to manipulate beats, samples, and melodies into hauntological paeans to the innocence of childhood and nature. The Scottish musical duo of Michael Sandison and Marcus Eoin infuse many of their compositions with the themes of nostalgia, memory, and loss. Named after the documentary films made by the National Film Board of Canada that they watched as children in the 1970s, Boards of Canada reimagine and recreate the naïve wonder children have when encountering the world and explore how this combined youthful awe, curiosity, and fear continues to structure relationships between human beings, technology, and natural landscapes way past adolescence. Using both soothing and abrasive tones and rhythms, Boards of Canada use techniques such as time stretching to distort the pitch and length of their sounds, fragmenting children's voices and other vintage sound samples (public information films, number stations, even the rantings of cult leader David Koresh), weaving them in and out of the mix to create haunting yet eerily familiar moods and moments. Neither purely synthetic nor purely organic,

Boards of Canada eschew digital recording, embracing older forms of recording technology to give their music a 'warm' clunky feel. Albums such as *Music Has a Right to Children* (1998), *In a Beautiful Place Out in the Country* (2000), *Geogaddi* (2002), and *Tomorrow's Harvest* (2013) conjure spectral and natural sounds out of the past, encouraging the listener to remember the fascination and fear children often have when first exploring the world around us. Boards of Canada's hauntological aesthetic extends to the imagery presented across their releases and promotional materials, culminating in the front and back covers for *Tomorrow's Harvest*, which invokes the sun-baked haziness of classic seventies downer sci-fi films like *Soylent Green* (1973), *The Idaho Transfer* (1973), *Phase IV* (1974), *A Boy and His Dog* (1975), and *Capricorn One* (1977). The use of this 'feel' from films predicting technological social control, environmental disaster, and governmental/corporate conspiracies offers a strange type of nostalgia for a time when these worries seemed far off, as if those vintage fears of dystopian futures now seem naïve and sentimental in comparison with the bleak, never-ending, dead present that only seems to get worse. We have lost the need to fear for the future because, sadly, there is no future to bother imagining.

Similarly, the group Broadcast uses 'pop avant-garde', 'futuristic' sounds pioneered in the 1950s and sixties that are now considered anachronistically hallucinogenic in the twenty-first century, blended with electronic instrumentation and vintage production technologies. Accompanying their retro science fiction soundtrack aesthetic are haunting vocals by the late Trish Keenan that are childlike, dazed, and often affectless (reminiscent of Mia Farrow's "la-la-las" on Krzysztof Komeda's terrifying soundtrack to Roman Polanski's *Rosemary's Baby*), sounding like lullabies sung by a robotic flower child, juxtaposing the hippie past and the spaced-out future. Albums such as *The Noise Made by People* (2000), *Extended Play Two* (2000), *HaHa Sound* (2003), *Tender Buttons* (2005), and *Berberian Sound Studio* (2013, the soundtrack to Peter Strickland's unnerving, self-reflexive giallo-inspired thriller) suggest the two sides of the 1960s, countercultural sensual psychedelia and space age techno worship, crashing into each other. In a 2009 interview with *The Wire*, Broadcast compared the effect of their phantasmal music to the time-phasing art cinema of Chris Marker:

> I think the evocation of memory in our music could be seen as the residue of imaginary time travel. You can either go forward or back. You go back in order to change something in the now, to redesign the course of events for personal reasons. When you go back to a previous musical time you're trying to recall a memory that never happened to you, that is not stored so it would make sense that you hear a fuzzy dissolving sense of time and place [...] It seems to me that the past is always happening now, all previous events have positioned us here philosophically, geographically, and in the present, we are always in memory...[21]

Their most hauntological release (and perhaps the most hauntological in the entire field of hauntological music) is a collaboration with Ghost Box Records act The Focus Group, entitled *Broadcast and The Focus Group Investigate Witch Cults of the Radio Age* (2009), an otherworldly cut-up mélange of ethereal music, spoken word, occult ritual, and radiophonic effects that explores the Nigel Kneale-esque notion of the connection between science and the supernatural. In particular, the track Make My Sleep His Song, with its swirling voices, drones, and incantations, suggests the kind of music the ghosts in *The Stone Tape* would have imprinted on the sound engineers' computers. In memoriam to Trish Keenan, members of Broadcast and The Focus Group collaborated on the Children of Alice project, four songs that cross-stitch folk horror and hauntology into a web of spectral associations.

Moon Wiring Club's Ian Hodgson is on a quixotic quest to single-handedly save, celebrate, and recycle everything cool that ever ap-

21 Joseph Stannard, 'Unedited Broadcast', *The Wire* (March 2020), https://www.thewire.co.uk/in-writing/interviews/p=11070 [Last accessed June 3, 2024]

peared in England in the last 200 years. Broadcasting from the mythical Clinkskell, a lonely town in the bleak moors of northern England, Moon Wiring Club has built a plastic fantastic modular future for permanent juvenilia: a psychedelic garden social here, a Dionysian rave for ghost children there, cardboard sets for the TV show *Druids in Space* interlinking with the discothèque utilized for Victorian robot shindigs. Starting with 2007's *I'm More than a Memory Now*, Moon Wiring Club's releases are sonic Ouija boards calling forth all the best spectral movements in art, fashion, music, and literature, along with the more obscure cultural artifacts that are often found in a hauntologist's kit bag: creepy children's TV, the occult, psychogeography, utopian daydreams, antiquated technology, anachronistic folk customs, and kitchen sink surrealism. Unearthly albums such as *A Spare Tabby at the Cat's Wedding* (2010), *A Fondness for Fancy Hats* (2013), *Psychedelic Spirit Show* (2018), and *Ghost Party Delirium* (2022) spill out of their musical containers into posters, videos, magazines, calendars, and even card games. Hodgson wields a diverse palette of musique concrete to ambient to electro to techno to acid house to downtempo to breakbeat, over multiple versions of releases, remixes, extended dance variations, and alternate forms that all coexist equally. Moon Wiring Club's masterpiece may be 2011's *Clutch It Like a Gonk*, which is self-labeled as 'Confusing English Electronic Music', as Hodgson conducts Dr Phibes' Clockwork Wizards automaton band, who are running riot in Kraftwerk's Kling Klang studio, triggering strange samples and eerie tones. Warped and woozy, freaked and funky, looped and loony, Moon Wiring Club emanates vital BPM: beats plus magick.

A major theme and method in hauntological music is 'broken' recording media and fractured time. Crackles, hisses, snaps, pops, slippage, static, and distortion are all pushed to the fore rather than covered over, muffled, or removed with contemporary digital editing, a 'nostalgie de la boue' (the yearning for mud) as Séverine Serizy might say. Ian Hicks, recording as Mordant Music, has an interest not only in lost recording media but lost recordings themselves. In the days before cable, satellite, the internet, and digital platforms, one could pick up weird TV channels or pirate radio waves through bent antennas and imprecise positioning, resulting in imperfect sounds and images, fuzzy, staticky transmissions, and interference that relied on the imagination to fill in the gaps of what one was seeing or hearing (or thought one was seeing or hearing) that seemed beamed from another world or time and now only exist in foggy childhood memories. Mordant Music's vivid 2006 album *Dead Air* is centered around the idea of an abandoned TV station that is still broadcasting, an ethereal symbol from outside of time, a ghostly beacon sending out degraded yet intriguing sounds haunting the ether. *Dead Air* utilizes the broadcasting voice of Thames TV announcer Phillip Elsmore from the 1970s and eighties to lend a further level of verisimilitude to this anachronistic media forgery. Even the packaging of the CD looks like some strange 'futuristic' product introduced in the 1970s. Mordant Music's works evoke something vague, elusive, happy, and sad at the same time, dipping in and out of the audient void. Hicks' influence can be directly related to the Broken Transmissions/Signalwave microgenres of Vaporwave, a music, art, and internet cultural movement that focuses on 'dead' genres, technologies, institutions, and pop culture fads, a more vapid than wistful look back at the promises of commercialism and the 'greed is good' ethics of the eighties as well as the information superhighway utopias of the nineties.

Following in the footsteps of Drew Mulholland, Mordant Music also recorded in Kelvedon Hatch at a declassified nuclear bunker that is now a tourist attraction, a symbol of a once horrific future now transformed into a place of morbid curiosity, historical kitsch, and second chances. In 2010, the British Film Institute commissioned Hicks to re-score several 1970s and eighties public information safety films (compiled on the DVD *MisinforMation*) with the results being comical, poignant, and disturbing, an ode to a past in which government actually seemed to care about the health, safety, and wellbeing of its citizens and were not hesitant to scare the bejesus out of them to ensure compliance. Mordant Music is extremely self-aware of his own status as a known commodity in this specialized musical genre, titling one of his compositions The Hauntological Song. Hicks continues his hauntological and psychogeographical exploration through sound via his *Travelogues* series of releases.

William Bevan's Burial also utilizes the ghosts of recordings and recording technologies, incorporating the random errors and mistakes when using these flawed media into his own compositions. Like Mordant Music, Burial is fascinated with pirate radio stations and unlicensed broadcasts that were free to roam the largely unregulated airwaves of the 1960s and seventies. Burial's music violently crackles and hesitates, distorted, messy, grimy, with nothing pristine or pure about it. Manic drum-and-bass beats slam into slurred garage rhythms existing right on the verge of pure noise, soundtracking the smeared time zones of the urban wyrd. Releases such as *Burial* (2006), *Untrue* (2007), and the *Ghost Hardware* EP (2007) are menacingly haunting tributes to lost transmissions, damaged gear, and accidental discoveries that have been erased by the corporatization of media and the quest for technological perfection at the cost of exorcizing the necessary ghosts that inhabit mechanisms. Burial's quest to recreate the feeling of being haunted, of being disoriented in time and place, of discovering we are living ghosts, continues on *Antidawn* (2021) in which eerie voices, mysterious samples, and fractured field recordings expose 'a wintertime city, and something beckoning you to follow it into the night. The result is both comforting and disturbing, producing a quiet and uncanny glow against the cold'.[22]

This psychogeography of the spectral postmodern landscape can also be heard in Chris Sharp's hauntological electronic project Concretism, which recreates music one might have heard in public service announcements, educational scholastic programs, and film strips

22 Hyperdub, Press Release: Antidawn, 2021.

in classrooms across both Britain and North America. In what is becoming a hauntological musical rite of passage, Sharp has played a concert in Kelvedon Hatch, perhaps the most switched-on, happening derelict nuclear bunker in the western world. This former symbol of technological Thanatos has been recommissioned as one of utopian Eros through a 2017 multimedia hauntological festival (at which Concretism played), transformed through the auspices of Buried Treasure Records label magus Alan Gubby and his wondrous occult conspiracy thriller *The Delaware Road* project. Concretism's *Teliffusion* (2021) is a paean to the early days of video recordings and the home video revolution, now superseded by streaming and non-physical digital media. The tracks on *Teliffusion* are jaunty retro electropop layered with synths, loops, beats and samples from Betamax video tapes (itself a technology that was abandoned by the home video industry), a remembrance and celebration of top-loading VCRs, rewinders, and adjusting the tracking. On the other side of the pond in another 'burned over district', situated in the rust belt city of Buffalo, New York, Matt Donatelli's Survey Channel taps into upstate New York's Victorian occult history, socialist dreams, and its Tofflerian industrialized visions of a fully automated post-third wave society in releases such as *Along the Wind Spear* (2020), *Silent Graphs* (2021), and *Canvas Doubles* (2023).

Inspired by the haunted ballroom scenes in Stanley Kubrick's *The Shining*, James Leyland Kirby records his electronic manipulations of antiquated vinyl records, found sounds, and downtempo soundscapes as The Caretaker (another *Shining* reference), sonic séances that contact the spectral revelers who endlessly celebrate July 4 in the Overlook Hotel. Amazing releases such as *Selected Memories from the Haunted Ballroom* (1999) and *A Stairway to the Stars* (2001) use orchestral and dance hall 78 LPs (a truly anachronistic and decaying medium) as source materials that are slowed down, sampled, resampled, distorted, and phased in and out of the mix like ghosts disappearing and rematerializing on a whim. Kirby's musical focus has now shifted to another hauntological theme, that of the rhetoric of memory, remembering, and misremembering, of how our perception is our reality and nothing exists outside of what we recollect with our faulty, fragile minds. Informed by his research into amnesia, fugue states, and Alzheimer's disease, works such as *Sadly the Future is No Longer What it Was* (2009), *Theoretically Pure Anterograde Amnesia* (2006), *Additional Amnesia Memories* (2006), *Everywhere at the End of Time* (2016–2019) and *Everywhere, an Empty Bliss* (2019) suggest that, like Samuel Beckett's *Krapp's Last Tape*, the brain is the ultimate imperfect, degrading recording medium, a haunted house filled with ghosts and selves of the past, the present, and the yet to come, playing the same tapes over and over until the batteries run out. Kirby's most evocative work must be his soundtrack to Grant Gee's documentary on the enigmatic, melancholic scribe W G Sebald. *Patience (After Sebald)* (2012) takes inspiration from the forlorn drifting interlocutions and ghostly recollections of Sebald's *The Rings of Saturn* as well as Franz Schubert's forlorn song cycle *Winterreise*: notes, loops, and voices hover, fragment, and vanish into the void. Most poignantly, Kirby recorded the aggrieved *Take Care. It's a Desert Out There...* (2017) in memory of Mark Fisher.

The genre of ambient music is a perfect platform for hauntological music as it is not concerned with the same kind of rhythms that most music utilizes to emotionally and physically engage its listeners. Ambient music is meant to unfold slowly, filling a space, creating an atmosphere, becoming a part of rather than becoming distinct from the environment within which it is played. Ambient music floats along, just at the threshold of hearing, sinking into the subconscious, background sounds taking their place along with all the other diegetic sounds in the listener's space. Wistful, like half-remembered reveries, the tones and keys of ambient flit through one's memories, calling the listener to days of futures past. It is a different listening experience than most music, which insists on its reason for being; ambient is ghostly, gently haunting a space and the listener, and yet its ethereal nature makes it as passive and fragile as a summer breeze.

Artist and musician Tor Lundvall creates some of the most spectral ambient music in the field of hauntology through opening spaces in his compositions so that the ethereal sounds of the past can seep through (Lundvall himself calls his music 'ghost ambient'). His music hovers between waking and dreaming, and, much like his paintings, conjures up serene environments with an underlying sense of darkness and dread, populated with beings straight from youthful daydreams and nightmares. Lundvall's music invokes childhood, nature, and desolate places, haunted by innocence, but just on the cusp of menace and loss, as time seems to slow and temporarily stop, allowing for the quick remembrance of past reveries before the coming of a long, cold night. His release *Field Trip* (2016) recreates the ghosts of school trips past: the initial excitement of leaving and the inevitable disappointment of returning once the trip has ended, while his collection of seasonal works *The Seasons Unfold* (2011) hints at a connecting cycle of nostalgia, natural forces, and landscape. Another ambient artist with hauntological leanings is Andrew Chalk. Chalk creates shimmering, crystalline minimalist sounds using the barest of source materials: plucked strings, piano notes, and echoed tones. Releases such as *The Cable House* (2009), *Ghost of Nakhodka* (2015), and *The End Times* (2022) exist in an era of their own yet are vaguely familiar, hauntingly lush soundscapes that call the ghosts out of the shadows, hovering in the ether, and lets them quietly fade back into the gossamer.

Hauntology has not only inspired music artists, but also labels and multimedia projects as well. Cultural archivist Stephen Prince's A Year in the Country began as a blog in 2014 documenting a year-long journey through the haunted English countryside, encountering the ghosts of the 'bucolic countryside dream' as expressed through neglected history, dismissed folklore, and forgotten people and places. Using photographs, reports, narratives, fiction, field recordings, research, ethnographies, visual art, and musical interpretations, A Year in the Country represents the collective mapping of the blurring of fact and fiction as it relates to rural England, experiences and séances that attempt to bring to light an alternative history and geography as well as a haunted lexicon of TV shows, films, music, literature, and graphic art. Wandering into these ethereal areas, Prince and the artists that contribute to A Year in the Country imagine the countryside as both idealized and demonized, a place of pure innocence and primeval brutality. Traditionally, nature and 'the country' have been romanticized as places of escape, simplicity, beauty, and wholeness, but they have also been vilified as places of isolation, ignorance, violence, and abjection, a both/and perception that makes the rural a particularly important hauntological trope. Attuned to the cycles of nature and the way the seasons affect life in the country, the project has spanned over eight years of delving into the 'unsettled'.

In addition to the blog and the books *The Marks Upon the Land, The Corn Mother, Straying from the Pathways, The Shildam Hall Tapes, Cathode Ray and Celluloid Hinterlands, Lost Transmissions*, and *Wandering Through Spectral Fields*, A Year in the Country released themed music compilations containing songs and sounds by other like-minded hauntological artists focusing on a central theme that reflects an aspect of the project covering rural, urban, media, and technological memories. Two of the most fascinating releases are *The Restless Field* (2017) and *The Quietened Village* (2016). Both releases are exquisitely packaged tributes to haunted places and the myriad of ghosts that still exist there. *The Restless Field* explores the murky, ominous hidden areas of the countryside that are imprinted with both the wondrous and tragic events that occurred there. The spectres of historical conflicts, struggles, protests, resistance, escape, and miracle are expressed in songs by artists such as Field Lines Cartographer, Vic Mars, Bare Bones, Grey Frequency, Endurance, Listening Center, and Depatterning.

The Quietened Village is a reflection on the lost, displaced, abandoned, and disappeared rural settlements, homes, and hamlets that have dropped off the map and become ghost towns. The English countryside has many abandoned as well as submerged villages, swallowed by the sea, reclaimed by nature, lonely, desolate spots, their inhabitants long gone but their fears and desires left behind. Artists such as The Rowan Amber Mill, Cosmic Neighbourhood, Sproatly Smith, The Soulless Party, Time Attendant, The Heartwood Institute, Keith Seatman, and Polypores memorialize these forgotten pasts, absent presents, and lost futures. The music on both compilations runs the gamut from unsettling electronics, tape manipulation, folk songs, found sounds, drones, ambient, trance, and pop music. Other labels such as Folklore Tapes, Finders Keepers, Woodford Halse, Clay Pipe Music, Castles in Space, Modern Aviation, Whinny Moor, Trunk Records, Buried Treasure, and Obuh Records also document spectral histories, alternate times, neglected subcultures, parallel worlds, and haunted sites, but none did it with such thoroughness and panache as A Year in the Country.

Another multimedia hauntological project is Andy Sharp's English Heretic. Self-described as 'a creative occult organisation dedicated to the reification of malefic energy spectres and the adumbration of a modern qliphoth', English Heretic unearths the ritual histories and magickal geography of pop culture, focusing on haunting occurrences of Carl Jung's synchronicity that connect the high and the low, the sacred and the profane, the living and the dead. Sharp commemorates these strange confluences with plaques that locate and historicize the uncanny connections and strange doubling in the actual places that resonate with these energies. Using music, lectures, performances, literary journalism, and field reports from the outer limits, the English Heretic agenda encompasses witchy electronics, folk skulduggery, absurdist wit, and preserving the weird currents of British supernatural history. And yet English Heretic is not only focused on the marvels of a distant age as more contemporary alchemists like Michael Reeves, J G Ballard, C S Lewis, The Beatles, and Iain Sinclair are connected in the cosmic continuum that unites past, present, and future as overlapping, recursive realities. Site specific musical/literary/visual/spoken word workings as well as artifacts such as *Temple Of Remembrance* and *The Sacred Geography of British Cinema* (2005), *Mondo Paranoia* (2013), *The Underworld Service* (2014), *Wish You Were Heretic* (2017), and *Summer of Blood* (2017) invoke, exorcize, and form new zeitgeists from across the spectrum.

The most recognizable hauntological music label is Ghost Box Records, a group of similar minded artists and groups inspired by rural occult horror, 1950s and sixties sci-fi, weird 1970s television, and the post-WWII promise of a better future through science, education, and socialism. They seek to recreate the odd mixture of the supernatural and the technological that became strange bedfellows in 1970s pop culture. Ghost Box Records mimics an institutionalized stance towards the paranormal and the weird, as if they are music scientists/researchers/technicians attempting to contact the other side through sound, documenting the ghosts of yesterday, today, and tomorrow. Ghost Box Records was founded in 2003 by graphic designer Julian House and architect Jim Jupp, who shared an interest in vintage electronic instruments and library music (music created by anonymous musicians to be used uncredited in films and TV shows) from the 1960s and 1970s. Much like Iain Sinclair, Peter Ackroyd, and Alan Moore, House and Jupp try to rediscover a hidden, lost England, a country and culture caught between a refined, rigid past and a future that promised much but delivered very little of what was expected by its citizens. Beneath, above, and next to these two poles exists the Ghost Box universe. The label has cemented its links with hauntological music not only through its stable of artists, but also through its collaborations with such hauntological pioneers as John Foxx, Broadcast, and Drew Mulholland. Ghost Box Records celebrates modernism, pop art, Nigel Kneale, *The Prisoner*, space age bachelor pad music, Moog mood albums, horror film soundtracks, music from educational film strips, *Doctor Who*, televised exposés on the supernatural and occult, the tales of Lovecraft, Machen, and Blackwood, local folk legends, and terrifying children's shows.

A crucial influence on the Ghost Box Records sound is the BBC Radiophonic Workshop, a collective of electronic musicians, engineers, and composers who composed incidental music, opening themes, sound effects, and atmosphere for the BBC's science fiction and horror television programs from the 1950s to the 1990s. The work produced by the BBC Radiophonic Workshop still sounds otherworldly even after fifty years, and the blend of awe and terror that their compositions provoked in viewers of the *Quatermass* serials and *Doctor Who* is actively pursued by many artists on the Ghost Box roster, attempting to invoke the same haunted déjà vu for Ghost Box's contemporary listeners. The music of the Ghost Box collective acts both as an aural time machine and a sonic Ouija board, portals to half remembered pasts, imagined futures, and spectres that lurk at the intersection of pop culture, science for the masses, and the occult. It is not only the music that creates these experiences but also the album art and aesthetics of the record label that pull on the memory strings of a certain generation of Briton.

Both Jupp and House are visual designers and so the look of Ghost Box's releases are very much part and parcel of creating the feeling of receiving an artifact from a disjointed time, an alternate 1970/1980s. There is a uniformity to the appearance of many of the albums and singles, as if they were all part of a series of esoteric paperbacks, educational guides, or textbooks for a ritualistic science class. (The covers of Penguin Books' Pelican line of informative socio/scientific/political/cultural/public health treatises on diverse subjects such as *The Stagnant Society, Derelict Britain, The Menstrual Cycle, Communities in Britain: Social Life in Town and Country, Changing Man's Behavior, The Hidden Persuaders, Electronic Computers, America's Receding Future*, and *The Strange Case of Pot*, aimed at a mass market, seem to be the aesthetic touchstone for the covers of early Ghost Box releases.) Ghost Box Records is not simply releasing music, but attempting to create a parallel, alternative world, both oddly familiar and hauntingly strange, reaching back to both primal and pop culture collective unconsciousness.

Three groups are the cornerstone of Ghost Box Records: Jim Jupp's Belbury Poly, Julian House's The Focus Group, and Cate Brooks' The Advisory Circle. Belbury Poly takes its name from a town in C S Lewis' *That Hideous Strength*, which details a government plot to experiment on the inhabitants of a town called Belbury inspired by the idea of 'the abolition of man'. The use of the term 'poly' comes from the belief in the democratization of knowledge and science through the practice of the polytechnic college. Incorporating both the beneficial potentialities and ominous control of institutions in its name, Belbury Poly is the Ghost Box Records group that is the most methodical and eclectic in its myriad uses of diverse sound, instrumentation, and musical genres: a daftly eccentric archeologist of the past but of the future too. Albums such as *The Willows* (2005, a reference to Lovecraft's favorite weird tale by Algernon Blackwood), *The Owl's Map* (2006, referencing the Alan Garner novel and TV series *The Owl Service*), *The Belbury Tales* (2012), *New Ways Out* (2016), *The Gone Away* (2020), and *The Path* (2023). Belbury Poly takes an academic approach to the strange sounds, alien moods, and jaunty tones that are explored and analyzed, almost as if a professor of hauntology was presenting musical proof for simultaneous time-transcending experiences. With each release, Belbury Poly get more expansive in their geographies, pulling in more and more archival allusions and intonations. Vocal samples, electropop, analogue synthesizers, rural folk, progressive rock, and processed reverberations help Belbury Poly interweave the ancient and modern, the dark and the light, as the listener drifts between two worlds and two modes, never quite settling in one or the other. Jupp is also responsible for *Ouroborindra* (2005), released under the Eric Zann alter ego, a droning, dark ambient symphony of Lovecraftian/Machenian madness, recorded, I believe, in an abandoned apartment building on the Rue d'Auseil.

Julian House's The Focus Group uses similar types of hauntological sounds and textures but instead of the lingering, uncanny submersion of Belbury Poly, The Focus Group's splice-a-delica constructs giddy, anarchic collages and montages, desynchronous sounds to conjure up disquietingly beautiful compositions, a familiarly quirky sense of otherness. Much more fragmented than Belbury Poly, The Focus Group's music shifts from sound to sound, ghost to ghost, and time period to time period effortlessly, sometimes in the same song. Referencing the occult and Euro-horror explosion of the late 1960s/early 1970s as well as the more obtuse children's television programs of the same era, The Focus Group digs deeper into the shadows cast by the hippie dream that crumbled into the punk nihilism of the late 1970s. Non-musical sounds and sources often take precedence over melody, but never overstay their welcome as they drift in and out of the mix like half-remembered dreams. The Focus Group's releases such as *Sketches and Spells* (2004), *Hey Let Loose Your Love* (2005), *The Elektrik Karousel* (2013), and *Stop-Motion Happening with the Focus Groop* (2017) offer dark surrealistic psychedelia collaged with joyful electronic noises, as splintered as his design work for Broadcast, Primal Scream, Stereolab, and Can. Appropriating both high and low culture, The Focus Group's masterpiece is *We are All Pan's People* (2007), a ritualistic kaleidoscope of carnival-esque lullabies and pastoral idylls that equates trashy TV dancers from *Top of the Pops* with the frenzied, body-rending ritual of Dionysian bacchanalia.

The final 'group' of the Ghost Box Records trinity is Jon Brooks' The Advisory Circle. (Jon Brooks is an alias for artist Cate Brooks.) While most of the label's roster tiptoe into the darkness at the heart of British culture, The Advisory Circle dives headfirst into the austere and menacing with the use of government warnings, noise, and mechanical drones. The Advisory Circle exudes sprightly authoritarianism: the juxtaposition of bouncy electronics, strict spoken commands, imperative titles, and firm rhythms offers an astounding sense of modernist anxiety and future shock dwelling underneath simple tones: banal façades can often hide 'benevolent' totalitarian control. The Advisory Circle's ghosts are neither quaint Victorian spirits nor Carnaby Street swinging spectres, but, rather, 1984-esque trapped revenants, much like the victims of nuclear holocaust whose screams reverberate in the haunted woods of Nigel Kneale's *The Road.* Releases such as 2011's *As the Crow Flies* (its cover invoking the strange opening aviary credits for seventies children's shows *The Owl Service* and the second season of *Shadows*), *From Out Here* (2014), *Ways of Seeing* (2018), and *Full Circle* (2022) dismantle any notion that either a futurist technological utopia or an ancient pastoral paradise can offer an escape from reality as both concepts have been rendered obsolete and futile in the face of post-humanist indifference and a heartless but endearing machine pulse.

viii. Conclusions

> 'Because it has always already begun, representation therefore has no end. But one can conceive of the closure of that which is without end.'
> —Jacques Derrida, *Specters of Marx: The State of the Debt, the Work of Mourning and the New International*

AS JACQUES DERRIDA wondered if an autopsy needed to be performed on communism, one has to wonder if hauntology itself has become a ghost, a nostalgic, spent force merely haunting pop culture and academia as a hip term to drop, no longer a vital critical field of inquiry, but, rather, a fading phantom. Critics claim that hauntology is actually culturally conservative and artistically retrograde; hauntology's yearning for the 'innocence' of the past and the nostalgia for promised futures vilify necessary progress as if the original sins of change and innovation have once again exiled us from the Garden of Eden. With the suicide of its leading thinker and proponent Mark Fisher in 2017, one may worry whether, without a specific direction and a spokesperson, hauntology will stay topical and on the academic/cultural radar with so many current, past, and future critical frameworks, lenses, theories, and philosophies competing for adherents? Fisher had done work on the metaphor of mourning as well as mindful exiting as a form of political, social, cultural, and economic resistance, a conscious refusal to accept what globalization and consumerism have constructed as the only reality possible in the twenty-first century. Fisher's body of work is heavy with personal, cultural, societal, and historical spectres, but at the heart of these uncanny manifestations is a cautious optimism that if we can imagine, dream, and create visions of futures yet to come, there's still hope. Because its central metaphors of ghosts and hauntings are so universal and have informed so many beliefs and forms of expression, as long as the spectral is still a topic of discussion and fascination, hauntology can be assured that its symbolism will not go away any time soon. As new academic movements push hauntology to the fringes, perhaps that may be the best thing for it. Maybe that's where hauntology belongs: on the periphery, along the borderlands, speaking for the abandoned, the forgotten, the lost, the neglected, the dead but not entirely gone.

Memory and history have become more and more contentious in the Digital Age, an irony in the sense that never have human beings been filmed, documented, mapped, and recorded more than in the twenty-first century. Do we even need memory anymore with Google, YouTube, iCloud, and iPhones that allow users to take almost endless photos and videos, stored forever in a virtual cloud? (One would hope for something more stable and material than billowy condensed water vapor to hold onto all that important data but diaphanous metaphors seem to be apt when discussing both memories and our ability to confine them.) The private emotional, psychological, and aesthetic processes that were once thought necessary to experience nostalgia and deep memory seem to so easily be replaced by the endless deluge of communicable memes and 'Throwback Thursdays' that have infected social media and online culture.

With the 'Fourth Industrial Revolution', 'the Metaverse', 'The Great Reset', post-singularity, and crypto-economies as the driving ideologies of twenty-first-century globalization, issues such as increasing time/space compression, 'the eternal now', 'capitalist realism', machine consciousness, and the commodification of virtual lifestyles make the questions that hauntology raises perhaps even more crucial now than in the aftermath of the fall of the Berlin Wall (which opened up a separate current of hauntological study: the crumbling, abandoned remnants of the Soviet Union's lost socialist utopian future as can be heard on x.y.r.'s mesmerizing *Memory Tapes*). Will nostalgia be a fruitful defensive reaction against post-singularity? If it's just another capitalist scheme that trades on banality and cliché, then probably not. Hauntology is the memory that works both ways, as the Red Queen in *Through the Looking-Glass* so astutely and ambiguously observed.

The main current of utopian thinking in the early twenty-first century is 'Longtermism', an ultra-utilitarian techno imperium concerned with engineering 'posthumans' and 'digital people', notions that seem right out of the most depressing seventies dystopian sci-fi flick you could ever dream of.[23] The harmless sounding 'chatbots' seem poised to take away every vestige of creativity and authentic communication we have left. With the advent of AI-generated stories, novels, music, poems, and paintings, are emotional attachment and nostalgia still necessary elements to creative expression in the twenty-first century? Do virtual, mechanized, algorithmic 'artists' feel trauma or nostalgia? Will posthuman art be haunted by ghosts or just digital glitches that can be 'fixed' and then erased? When the spectres of memory, longing, and lost futures are no longer conjured and materialized though creativity, where will they go?

23 The company DeepBrain AI offers a full immersion into AI living: 'Here at DeepBrain, we believe that artificial intelligence can help focus and accelerate the growth of every talented individual. Technology can never replace people, but rather assist them to focus on maximizing their personal capabilities. We only exist to advance the quality of human life by creating user-friendly AI systems.' Their services include 'Conversational AI Humans', 'Hyper-Realistic Digital Humans', 'Full-Body Avatar with Gestures', and 'Versatile AI Human Styles' to align with your business and corporate needs.

With the internet, social media, and virtual information deluge only increasing in the twenty-first century, the flattening of all experiences to the same level, the same feel, the same value, and the same effect, one must wonder if the production of memory and nostalgia, the very acts of remembering and reminiscing, will dissipate and atrophy like an unused vestigial organ. And what of the ghosts that accompany recollection, reflection, and recall? Instead of forgetting the ghosts of trauma, fear, hope, and otherness, the social, cultural, political, economic, and historical hauntings of the past seem more crucial now than ever, and so these spectres are more in need of investigation and interaction than, conceivably, when Derrida wrote his visionary essay in 1989. Perhaps, at this point in history, we are at the moment prophesized by Willie Brown's Future Blues: "Can't tell my future, and I can't tell my past/Lord, it seems like every minute, sure gonna be my last." Just as the materiality of wealth and power were re-spatialized and materialized into new forms during the continuous bourgeois/industrial revolutions, so it is happening again for the auto-technocrat/digital/post-singularity revolution. Presence, whether physical, material, virtual, or geographical, has also become a contested mode of being and authenticity, and so the ability to haunt, to dwell, and to be seen, heard, remembered, and acknowledged are now acts of resistance.

Perhaps what hauntology has identified for us is that nostalgia is not a one-size-fits-all experience. There's the nostalgia that comes from the inevitable passage of time and then there's the nostalgia that comes from our own past failures, mistakes, hopes, and reveries. One is felt through mourning and yearning, the other through remorse and regret. One is an existential burden, the other a personal one. These ghosts come in all shapes and sizes. Then there is the marketing strategy/ideological scheme that uses a generalized yet strategic visual discourse to signify a collective nostalgia that can be re-experienced through buying certain products or services. Of course, this nostalgia is ultimately unsatisfying due to its depersonalized origin and lack of any authentic emotional connection to an individual. Thus, nostalgia becomes just another reified commodity in the global market: bought, sold, possessed, appreciating and depreciating like stocks and futures. These aren't ghosts because they never really lived.

Unlike most academic movements, hauntology has benefited from being adopted (albeit in a loose form) by popular culture, either explicitly or implicitly. Hauntology's flexibility in being applied to both the personal and the collective, the micro and macro, the ghosts of the individual and the ghosts of history, make it a framework that allows for multiple applications and experiences. The anachronistic aesthetics of the found footage genre are being appropriated into the amorphous characteristics of the hauntological film: witness the ambient, analogue horror of Kyle Edward Ball's hypnogogic reverie *Skinamarink* (2022)[24] where hazy, refracted childhood trauma, impaired perception, and shadowy leaps of time and imagination are just as terrifying as supernatural entities or unkillable killers. The cultural genres of folk horror and the 'urban wyrd' have found much crossover and convergence with hauntology as artists from one area often borrow from, innovate, and crosspollinate into others. In particular, Mark Jenkin's 2022 *Enys Men* eerily combines landscape (a resonating megalith), personal and historical trauma (ghostly images of ordeals and sufferings), and disjointed yet cyclical time patterns in a potently atmospheric film. The concept that unites hauntology, found footage, the urban wyrd, and folk horror is the shared practice of finding, unearthing, and revealing the lost, the forgotten, the ignored, and the repressed. Even hauntological satires and tributes such as the television show *Look Around You*, Richard Littler's *Scarfolk* project, *Scarred for Life*, *The Haunted Generation*, *The Occultaria of Albion*, J W Bohm's *This Wounded Island* series published by the 'Institute of Liminal Landscape Studies', and Agnes Carew's *In Place of Memory* have emerged through the ectoplasm.

24 While *Skinamarink* might be the most high-profile ambient horror film, it is with Jane Schoenbrun's *We're All Going to the World's Fair* (2022) and *I Saw the TV Glow* (2024), that the genre has found its auteur.

Perhaps in the posthuman era, cultural history itself will becor fully hauntological, marked not only by what was accomplished, b also haunted by what slipped through our fingers. Jóhann Jóhann: son's austerely elegiac 2017 film adaptation of Olaf Stapledon's nove of cosmic tragedy *Last and First Men* (1930) is a cinematic memoria for epochs of vanished futures, demonstrating not so much the futility of humanity, but, rather, a requiem for the unrealized potentials of our entire species. Jóhannsson brilliantly illustrates these lonely, eroded ideals through his eerie focus on Spomenik monuments (futurist utopian public works in the former Yugoslavia that celebrated those who sacrificed their lives in WWII to get their comrades to the impending communist paradise), that are now abstract commemorations for our doomed kind. Sadly, this would be Jóhannsson's only film as a director; the multitalented composer died only a year after his film's debut (another tragic loss of an artist on the verge of exploring new creative expression).

Although hauntology has been largely a UK-based movement, the US-centered phenomenon of 'dead malls', a Ballardian concept of abandoned, decaying suburban shopping centers haunted by material capital and antiquated consumerism, is a major interest in the urban geography field. A genre of electronic music called Mallsoft layers samples of smooth jazz, Muzak, advertising jingles, and infomercials, reverberating to the ghosts of acid-washed teenagers hanging out at the food court trying prefab sushi for the first time: a piped-in, extinct soundscape that is as immersive as it is generic. Weirdcore is an internet cultural movement that celebrates an antiquated, lo-fi, poor quality, over-compressed, amateurish visual aesthetic harkening back to the sense of vague innocence and innovative bizarreness of the earliest days of the internet.

In the musical arena, the genre of hauntological folk connects moody post-rock, electronic instrumentation, slurred hip hop beats, and analytical production with the evocative content and gloomy feelings of eroding folk traditions, customs, and landscapes in such works as .O. Rang's *Fields and Waves* (1996), Hood's *Rustic Houses, Forlorn Valleys* (1997) and *The Cycle of Days and Seasons* (1998), Misty Dixon's *Iced To Mode* (2003), The Declining Winter's *Haunt the Upper Hallways* (2009), Mamiffer's *The World Unseen* (2016), Juana Molina's *Halo* (2017), Charles Vaughan's *Pylon Reveries* (2017), and Wooden Tapes' *Music from Another Place* (2023). The cryptic 'Gespensterland' cadre of artists sing in their native German about the eerie, the phantasmic, and disappearing folk traditions, caught between a mythic Romantic past and an uncertain future. Their wistful, nostalgic music expresses Teutonic longing against a backdrop of contemporary electronics, old-fashioned instruments, and unpredictable sound poltergeists. Chiptune, a musical style that uses the medium of obsolete 8-bit CPUs and démodé handheld gaming consoles, seeks to resurrect the sounds of antiquated video game soundtracks, discarded audio programs, and outmoded computer models in order to create the feeling of exploring a lost world of misfit electronics and nostalgic gaming.

The horror television genre is also starting to include more explicit aspects of hauntology in its creations. Analog horror, a subgenre of the found footage film, broke into the mainstream with 2022's *Archive 81*, a highly entertaining but intellectually shallow Netflix series that presents a postmodern mélange of urban wyrd tropes borrowed from *The Seventh Victim*, *Rosemary's Baby*, and *The Sentinel*, *Blair Witch*-esque found footage camcorder recording aesthetics, and hauntological clichés including anachronistic technology, degrading data, ghostly memories, glitchy time anomalies, and the two-sided coin of science and the supernatural. Unfortunately, *Archive 81* also adds snarky humor, stereotypical horror character traumas, and clichéd nineties nostalgia to dumb down a potentially innovative addition to the hauntological TV category.

Hauntology might even be coming to the usually vapid, virtual halls of celebrity culture, as it has been reported that the MTV Video Music Awards, Teen Choice Awards, People's Choice Awards, and Latin American Music Awards winner (and Guinness World Record holder) Demi Lovato sang a lament for Carmen, a ghostly presence that haunts a brothel in the abandoned Arizona ghost town of Vulture City. According to legend, Carmen was a sex worker at the brothel who was exploited by the men in the town during the Arizona Gold Rush of 1863. The reason why Lovato sang for the spectral woman was right in line with the tenets of hauntology: "Oh, I get that a lot. She has trauma. That's why she doesn't like men. I have trauma, too, so I feel you and I get it."[25]

Hauntology's emphasis on temporality and spatiality may also encourage academics and artists interested in postmodern chronology and critical geography to utilize it as a way to dig deeper into the past and insist on a future. The spectres of space and place, of past, present, and future, will continue to haunt all of us, and yet this is not necessarily a negative or pessimistic experience; perhaps the need to listen to, confront, and exorcize our personal and collective ghosts and the nostalgia that calls forth such ghosts is the only way to heal personal and collective traumas, to practice resistance, to find justice, and to progress into a more empathetic, ethical, and equal way of being. Hauntology suggests it's never too late to identify the perpetrators of historical crimes, address the sufferings of the exploited, and make some sort of amends in order to heal and move forward in a just, conscientious, and inclusive way. Perhaps what hauntological art can best do is offer some sort of recompense to those who were traumatized and forgotten, uncovering, recalling, and preserving memories, people, places, times, ideas, and events that help us live with and learn from the ghosts of yesterday, today, and tomorrow. Hauntology recognizes and affirms the humanity of all historic causes and future solutions. The echoes of futures past and the spectres of historical and personal trauma remind us individually and collectively of the unfulfilled promises that democracy can still deliver: paying it forward and back. Hopefully, by letting the dead speak and listening to what they

25 Unidentified interviewer with Demi Lovato (September 30, 2021), https://www.youtube.com/watch?v=vnfXeffcdCM [Last accessed June 3, 2024]

say, we can all live better, more just, lives in a more equitable future. Nostalgia for this kind of life and way of living is much more than naïve sentimental yearning: it is the stuff that futures are made of.

> 'But they never last, the golden days. And it can be sad, the sun in the afternoon, can't it? Yes, it can be sad, the afternoon sun, sad and frightening.' —Jean Rhys, *Good Morning, Midnight*

Interview: James McKeown (Hawksmoor)

JAMES MCKEOWN IS an artist of many names and many talents. Recording under various monikers as Hawksmoor, Frugal Puritan, The Dead Astronaut, and his own name, McKeown's electronic, acid folk, psych rock, and dream pop works reach across genres and atmospheres, combining the melancholic futurism of hauntology, the progressive music of the sixties and seventies counterculture, and the ambient presence of psychogeography. McKeown's masterpiece is *Hawksmoor*, a moody sonic mapping of the occult patterns formed by the stark Dionysiac architecture and sacred geometry of Nicholas Hawksmoor's six churches. Urban explorer and sound alchemist, James McKeown is poised to enter the world of 'pagantronica' with the single The Boy From Space being released by the Library of the Occult label, a full-length album *Saturnalia* also out on Library of the Occult, and *Head Coach* on Spun Out Of Control, inspired by the druidic, Solstice-referencing layout of Milton Keynes. 2023's *Telepathic Heights* is his most hauntological release yet, heralding a different kind of space age, inner and outer journeys that send us back as well as forward in time, emboldened yet forlorn. His fascinating releases can be found at https://hawksmoor.bandcamp.com/, https://spunoutofcontrol.bandcamp.com/, and https://soundsoftheuniverse.com/product/telepathic-heights.

William Burns: What are your key TV/film/music memories that you think helped form your artistic identity?

James McKeown: Musically, from my childhood, early eighties, I remember feeling an eerie sense of dread from hearing my Dad playing Eleanor Rigby, as he was a big Beatles fan. Also seeing the cover to King Crimson's *In the Court of the Crimson King* and being quite freaked out yet fascinated. Film would be *Star Wars* as I'm of that generation, but also things like *The Snowman* and even the Raymond Briggs nuclear fallout cartoon, *When the Wind Blows*. As the result of a quite traumatic childhood, I was a very serious, deep-thinking kid.

TV-wise, although I'm not sure if I ever actually saw it, maybe it was just the trailer? There was a Channel 4 adaptation of *Nineteen Eighty-Four* that seemed to lodge in my brain, also watching the first Space Shuttle launch and, later, the adaption of John Christopher's *The Tripods* really stuck in my head, as did the many public information films/advertisements warning children not to get close to power lines or play on railway tracks etc. The impact of wider technological advances at the time also made an impression — the first home computers etc.

Another major influence as a kid (and now) that really taps into the whole English, folk horror, and a sense of pagan strangeness: *Watership Down*, from the melancholy of the Bright Eyes theme to the strange animation with the sun and the 'prince of a thousand enemies' section. Also, it's pretty violent and visceral for a kid's film as I remember.

In the 1980s the British artist Kit Williams produced a book called *Masquerade*. It was a kind of treasure hunt which, through solving clues in the pictures in the book, would lead to the discovery of a golden hare buried in a secret location. The images in the book are extremely evocative, and what I would now associate not only with Mark Fisher's aesthetic category of 'weird and eerie', but also with what has become known as the folk horror genre.

WB: Your work is very connected to urban landscapes. Does the environment of Bristol find its way into your music?

JM: Absolutely. I have lived in Bristol all my life and many years of it on the outskirts near the countryside, yet in an area where the path of suburbia has gradually eroded away elements of nature with the progress of expanded housing, shopping centers, and transport links. The sound of the M5 (a large, busy motorway) is always in earshot too and I love the juxtaposition of nature and the man-made, walking under the M5 bridges that span rivers, fields, and trees. Equally, there are unofficial landmarks, such as the telecommunications tower that is situated in an area called Purdown that looks over the city. I have always been fascinated with urban decay too, and in the early 2010s got into urban exploration, deliberately seeking out abandoned buildings, churches, old hospitals, and asylums. I enjoyed the sense of danger and forbidden trespass and got some interesting photos and a headful of ideas. Gareth E Rees (www.unofficialbritain.com) is a good insight into this sort of thing.

WB: You utilize a variety of pseudonyms (Hawksmoor, The Dead Astronaut, Frugal Puritan) in releasing your work. Why? Are there aesthetic differences found in the works of each pseudonym?

JM: Frugal Puritan was the first project released under a pseudonym. It was kind of tied into the urban exploration and I took lots of pictures of churches, particularly those built in a postwar modernist style. I was a bit frustrated with the pace of creativity of the band I was in at the time and wanted to make some music that was a parody/homage to Christian Acid-Folk music — often released as slightly unhinged, hubristic, amateur private pressings — and I came up with an EP of four tracks and put it on Bandcamp. A label called Folk Police in Manchester were interested and suggested I expand it into a full album, which I did. The pinnacle of success for this was Jarvis Cocker, who had a show on BBC6 Music, playing a track and Stuart Maconie on BBC6 playing a track on his show, *Freak Zone*. I've managed to get sporadic BBC airplay for nearly all my projects, which all feels like a major achievement often with little or no label backing, budget, or PR company.

The Dead Astronaut — once again named after a Ballard novel — was a very personal, melodic, and melancholic, introspective set of songs, primarily written as a form of therapy for a very difficult time in my life. I assembled a group of musicians including a cellist and trumpet player and 'produced' the album. It was picked up by a Dutch label who I think slightly misunderstood where I was coming from, and the album did absolutely nothing. Needless to say, they weren't interested in the follow-up either, which I then self released and, despite one track being played on BBC6 Music (a tribute to David Bowie who had recently died), I had lost all enthusiasm for the project and songwriting in general, in the traditional sense. It was the second TDA album on which I started to play with the Moog, which began to creep into the sound, recording, and production and made me want to explore the possibilities further. Which then led to Hawksmoor.

WB: Do you feel there are unifying themes that run through all your work?

JM: A sense of loss, melancholy, and hopefully beauty. In many ways I always want to make the most heartrending, sweetest, beautiful music I can. Which is a balancing act, as too much sugar destroys the intention. That said, I think my lo-fi techniques and lack of musicianship probably provide the counterbalance.

WB: What are your musical influences and how do you incorporate them into your work?

JM: This would be a bit of a long answer to go into in any serious detail, so I'll simplify it to genres: Krautrock, prog, sixties psych, post-punk, electronica, and one or two bands or artists that deserve a standalone name check; Pink Floyd, Talk Talk, Kraftwerk, Bowie, Kate Bush, Terry Riley, Eno, Joni Mitchell, Alice Coltrane.

WB: Do you feel any connection to the hauntological genre and its philosophy?

JM: Absolutely. The problem now is that the term has been corrupted and almost commodified into a brand, as nearly always happens with ideas in music, and has now strayed into pastiche and parody, so that anyone with a modular synth and a few samples is 'hauntological'. Taking it back to Derrida's original concept — and let's not forget this was a linguistic play on ontology — hauntology is about the *lack* of being, the 'uncanny' and strange, and I hope that in parts some of my music taps into this aspect either sonically or in the themes and concepts behind the music. Mark Fisher's critical theory and essays in *The Weird and The Eerie* give the best descriptions of hauntology across the arts, be that literature, film, or music.

WB: *Sublime Knight Elect* has a cosmic and mystical feel to it, almost Lovecraftian. Are you interested in the occult, the supernatural, and metaphysics?

JM: Aspects of all of this, yes. Of my earlier material, this is the only one I think still stands up. The title *Sublime Knight Elect* is a Masonic term that relates to a rank of Freemasonry. Musically, in many ways it was a precursor to the ideas I would later exploit thematically in Hawksmoor material. It's all instrumental and uses a palette of acoustic and electric guitars, tape manipulation, delay effects, and even Brian Eno's Oblique Strategy cards to make creative choices. The inspiration was very much rooted in alchemy, astronomy, and local Neolithic ceremonial sites such as the stone circle at Avebury and Silbury Hill. It's probably the only material from this time that I still feel really stands up, and could almost be re-issued under the Hawksmoor name.

WB: I first became aware of your work with 2018's *Hawksmoor* album. It's the perfect soundtrack to reading Iain Sinclair, Peter Ackroyd's novel, and Alan Moore and Eddie Campbell's *From Hell*. What was your inspiration for this release? How did you approach recording it?

JM: The interest in *Hawksmoor* initially came from Iain Sinclair's *Lud Heat*, which is a sort of diary, prose, and long-form poem about his time working as a gardener in London churchyards as a way to supplement his income as a burgeoning writer. It also features a drawing which maps the strange cartography that links the six

Hawksmoor-designed churches in the form of a loose pentagram across London. This book was the inspiration behind Peter Ackroyd's novel and once I had read that too I knew I wanted to make some music that used this idea as a concept. I approached the recording by restricting myself to using the Moog Sub37 to produce all the initial sounds: pads, drum sounds, fx, and melodies. I then began to build the tracks up and added some real live bass and a few software synths which I then ran out to an old four-track tape machine to give them more analogue tone, hiss, and character. I was thinking along the lines of William Basinski's *Disintegration Loops*. I worked quite quickly, over the Christmas break, and then eventually took the results into a studio to mix in early 2018.

WB: Did you do any field research at the actual sites of Hawksmoor's churches?

JM: Yes, I spent a day tracing the six Hawksmoor churches in London, mainly on foot and taking photographs. My favorites were Christ Church, Spitalfields, and St Annes, Limehouse as it also has a pyramid in the grounds. It was a very long day as they are not closely located, but I'm glad I did it!

WB: Is the field of psychogeography of interest to you? If so, how do you translate this experience of place into your music?

JM: Much like hauntology, psychogeography, or the idea of it, has also been a bit exploited of late, although I would say that the two are intrinsically linked. As previously mentioned, about my love of urban exploration, I do enjoy walking and exploring and many of the projects I have created as Hawksmoor (most specifically the debut) reflect a sense of place or are inspired by the concept of a specific location or the application of Guy Debord's 'dérive' theory to explore a new place. I have just finished a new album that links neatly with this, relating to the pagan/druidic links associated with the 'new town' of Milton Keynes. The town planners constructed the city using the concept of solstice alignment and there are points in the city that reflect this through monuments and street names.

WB: *On Prescription* focuses on the clinical and medical obsessions that have taken over the world's attention. How has the pandemic and the social, political, economic, and scientific consequences of current affairs affected your work and its aesthetic?

JM: Well, in truth it wasn't about the pandemic; it was about an issue much closer to home. Here's the liner notes that explain the background — partnering with Spun Out Of Control we raised £650 for Cancer Research UK.

> When someone very close to me became seriously ill they asked me, in uncharacteristically macabre humour, if my next album would be 'the cancer album'. I dismissed this outright mainly because I couldn't find it in me to trivialise the situation and was too wrapped up in fear and sadness to even think of music. The creativity did eventually creep in from an unexpected angle. Drugs. More specifically drugs, *On Prescription*. The strange paradox of chemotherapy is that the medicine that will hopefully mend you, initially becomes a source of terrible illness. You need to get sick to get well. This contradictory remedy also comes bundled with a variety of mind and body bending side effects — uppers, downers, lose-your-mind-playgrounders. The science of Oncology is, frankly, mind-blowing and the cocktail of super strength pharmaceuticals administered is unfathomable, further compounded by their weird and mostly unpronounceable brand names. Creatively this was the trigger. I could only justify making an album with this as my source of inspiration if in doing so there was going to be some greater utility from my creative exploitation, and so decided that if the music could be enjoyed by others, then any profits made should be directed to charity.

WB: *Methods of Dreaming* and *On Prescription* were both released on cassette by the label Spun Out Of Control. Why this medium? Do you have a preference in terms of how your music is released and experienced?

JM: Spun Out Of Control are primarily a boutique cassette label. I liked their aesthetic as they have some interesting artwork which is in the style of 1980s VHS tapes or film posters and Italian giallo film artwork. People tend to listen digitally through Bandcamp but like to have a physical artifact to collect too, so this is a neat way to present it. I don't have any specific affinity to cassette and have also released Hawksmoor material on CD and vinyl, although cassette can add an extra sonic quality to some music, particularly with albums like *Methods of Dreaming* which has a more overtly psychedelic and ambient feel.

WB: How did your collaboration with The Heartwood Institute happen? Do you feel an affinity with their aesthetic smash-up of folk horror, supernatural science, and hauntology?

JM: Definitely. Jonathan and I hooked up over Twitter and began discussing the possibility of a collaboration. We began by sharing files and playing a musical game of 'exquisite corpse', swapping ideas and sketches until we had a body of work which we had begun to fit around the concept of Ballard's *Concrete Island*, and it seemed to work well as an imaginary soundtrack.

WB: Your releases *Concrete Island* and *Crystal World* suggest the influence of J G Ballard. What is it about Ballard's work that you feel has had an effect on your music?

JM: I am influenced by Ballard and do feel a great affinity with his writing. Something taps into the sense of the banal and melancholic British suburban life, but through a slightly strange lens, and it is that warped subtlety which makes it even more unsettling and goes back to the notion of the 'uncanny'. This, often combined with the protagonist's sense of mental collapse in the face of day-to-day reality, makes a heady concoction which I find irresistible in his fiction. Ballard was a genius and a modern-day soothsayer in his predictions of society, politics, and technology, particularly in a world where we now live and determine our lives through our smartphones.

WB: What would your dream project/collaboration be?

JM: I am a huge fan of Ben Wheatley's films and would love to work on a soundtrack commission.

WB: I love your live release on the Sleep Fuse label. How important is performing live to your creativity?

JM: Thanks! I find it quite stressful to be honest and I don't feel that I've really arrived at a set-up that I feel completely satisfied with for live shows. I don't want to just play out a set from a laptop, I like to be a bit more musically 'hands on' and creative when playing live. That set was good, but I would like to capture a better live recording with a refined set-up at some point and will aim to play live again when completely safe to do so, post-pandemic.

WB: What is in the future for James McKeown?

JM: Finish my degree and see where that takes me next, into further study or aspects of academia. Continue making music with the aim of collaborating on a real soundtrack, or as part of an art exhibition or installation, and possibly write something in some form too. My current fascination is with [monastic order] Aghori sadhus, which may turn into musical inspiration?!

James McKeown Discography

Hawksmoor

201984 (2018)
Recorded Live at Environmental Studies Research #1, The Cube, Bristol, 7th September 2019 (2019)
Methods of Dreaming (2020)
On Prescription (2021)
Concrete Island (with The Heartwood Institute) (2021)
Crystal World (2021)
The Boy From Space (2021)
Saturnalia (2022)
Head Coach (2022)
'Cycloid / Synesius' (2023)
Telepathic Heights (2023)

James McKeown

James McKeown (2010)
English Dream (2012)
Sublime Knight Elect (2013)
Drawninward (2016)
Hawksmoor (2018)

The Dead Astronaut
The Dead Astronaut (2015)

Frugal Puritan
Frugal Puritan (2013)

Hi-Fiction Science
Hi Fiction Science (2011)
Curious Yellow (2014)

Interview: epic45

TIME. Change. Loss. Recovery. All these experiences and states of being inform the work of epic45, a musical project that balances beauty and melancholia through seasonal imagery, memories, and the inevitability of decay. For over twenty years, Ben Holton and Rob Glover have been creating haunting and deeply moving music, leaving the listener floating between the bliss of lush dreams and the harsh realization of waking into a world that can never be what we wanted it to be. The escape is momentary as we all must return and face our futures, whatever they may be. In releases such as *Against the Pull of Autumn*, *In All The Empty Houses*, *Weathering*, and *We Were Never Here*, Holton and Glover construct sounds that reflect the consequences of change and returning through the weary awareness of seasons cycling, the relentless landscape development of the English countryside, and the passage from childhood to maturity, ghosts fading into nothingness as individual and collective memory ebb and dwindle. Ben Holton also records under the names My Autumn Empire and Birds in the Brickwork, as well as running the Wayside and Woodland record label with Rob Glover. Expect the highly anticipated new epic45 album *You'll Only See Us When The Light Has Gone* in 2024. Their releases can be found here:

https://digital.waysideandwoodland.com/

William Burns: What are your key TV/film/music memories that you think helped form your artistic identity?

Ben Holton: I was brought up in a very musical household for which I am eternally grateful. From both my mum and dad, I got my love and fascination with The Beatles and, also from them, a love of folk music. I spent lots of time in folk clubs and festivals and that all seeped into my consciousness for sure. Then I had two older brothers, the oldest of which exposed me to artists like Public Enemy, R.E.M., and Neil Young, and the younger — and possibly most importantly to the early days of epic45 — New Order, The Wedding Present, Depeche Mode, and Pet Shop Boys, as well as the sounds of drum 'n' bass, rave, and acid house. As well as all this, I developed an early interest in recording sounds on my tape player, ranging from me doing silly voices and recording sounds from around the house to embryonic song ideas made by singing (and occasionally rapping) over tunes my brother had made on his Commodore ST or Amiga. Later, I got hold of an old midi hi-fi system with a twin cassette mechanism that didn't work properly and allowed me to 'overdub'. I was able to crudely loop a beat then layer on 'samples' (voices from children's story tapes).

As for TV, *Doctor Who* was a big influence with its incredible theme tune and weird incidental music. Also, I was always strangely obsessed with school programs and their mixture of grainy film footage and mysterious music. There were so many haunting theme tunes growing up in the eighties that have stuck with me all these years: *How We Used to Live*, *Emmerdale Farm*, *Teabag*, *Ever Decreasing Circles*, etc., etc.

WB: Your work as epic45 is very connected to the English pastoral landscape. How does geography inform your music?

BH: I guess very simply because myself and Rob grew up in a small village surrounded by countryside. It wasn't a 'posh' idyllic kind of place, not like a picture postcard or anything. But it did lead us to having many an adventure out in the fields and woods, a love for which has never faded. However, as time has passed, we've witnessed the continued evolution of the countryside and how you can experience loss from watching places change. That became an element of epic45 from a very early stage. The encroachment of 'progress' upon ancient land. It's an inevitability, of course, but some seem to feel the loss side of it more keenly than others.

I was always obsessed with seeing depictions of the English countryside in TV and film too. It's hard to pinpoint what this means, I feel. Also, it's important to note, the countryside angle is not a binary, countryside: good, town/city: bad. I'd like to think we draw upon and reflect some of the less talked about realities of the rural world. The isolation, the loss of community in some areas, the poverty in some cases. The sense that the working class were expunged from the countryside and replaced with the well-to-do middle class has also been an interest.

WB: How does epic45 'work'? What are your artistic/musical goals?

BH: How we've worked has been a shifting process over the years since we started. In essence, epic45 is an entity formed by Rob and I, which has shifted focus from being a live band, working out songs together, to a home recording project to be translated into a live setting at a later date. That transition happened fairly early on, but it was never laid down in stone, leading to years of confusion, frustration and, at times, acrimony between certain members. I think we've found ourselves, after so many years, in a place where we all pretty much know what our roles are and are happy with that. I say that in terms of epic45 being myself, Rob, and James Yates (drums, percussion, production, etc.). We're finding it enjoyable to, broadly, take ideas laid out by myself and Rob, work on them as a three piece in the studio, then take them away and finish them. It feels a lot more collaborative now.

As for goals, in simple terms it would be to just continue while it feels there is something to say in the music and it's still enjoyable. The goal would be to reach more people, if anything.

WB: What are your musical influences and how do you incorporate them into your work?

BH: There's no way round it, Mogwai were a massive influence on us in the late nineties. Before that, the music we listened to didn't feel like the music we wanted to make. It felt like copying. I was very much influenced by Beck as a recording artist, inasmuch as he seemed not to be tied to any particular genre, plus in his early work (*Stereopathetic Soul Manure*) it was obvious he was recording using a four-track, Dictaphone, and other 'lo-fi' equipment. That was what made me first start thinking that we could make and release something like our heroes (The Beatles, Pet Shop Boys, New Order, etc.). Maybe it was the idea that it didn't even need to be that good! A bit of a 'punk' moment. And that was the same with Mogwai. We'd been jamming about without bothering to add vocals and seeing Mogwai on the NME Brat Awards show was a revelation. We didn't need to add vocals. In hindsight, it was me running away from that responsibility too, as I love singing. I'm glad I didn't sing too much, though, as I'm sure the lyrics would have been rubbish.

The next big thing was hearing the band Hood, who sounded like people we knew. They sang about the fields and skies in this slightly angsty way that hit me like a ton of bricks. The first record I heard was *Rustic Houses, Forlorn Valleys*, which is a moody, beautiful album of Northern spoken word and mysterious music akin to Bark Psychosis, Talk Talk, Movietone, and Crescent (all bands we were unaware of at the time). Then, I dug back and got the album *Silent '88*, an album of scratchy guitar pop, ambient electronica, drum 'n' bass and melancholic slowcore. That was it, they were now the best band to have ever existed and, quite frankly, still are.

Nowadays, I don't tend to consciously use other music as an inspiration, certainly not what might be contemporaneous to us. Of late, though, I have been listening to certain artists from the ECM label, Eberhard Weber, Terje Rypdal, and Ralph Towner, particularly their work from the 1970s and eighties. That is possibly making its way into some of the music. Less so the copious amounts of extreme metal I also listen to, although you never know.

WB: There is a lot of crossover between epic45 and July Skies as you and Rob are members of July Skies and Antony has guested on epic45 releases. How would you differentiate epic45's sound and aesthetic from July Skies?

BH: Not too long after we released our first 7" in 1999, we became friends with Antony, who reached out to us after purchasing that record and possibly seeing us live(?). He sent me his debut 7" and I instantly fell in love with the sound he made, it floored me. Ant is a master of conjuring a dreamlike state in his songs. Aching melancholy and the most poignant melodies and tones. His music was, to me, an abstraction of the 'shoegaze' and dreamy guitar pop of the late eighties/early nineties, a spectral form. It wasn't too long before we were playing together and contributing to each other's music as we were very much on the same page with our thought processes.

I would say, though, the main differences between us are that epic45 bring more of the 'now' into the sound. I always see what we do as navigating the push and pull of nostalgia and modern reality. We'll flit between a dreamlike state and the harshness and cold light of day of the present. But there are not many artists I know of that can conjure that sense of a lost past, childhood, sense of place, and the passage of time quite so brilliantly as Antony can. It's an honour to be a small part of that process.

WB: You were working in the hauntological mode even before the genre was defined as such. Do you consider yourself a hauntological artist? Is the label helpful or hurtful to the recognition of epic45?

BH: A great question and one I have been writing about recently. I would say I don't consider epic45 (or myself in other guises) as a hauntological artist in the sense of how it has solidified as a 'genre'. Just as I wouldn't now refer to epic45 as 'post-rock'. These tags do, ultimately, become a nuisance because they cease to explain anything about the music, only surface details. Those who set out to create music in a certain genre are doomed to corner themselves artistically. If it works for them on some level, though, either financially or is simply self-gratifying, then of course it has a certain validity for the creator and fans. I see epic45 more as part of a lineage of artists who cover a wider area than just 'nostalgia' and/or pastiche.

As to whether it has been helpful or hurtful to epic45, it's hard to gauge. I certainly don't think we fit comfortably into hauntology so probably weren't able to capitalise on it as such (not that we've ever been motivated in that sense) but have been swept along with it to some extent. Simon Reynolds, who first attributed the term to a musical movement, had said that epic45's *Weathering* had 'hauntological elements' and included my side project Charles Vaughan in his summary of 'Undead Hauntology' in a 2011 *Wired* article.

However, from a personal viewpoint, I have found hauntology to have become another catch-all genre tag, which people have fed with almost identikit musical projects that 'fit the bill' so to speak. Which, as I say, is fair enough but just doesn't excite me personally. Indeed, I have found the cornering the market of a certain type of postwar nostalgia a little dismaying on the whole. I loved it when it wasn't so centralised, before people could say 'that's a bit Ghost Box, isn't it?', and such strange TV-related memories were discussed on long walks or pub corners with close friends. Even in the early internet days, such esoterica was reserved for obscure forums and crude websites. I just feel like some of the magic has been lost.

That elusive sound, those elements that stirred the imagination as a child via hearing incidental music on TV, could once be found in artists such as Aphex Twin, Boards of Canada, Position Normal, etc. not as a raison d'être, but simply as a part of the tapestry that said artist was creating. It was one facet of an approach. Now the idea of creating a pastiche or explicit homage to library music and incidental music has become a genre in itself and as a result has created yet more genre-locked artists.

It's still a lot more fun to discover those peculiarly evocative sounds by delving into things yourself: YouTube uploads, severely uncool eighties pop music, eighties jazz, New Age, etc. In that sense, even though it's considered a 'dead genre' I find Vaporwave and its many offshoots still quite a rich seam to mine and enjoy. This is also partly down to the fact that my generation falls between the so-called 'Haunted Generation' of sixties, seventies, and eighties TV with its terrifying public information films and spooky children's shows, and the dawn of the ubiquitous home computer and internet age. Somewhere between *Chocky* and Windows 95.

WB: How did you decide to start epic45? What does the name epic45 signify?

BH: epic45 grew from three schoolfriends learning their instruments together at the age of thirteen. The name came about sometime in 1997 and, if memory serves, was made by simply adding the 'Epic' record label to the '45rpm' on the vinyl. It was the idea that a small piece of plastic could sound huge and life-changing. Very naïve and, ultimately, a bit cheesy. I honestly think the name has held us back over the years. Funnily enough, in an interview with a Japanese website many years ago, they asked if it was anything to do with the end of WWII, to which I replied that it was. It just sounded better.

WB: How did you approach your early work contained on the Shorebound single?

BH: To be brutally honest, the title song is very inspired by Mogwai, specifically the song Tuner, and was simply a stage in our development, getting closer to making something unique to us. The Overwhelming Feeling is more interesting as it stemmed from a song that was pretty much a grungey Nirvana-type thing which Rob and I then transferred to synth and delayed guitar. We then took that to our drummer, Mark, and the final song took shape. Again, trying to be like the 'post-rock' of the time but not quite getting it 'right'. Sunset Over Sea was all Rob, another Mogwai tribute but one created from samples and guitar, a signpost to the methods we would later employ fully and more effectively.

WB: Your first two full length releases *Secrets, Signs, and Threats* and *Reckless Engineers*, establish two of your primary motifs: the inevitable end of seasons and the flowing away of water through tidal movements. Why this imagery?

BH: I would say this imagery is rife in those recordings as we were pulling very much from our immediate surroundings and places that were (and still are) very special to us. As stated before, the countryside was integral to our art. Added to that, the frequent trips to the coast from childhood onwards, either on holidays or visiting relatives in Wales, something Rob and I shared. I think the natural world and the landscape is and always will be ripe for converting into music, if you can tap into that, which we seem to have been able to.

WB: epic45 has released many singles and EPs. What do you like about this format? Is it its practicality or a harking back to more anachronistic forms of music distribution?

BH: In the beginning, the 7" vinyl format was, believe it or not, a cheap way to create a physical release. We'd always been fans of 7" singles and EPs, yeah. There's a conciseness to them that an album can easily lack. It's sad that the format, vinyl in general, has become this elitist, almost luxury, item that is fairly financially crippling to manufacture.

WB: I think *Against the Pull of Autumn* is epic45's first masterpiece. How did the recording of this album come about?

BH: This album was a very different process to the preceding ones as we were attempting to unify the separate elements of epic45 together a little more than we had before i.e. Rob's home recordings, my home recordings, and the work we created as a band (which was the stuff we'd play live). I just wanted everything to be under one banner, I didn't see why it couldn't be, and side projects seemed like a waste of energy. So, with that in mind, we initially pulled together a few tracks that had been worked on separately and started to flesh them out as a band. At the time, we had a keyboard player, whose house we could use to record, so most of the final recording sessions happened there. Ultimately, though, for many reasons, this didn't work the way it was intended and that iteration of the band broke up not long after.

The songs have made more sense in retrospect if I'm honest, I can see it now as facing the future, growing up, being uncertain. Using the allegory of the passing of summer, the leaving behind of childhood, across the span of the album.

WB: How important is collaborating with outside musicians for epic45? Is it difficult to keep the purity of your vision when many people are involved?

BH: It is something that has become a lot easier as the years have passed and I've grown more confident in both what I want to ultimately achieve on the project and how confident I am in communicating that. There have certainly been times in the past when a collaboration has happened where communication has broken down and the end result has been compromised, but it's part of learning and progression, I think.

We find ourselves in a position now where collaborating is a pure joy and something we would like to do more of in the future.

WB: Was the *England Fallen Over* EP an outgrowth of the *Against the Pull of Autumn* sessions?

BH: No, there was no connection to *Against The Pull...* at all, apart from retaining Matt Kelly as a band member. In fact, in the timeline, you have *Slides* between the two, which represents a period of extreme flux and uncertainty with epic45. We'd lost our drummer and were operating mainly as a duo with people helping out here and there, the focus was lost somewhat. The music was getting darker and more desolate. This changed when Matt came back from uni with a fresh head, leading to the brighter sounds you hear on *EFO*.

WB: Do you think that England still has elements of its past 'quaintness' in the twenty-first century?

BH: I'm going to have to try and rein myself in a little here. I think any notion of 'quaintness' is a projection, usually from the privileged, foisted upon rural life. It's true that there are areas of England that still look like chocolate tin decorations or illustrations from the 1950s, but I see them, as pretty as they are, as a work of aesthetic preservation and little else. The countryside, after years of being inhabited by hard-working people living tough, often miserable, lives was slowly gentrified as the workers were sent into the towns and cities to work in factories and live in tower blocks. I've also noticed a trend in some areas of popular culture to somewhat fetishize the countryside and rural history. To use it as yet another element of their artistic personality. As someone who grew up in a scruffy village in the middle of nowhere I knew and still know farmers and field workers who would balk at the idea of their lifestyle being seen as 'quaint'.

Even so, the imagery works in some respects, as a dreamlike idea, an idea of an imagined way of life, an unreachable ideal. It ties in also with ideas of the apparent death of the future as it was seen post-WWII. In that sense, the dreamlike countryside portrayal is ultimately very heartbreaking and haunting. It works as a metaphor for the loss of childhood simplicity and the naïve ideals that die over time.

So, quaintness can seem a little like a betrayal of our rural heritage. In this respect I would cite *Requiem for a Village* by David Gladwell and *Akenfield* by Peter Hall as good examples of how to represent some of the realities.

When I see a thatched cottage nowadays, I simply wonder what kind of job the owner has that has allowed them to live in such a place. Not very romantic, really.

WB: The *Drakelow* EP focuses on England's role in WWII. The focus on bunkers and the war effort is similar to July Skies' *The English Cold*. Was there mutual inspiration or did these ideas arrive separately?

BH: I think, if memory serves correctly, we simply spurred each other on in these interests as we both were invested from an early age. The village where Rob and I grew up had a WWII airfield nearby which was a regular haunt of ours growing up. We visited there once or twice with Antony and, after a particularly powerful visit, came back to the house and worked on some of *The English Cold* tracks. Like I said, we found a kindred spirit in Antony.

WB: *May Your Heart Be The Map* has a tangible sense of loss, yearning, and place. Were there any specific influences (personal, cultural, or geographical) for this album?

BH: Unfortunately, I can't go into the specifics of what was happening around that time but, in many ways, the album was an attempt to engender and express hope in a dark place. Again, I think we were just charting the passing of time and the changes in our lives that were occurring. However, there was one other influence on the album and that was the 1970s TV series *Survivors*, regarding the exploits of a group of disparate people following a worldwide pandemic (oh, how prescient). I was watching this heavily at the time and, I think, took some comfort in the idea of a world depleted of people and a return to the rawness of nature. A naïve and selfish view, of course, but one which was helping me through the aforementioned trauma. It didn't turn out to be a concept album, but the theme of an abandoned world is dotted throughout the songs if you listen carefully, most notably on May Your Heart Be The Map, We Left Our Homes For Winter, and The Trees and Lanes. It was an allegory for escape, I think, a means to detach myself from the present situation.

WB: There is a definite 'ghostly' vibe to *In All the Empty Houses*. Are you interested in the paranormal or supernatural?

BH: As a child, both Rob and I were fascinated by the idea of ghosts and hauntings and the Usborne *Mysteries of the Unknown* book was a kind of bible to us. As I grew up, I became somewhat of a rationalist and therefore have no belief in a spiritual world, etc. However, when people talk of areas having an 'energy', whilst there is no scientific basis for this, I believe what is being experienced is, on a psychological level, still a valid and interesting thing. I think it's a mixture of how you perceive your surroundings in terms of their history, both recent and ancient. It's about allowing yourself to imagine a place (an abandoned building, an airfield, a set of 1980s garages, a worn-down council estate) at various stages of its existence. Who inhabited or passed through these places. In that sense, most places we visit or find ourselves in are 'haunted' in some way, you just have to be willing to perceive them as such.

WB: Can you discuss the DVD that accompanied *In All the Empty Houses*? How important is the visual to epic45's aesthetic?

BH: Visuals are very important to us, as can be seen in the artwork created by me and Rob. To me, photography and music go hand in hand and is something I'm increasingly trying to integrate. Videos, however, have been a sticking point and something we've struggled with a little over the years. Kind and incredibly talented people have helped out and we've been really flattered by that. However, I don't think it was until the video for Outside that we truly got something that resonated correctly with our music. And that, basically, was because it was an 'in-house' production. The idea with the *Empty Houses* DVD was, simply, to have a project where each song was accompanied by a video, to which we left it to the individual talents and concepts of the filmmakers themselves. I think it was largely successful i.e. I don't think we've ever had a 'bad' video, but it's definitely something we've struggled to be happy with.

WB: *Weathering* is another masterpiece. It's much more expansive and fully formed in terms of its compositions and themes of time, acts of nature, and the cycles of seasons and their effects on people, places, and memories. How did this album come about?

BH: It's the first album I was truly happy with and was definitely the beginning of the end of a certain chapter in our lives, another transition. The album came about after the relative failure in the success of *In All the Empty Houses*, a release we believed might mark a change in our fortunes after *May Your Heart...* was so successful. It didn't, so, after the semi-conscious decision to make *IATEH* a 'poppier' record, we just said to ourselves, 'let's make the best epic45 album we can'. As I said, it marks the beginning of the end of a chapter in our lives and in music. It's a somewhat downbeat and resigned album in places, which reflects where our heads were at around that time. There's a stronger element of the 'cold light of day' going on. It's about noticing the weathering of our surroundings, where we grew up, and of ourselves getting older. We also incorporated ideas of the sense of community breaking down in the village where we still lived at the time. The encroachment of new-build estates and the demolition of ancient buildings, it was all very heartbreaking. That's *Weathering*.

WB: *Weathered* is a remix album of tracks from *Weathering*. What are your thoughts on remixes?

BH: Initially we wanted *Weathering* to be released in conjunction with *Weathered*, as a double disc, but time was against us on that one. We loved the idea of taking the themes of decay and weathering and applying them to the songs from *Weathering*, so gave the artists we chose a sort of 'brief' to work with and I think it worked really well.

Remixes in general, though, I have become a little sceptical of as sometimes there just isn't a point to them. In the early days, I saw them as a fun exercise more than anything and we would do them for free and let others remix us for free. Playing around with like minds for the fun of it. When the *Weathered* concept came about something happened that chimed in nicely with the themes of change, decay, and loss quite poignantly. All of a sudden, friends of ours, fellow artists, were asking huge amounts of money for their services and this cold realization dawned on me that some people just weren't doing this for the fun of it anymore. It was a really sad and frustrating fact to accept and really colored my thoughts of collaboration for a while afterwards. I was naïve, again.

Having said all this, I still enjoy making remixes to a degree, especially for friends, and find the process of being given a load of musical stems and building something from them, without even hearing the original, a fun process. Sometimes adding quite a few extra original layers too. Though I think we may have confused some people with what they've received on occasion.

WB: There is a six-year gap between epic45 releases. Why?

BH: As stated before, after *Weathering* a lot of changes occurred, both musically and personally. Long-term relationships ended and the move away from the village began. The last things we recorded from this period were for a French 10" EP released in 2012, later released as the *Monument* EP in 2014. I chose that name and the artwork to directly reference that this was a monument to what had gone before. I still find it quite hard listening back to it if I'm honest.

It was never planned, but in retrospect, it was clear we needed a break from epic45, to gather thoughts and grow as people a little. Again, *Weathering* wasn't particularly 'successful' in a commercial sense, an expectational trap we had fallen into a little since *MYHBTM* and the following European tour had some abysmal turnouts, even though we were playing the best we had yet played as a band. James left us to pursue other things and that was also a big blow to us.

However, instead of abandoning everything, we simply turned to our side projects and carried on creating. Both of us were quite transparently indulging and paying homage to our musical heroes from childhood. With My Autumn Empire, on *II*, I was dealing with a break up via the medium of 'classic pop'. I think that album and the follow-up appalled some people, which I find quite funny. But what these projects did achieve was to hone our skills as producers and performers. Both of us were heading out and playing shows on our own and later with bands of friends and the confidence levels soared as a result. When epic45 finally began to happen again, as we both knew it would, we were ready for it, ready to begin a new chapter.

WB: It's interesting that epic45's 'return' album *Through Broken Summer* has as one of its themes the notion of returning to childhood times and places, as well as the breakdown of innocence in the face of progress. The album has been described as a view into a 'hazy' past. How did you achieve this haziness in sound?

BH: *Through Broken Summer* is us returning and saying 'hello, we're epic45 and this is what we do'. I see it as a kind of showcase of who we are in some respects, whilst also bringing in new sounds and new approaches. Some tracks were begun before the break, but I won't say which ones.

The theme of the album is about returning to the place we grew up after living away for some time, which fits in perfectly with the fact we were 'returning' to epic45.

Hazy sounds are just what occurred and, not wanting to get too bogged down in production speak, it was a continuation and refinement of methods we had been employing for years. Artificial 'ageing' of elements, processing, and filtering. Lots of tape was used, lots of 'hands-on' techniques, which are important to us in an age where certain sounds can be achieved by the click of a track pad.

WB: *Cropping the Aftermath* is epic45's meditation on the nineties. The track Buildings Aren't Haunted, People Are is particularly fascinating to me. Can you discuss its creation?

BH: With *Cropping*, we were directly referencing the sounds we experienced in the nineties and, instead of creating pastiche, we used these elements to build songs. So, for instance, Buildings... began as a programmed beat, in the spirit of how my brother would build a beat from individual hits and sounds using the 'tracker' Octamed on his Commodore Amiga. A method not uncommon to epic45, I might add. Then the song grew around it. Again, like I said before, we seem to end up contrasting the past with the present, so lyrically the song begins addressing the hate I have witnessed on the internet before concluding that hate has always been present, just in a different form.

WB: *We Were Never Here* is a beautifully mature contemplation of disappearance and fading away. How do you see the twenty-one-year evolution of epic45 from Shorebound to *We Were Never Here?*

BH: I think we've just simply become better at our craft and how we are able to express our ideas. It's been a slow, steady progression. From kids wanting to be Mogwai to just us making our music about landscape and the places where we live. I think we're able to conceptualize a whole project now and approach it with a certain outcome in mind.

WB: You released an accompanying photobook with *We Were Never Here*. What is the relationship between the book and the music on *We Were Never Here*?

BH: It was an attempt to finally marry the music and visuals in a more comprehensive way. To convey the feelings we have about these places in both how they are captured visually and how they are recreated sonically. We didn't go too literal this time, but we will see where the approach leads. It's still really difficult to convey quite why a certain place can resonate in such a powerful way. An electric substation, crackling quietly in a country lane or housing estate, a telephone exchange on the edge of a town, the view of tower blocks from a farmer's field. I can't really put it into words so it comes out in music and photography.

WB: Why did you establish your label Wayside and Woodland? Do you feel there is a unifying aesthetic amongst those artists on the label?

BH: The label came about in around 2006/2007 and was envisaged as a way to release things that didn't have to pass through the 'approval' of the Make Mine Music syndicate label of which we were part. Not that that would have been a massive problem, of course, I just think we liked the idea of these little releases being created and curated by us. Initially it was to release side projects from Rob and I, but, after we met Eric Heath, we decided some of his music was too good to not have on our fledgling label. Eric's approach definitely chimed with ours so he was happily on board. Later, our good friend and musical collaborator Mike Rowley put forward some of his music, which, whilst being a little different to the majority of the stuff we had put out already, still piqued our interest and was from a similarly observational place. In Mike's case it was the industrialized landscape of the Black Country in the West Midlands. We dallied with releasing other people's music for a while, people we admired and respected a lot, Oliver Cherer, Mark Van Hoen, and Richard Youngs, but ultimately found that approach to be more trouble than it's worth, especially in today's climate.

WB: You are quite prolific in terms of side projects and contributions to other artist's releases. How do extracurricular projects inform epic45?

BH: Like I said, the time that both Rob and I put into our other projects helped develop our production skills and approaches. I think it's possible that some of the other styles we have dallied with spill into epic45 here and there, but we usually try to keep them as separate as possible. With the last two My Autumn Empire albums, I found I was beginning to make more dreamlike, experimental stuff again and thought 'why not just start applying this to a new epic45 project?' That's when I knew it was time to return. It cannot be overstated, also, how working as a part of the live and recording side of July Skies has greatly influenced my approach to the guitar.

WB: Your My Autumn Empire work, *Dreams of Death and Other Favourites*, has a magickal, folk horror feel. Can you discuss the literary and musical influences on this project and how they are embodied in the music?

BH: I was reading the works of Robert Aickman at the time whilst also in a bit of a spot with my mental health so the two kind of merged into one another. I love how Aickman creates a palpable sense of unease with his stories by never being totally explicit with the threat, letting your mind fill in the blanks. If your mind is predisposed to such darkness then the effect is pretty powerful. There's a sense of the nightmarish and a distorted sense of reality with his stories that really got to me at the time. I was and still am a fan of M R James' ghost stories too, with their similar 'seen in the corner of your eye' spectres and presences. There seemed to me a beautiful metaphor there for the way our minds can turn against us at times in our lives.

Another influence was the TV work of Nigel Kneale, especially his series *Beasts*, which dealt, again, with ambiguous manifestations that could be taken both literally or metaphorically. It all seemed to fit with where my head was at the time. A pre-*Beasts* tale, 'Murrain', dealt with a woman who may or may not be a witch, a theme I was to return to a little later with an idea I had for a film, the completion of which has only resulted in an unreleased soundtrack.

WB: Can you shed any light on the mysterious Wayside and Woodland artist Charles Vaughan?

BH: Charles Vaughan was a character from the aforementioned *Survivors* TV show. His character was obsessed with charting and mapping the world left behind after the pandemic. He was also obsessed with repopulation but the less said about that the better.

He emerged as a musical entity around the time of *May Your Heart Be The Map* as a kind of distillation of the degradation techniques we had been using on epic45 material. His first album, *Documenting The Decay*, was completed around 2007 but it took ages for it to come out, annoyingly. He'd be a millionaire now.

Some say that Charles Vaughan is me. I will neither confirm nor deny this.

WB: What would your dream project/collaboration be?

BH: I must say, we've already been able to fulfil some dream collaborations already, namely working with the members of Hood, Disco Inferno, and Babybird. Stephen Jones (Babybird) is perhaps one of the most underrated artists in the UK today. His hits in the mid to late nineties have become a little like a millstone around his neck and not many people are aware that he had a massive body of work before this and has continued to be mind-blowingly prolific ever since. To work with Richard Adams, Craig Tattersall, and Andrew Johnson on *Weathering* was literally a dream come true and we were really pleased with the results. Added to that, Chris Adams has made one or two amazing remixes for us too.

In terms of dream collaborations now, though, the first person to spring to mind would be Robert Wyatt as I think he has one of the most wonderful voices ever. Others would probably just be musical heroes of mine from childhood. I'd love to make a track with Dave Gahan on vocals, or Neil Tennant.

WB: How important is performing live to your creativity?

BH: In terms of the creative side of things, it's probably not much of a factor to be honest, but what it can be is extremely fun and gratifying. Sharing the music with people in a room is a lovely thing. However, saying that, in purely pragmatic terms, we do have to get quite creative in how we think about reproducing the songs in a live environment as a lot of what we do is about the production. It can be difficult at times but we usually end up happy with the live recreations. Playing as a band also helps us tighten up the live element to the recordings, which is why we've focused a little more on that for the last couple of records and the one we are currently working on. If the core of a song is strong, then what it goes through afterwards will be all the better for it.

WB: What is in the future for epic45/Ben Holton?

BH: We are currently working on a new album as epic45, a quite strongly 'song'-oriented project referencing new housing estates built on marshland, English political and societal isolationism, and the ever-present influence of landscape, both rural and urban, on our ageing psyches.

As for me, I plan to continue with my photography and music project Birds in the Brickwork, again, a project of reportage on and reflection/reinterpretation of the landscape in which I live. The next release will be a small book/photo-zine and CD album, which documents the beginnings of the project. I'll also be looking into making prints of some of my photographs to sell as standalone items.

epic45/Ben Holton Discography

epic45

Shorebound (1999)
A Is An Alphabet (2000)
Secrets, Signs And Threats (2001)
Substracks #2 (Split with Laudanum) (2001)
Untitled (Split with 100 Pets) (2001)
Miranda Whiskey 27 (Split with Avaray) (2001)
Reckless Engineers (2002)
Slides (2004)
Against The Pull Of Autumn (2004)
England Fallen Over (2005)
Drakelow (2006)
May Your Heart Be The Map(2007)
In All The Empty Houses (2009)
Steps To Further Winter (2009)
Dandelion Sessions (2009)
Daylight Ghosts (2009)
Weathering (2011)
Weathered (2012)
Fragment #3 (2012)
Monument (2014)
Through Broken Summer (2018)
Sun Memory (2019)
Vanishing Britain (2019)
Cropping The Aftermath (2020)
We Were Never Here (2020)
Summer Broken Summer (2020)
Another Year (with Babybird) (2021)
Spring (2023)
You'll Only See Us When The Light Has Gone (2024)
A Beacon of Light (2024)

My Autumn Empire

2001–2005 (2007)
The Village Compass (2010)
The Toy Library Vs My Autumn Empire (Spilt with The Toy Library) (2010)
II (2012)
The Visitation (2014)
Blue Coat (2014)
Last Year's Leaves — Tape Reflections Vol: I (2015)
Dreams Of Death And Other Favourites (2015)
Oh, Leaking Universe (2018)
The Sound of Where It All Ended (2023)

Birds in the Brickwork

Twelve Months (2021)
Recovery (2022)
A Strange Peace (2023)
Three Years (2024)

The Balloonist

The Balloonist (2022)
A Quiet Day (2024)

Chapter 2

The Yearning to Return: Folk Horror and Nostalgia

It's Time to Keep Your Appointment With ... The Folk Horror Revival

> 'Far from feeling fear, I was possessed with a sense of awe and wonder such as I have never known. I seemed to be gazing at the personified elemental forces of this haunted and primeval region. Our intrusion had stirred the powers of the place into activity. It was we who were the cause of the disturbance, and my brain filled to bursting with stories and legends of the spirits and deities of places that have been acknowledged and worshipped by men in all ages of the world's history.'
> —Algernon Blackwood, 'The Willows'

A DARK, FOREBODING forest. An isolated, decrepit village. Strange, ancient occult rituals. Monstrous figures worshipped as gods. Ancient mounds. Stone circles. Hills of dreams. These are the tropes of folk horror, a sub-genre of horror cinema that has come back into malevolent style. As the found footage movement is finally showing signs of finishing, horror filmmakers are reacting to our overly technological, globalized, always online, cell phone-obsessed, TikTok virtual world through the rediscovery of the terrors of nature, eldritch beliefs, and those who inhabit those decaying rural lands that time and the internet have forgotten. This fascination with, yet distrust of, rural folk communities could be the result of the imperium of globalization, the 'Metaverse', and the 'Fourth Industrial Revolution' swallowing local autochthonic cultures and regurgitating homogeneous, consumerist virtual lifestyles. Folk horror is based on folklore: communal stories, songs, art, customs, memories, and myths that preceded the commodification of experiences and creative expression by the institutionalization of capitalism, consumerism, and the culture industry. Old ways die hard even in the age of Facebook and Instagram, and folk horror portrays the clash between antiquated and 'modern' belief systems, most often personified by the unusual survival of so-called 'pagan' rites (witches' sabbaths, sacrifices to obscure gods, fertility ceremonies) in the arrogant, scientific world of logic, reason, and materialism. The traditional bourgeois distrust of commoners because of their closeness to the soil, to what's underneath, grows into the class paranoia that these bumpkins possess secrets that no money can buy, giving them preternatural power over the sophisticated, educated, elite. (Perhaps folk horror is the soil from which hoodie horror germinated in the early 2000s?) The urban and suburban fetishizing of the 'realness' of rural life can become a commodity bought and sold on the open market, an exchange that may subsidize agrarian communities but also reinforce class boundaries. Folk horror is the place where secular humanism and capitalist liberalism meet defensive isolationism and druidical fundamentalism: the anxiety of the colonizer and the reckoning of the colonized; what author Gloria Anzaldua called the 'Borderlands/La Frontera: The New Mestiza'.

The birth of folk horror is traced to three iconic films released in the late 1960s and early 1970s, lodestones to which the majority of folk horror works are pulled: Michael Reeves' *Witchfinder General* (1968), Piers Haggard's *Blood on Satan's Claw* (1971), and Robin

Hardy's *The Wicker Man* (1973, no, not the one with the bees).[1] These three films reflected the turning away from the strife of current events and shocks of modern society like the seemingly endless Vietnam War, social upheaval, assassinations of public figures, and riots in the streets. Faced with this volatility, many in the counterculture chose to 'drop out', rejecting 'civilized' society, heading back to nature to live on distant communes far from the maddening crowd, burying themselves in a seemingly bucolic past before the Industrial Revolution and modernity. The economic crises of the 1970s in the US and UK also fed this desire to reject the present, as class fragmentation initiated by the transition in the western world into postindustrial societies was met with much fear, confusion, and angst. This discontented search for the 'old ways' and the authenticity of bygone times represent the resistance many felt (and still feel) towards not only the turbulence, but also the emptiness, inhumanity, and materialism of the nightmarish consumerist rat race that overwhelms so many of our lives in the contemporary world: that overwhelming need to find something or some place that is genuine, deep, and meaningful. Yet this turn to the rural and agrarian can also unleash the forces of fanaticism (pagan and Christian as *The Wicker Man* brilliantly exposes) and paranoia, pushing us towards the paths of superstition, fear, and ruin.

In an interesting bit of serendipity, just as folk horror was establishing itself as a genre to be reckoned with, Marxist critic Raymond Williams published *The Country and the City* in 1973. Part autobiography, part literary analysis, and part socio-economic critique, *The Country and the City* examines the relationship between the rural and the urban as metaphors and images that are usually divorced from genuine material and political conditions, and rather than representing binary oppositions, the concepts of country and city are caught in a symbiotic association. Williams is especially suspicious of the notion

1 Prior to these three films, it was never the expression of English folklore that was to be feared in proto-British folk horror movies, rather, foreign folklore that had been imported into England that was the source of horror as seen in films such as Hammer's *The Reptile* and *The Plague of the Zombies*. The 'unholy trinity' identified terrors homegrown in Albion.

that the pastoral ever was a real utopia and that 'the old ways' were handed down in a pristine, unadulterated manner to successive generations of folks. This nostalgia for the old innocent days of agrarian village life and the frustration over the loss of this imagined 'Golden Age' is not a singularly contemporary lament but has been a consistent theme in English literature since the 1500s. According to Williams, there never was one monolithic 'Merry Olde England', rather, a series of artificial constructs that acted as corrective revisions to actual social and economic historical conditions. These 'structures of feeling', based on discourses and myth rather than actual lived material experiences, assist in justifying and reinforcing oppressive geographic, class, and economic boundaries.

At the core of folk horror is the concept and lived practice of cultural heritage. Social scientists have identified four aspects to cultural heritage: cultural property (material objects created by members of a culture), intangible cultural heritage (customs, traditions, values, oral language activity of a culture), natural heritage (geography, natural features, and landscapes incorporated into cultural experiences and production) and digital heritage (online, digital cultural expression and preservation). These physical, intellectual, aesthetic, emotional, and spiritual relationships to the past and the negotiated associations between humans and nature express a complex network of ideas and actions that are central to cultural formation and social praxis as ways to understand and interact with the often-inscrutable forces that surround us.

The three key components of cinematic folk horror are:

1 Exploration of how natural landscapes, their isolated inhabitants, and cultural heritage intertwine;
2 Fanatical resistance to progress, materialist doctrines, and linear accounts of time;
3 Clash of belief systems resulting in violence.

For example, *The Wicker Man* meets these criteria in the following ways:

1. Director Robin Hardy films the wild landscape and insular inhabitants of Summerisle (the film's setting) in an almost documentary style. We are presented with in-depth views of the island's flora and fauna, its citizens and community social structure, as well as its history, customs, lore, and ideology. So close are the land and the people connected that Summerisle the location, Summerisle's population, and Lord Summerisle the character are basically one and the same, sharing the same oversoul.
2. There appear to be no cars, televisions, telephones, or contemporaneous (early 1970s) modern conveniences on Summerisle. The inhabitants of Summerisle live in both geographical as well as self-imposed isolation. Their society prescribes to a cyclical rhythm of life, privileging an agrarian tradition rather than one that conforms to linear time and elevates technological innovation. There is a communal conviction that there's more to human existence than scientific, secular humanistic, consumerist, and institutional Christian worldviews. The group philosophy of Summerisle is a transcendental, polytheistic spirituality that lives in symbiotic, corporeal reverence with nature rather than seeing natural environments as things to conquer and exploit.
3. In addition to the obvious Christian vs pagan religious conflict, *The Wicker Man* also illustrates confrontations between city and country, hedonism and asceticism, individualism and collectivism, as well as national state-endorsed notions of legality and justice opposing local community-based codes and authority. Poor Sgt Howie pays the ultimate price for standing up for his beliefs.

The need to escape and return to the old straight track was not only a social, cultural, economic, and/or political stance, but an aesthetic one as well. Most folk horror aficionados are aware of the concurrent acid/wyrd/freak folk revolution, but the search for the campestral also went beyond the cinematic and musical. A group of UK painters led by world renowned pop artist Peter Blake (designer of the iconic cover for The Beatles' *Sgt. Pepper's Lonely Hearts Club Band*) formed the Brotherhood of Ruralists in 1975, leaving the urban behind to find inspiration in the pastoral outside of Bath, a fecund motion of the soul. This was not only a geographical move but also a creative one. According to Blake, the Brotherhood of Ruralists' artistic goals were 'the continuation of a certain kind of English painting. We admire Samuel Palmer, Stanley Spencer, Thomas Hardy, Elgar, cricket, the English landscape and the Pre-Raphaelites'.[2] Although the participants did not share one unified technique or style, they all took inspiration from an almost atavistic connection to the English countryside and the metaphysical kinship between the rustic inhabitants and nature. In particular, the works of Ruralist painter David Inshaw echo the same strange yet familiar nostalgia found in folk horror, landscapes of ominous beauty and Arcadian mystery, while later Ruralist Joseph Hewes' *Standing Stones* could have been sold in the gift shop of Milbury's Natural History Museum. Drawing inspiration from the earthy grotesque and brooding expressionism of such dark mages as Samuel Palmer and Arthur Rackham, the Brotherhood of Ruralists sought to till the fertile ground of 'old weird Britain', excavating and renovating an enduring English condition that grew out of landscapes both actual and fantastic, as portrayed in David Gladwell's docufiction/visual elegy *Requiem for a Village* (1976) and Elisabeth Kozmian's *Two Houses* (1980), which was soundtracked by BBC Radiophonic genius Delia Derbyshire. Following a lineage from the Romantics and the Transcendentalists, the Brotherhood of Ruralists were criticized for being naïve, idealistic, and even colonial in their sentimentality towards and glorification of the bucolic lifestyle and those who have no choice but to live it.

2 "'For instance, now, there's the King's messenger…'", The Victoria and Albert Museum, https://collections.vam.ac.uk/item/O1038285/for-instance-now-theres-the-screenprint-sir-peter-blake/ [Last accessed June 10, 2024]

Although nature has often been portrayed as an idyllic, innocent paradise, folk horror suggests that the natural world and those who live in close proximity to it are not always the mellow, peace-loving tree huggers they appear to be. The feminine is a force that is both worshipped and damned as an uncontrollable dynamic that is beyond total submission and dominance. Witchcraft is secret knowledge, the nexus of hidden power. The figure of the witch is perhaps folk horror's most fearsomely potent symbol, taken to its apex in Barbara Hirschfeld's clandestine *Transformations* (1976), depicting a feminist coven leaving behind the patriarchal world through an organic ritual that connects them to the ceremonies and traditions of the wise woman. (Wouldn't Aghast's *Hexerei im Zwielicht der Finsternis* be the perfect soundtrack to this film?) Though it feels we are epochs away from backwards social panics like the centuries-long witch-hunting genocides that ravaged rural communities, the potential of social media to spread social contagions could very easily devolve our high-tech digital personas into atavistic beasts baying for blood. Irrational, darker impulses are allowed to run wild as regression to the primal somehow bypasses the survival of the fittest. It was not only in art and popular culture that these urges and impulses were stirring, as even the Bishop of Exeter's 1972 report on exorcisms mentioned the daemonic influences of locus terribilis. In a particularly chilling exercise of PSYOPs, folk horror was even weaponized by the US Army during the Vietnam War in Operation Wandering Soul, playing the unearthly *Ghost Tape Number Ten* in the jungles to suggest that disembodied, deceased ancestors were imploring the Viet Cong to give up.

Violence, ignorance, supernatural darkness, and the unrestrained power of natural forces are all to be found in the disturbing world of folk horror as naïve outsiders intrude into situations that have been hidden behind the façade of beautiful flora and fauna, charming cottages, and benevolent rustic townspeople. Landscape plays a crucial role in folk horror, as the countryside provides an uncanny, eerie environment far removed from the urban and suburban, where anything can and will happen. There are no security cameras or digital surveillance systems to observe and safeguard one's every move. What we know of nature is always filtered through our limited awareness, perspectives, and structures of feeling: what we can collect and control, what we can define and destroy, what we can map and molest. Not only do we project ourselves and our inner realities onto the countryside, the reverse is also true as well; material conditions and topography impact our own physical, psychological, emotional, and spiritual identities. Nature doesn't have an ideology; humanity almost always does, and whether that belief system is primitive or ultra-modern, it is not a reflection of the natural world's 'agenda', but of the folk ourselves. But where does this notion of reverting back and returning to previous ways of existing end? Is it only the desire to escape the pressures of modern society or does this craving go deeper into our collective ancestry? There is both a fear of and attraction to devolution and dissolution, past the animal back into the protoplasmic primordial ooze, the 'oceanic consciousness', like the fate of Helen Vaughan in Arthur Machen's *The Great God Pan* (1894) and the near fate of Dr Edward Jessup in Ken Russell's 1980 phantasmagorical adaptation of Paddy Chayefsky's novel *Altered States* (1978).

These gorgeous yet haunting settings provide the perfect backdrop to the concealment of primeval secrets, seething brutality, mysterious cults, and creatures that should not be but are: a fury that festers just beneath the skin and the field. It's a hard life in the country, especially for those who exhibit the arrogance of the urban, the 'educated' class, the 'civilized' who are not smart enough to realize that knowledge and place are intrinsically linked, and that, in certain spaces, lore is more insightful than book learning. Folk horror often indulges in parallel stereotypes about both city and country dwellers, but it is the rustics who often come out on the wrong side, either represented as ignorant, backwards cretins or enlightened, free-spirited demigods. Of course, there are a lot more nuances than these two tropes to accurately depict the realities of agricultural living in the hinterlands of the past: 'The ordinary Georgian working family did not bask in a folksy golden age; neither, however, did it have one foot within the refugee-camp.'[3]

Folk horror excavates forgotten layers of myth, magic, and subsistence that informed the everyday lives of so many of our ancestors across time and geography. This fascination with the ancient and the traditions of days gone by has returned with a vengeance to revitalize contemporary horror culture in a plethora of fascinating ways (even *Bob's Burgers* had a folk horror-influenced episode). In the last few years, movies such as Robert Eggers' *The Witch* (2015), Ari Aster's *Midsommar* (2019), David Lowery's *The Green Knight* (2020), Alex Garland's *Men* (2022), Goran Stolevski's *You Won't Be Alone* (2022), and Mark Jenkin's *Enys Men* (2022) have brought folk horror back into the mainstream, but it is in the works of British director Ben Wheatley that the folk horror revival has found its spokesperson. Wheatley's films such as *Kill List* (2011) and *A Field in England* (2013) have added contemporary (and psychoactive) twists to the folk horror formula. His newest film *In the Earth* (2021) might be his folk horror masterpiece; Wheatley conjures up the ritualistic equivalent of *2001: A Space Odyssey* as scientists trying to find a cure for a pandemic step through a psychedelic portal opened by magic mushrooms and a monolithic stone, encountering the terrifyingly alien energies of nature that are beyond human comprehension, experiencing the thrilling yet horrifying awe of the unknown. *In the Earth* reflects a triad of Algernon Blackwood, Arthur Machen, and Carlos Castaneda.

Folk horror makes sense in a world in which we are increasingly faced with the disturbing acknowledgement that there is no escape from the social, technological, and environmental disasters that we have unleashed upon ourselves.[4] In addition to these macro problems, folk horror also engages with contentious issues of cultural

3 Roy Porter, *English Society in the Eighteenth Century* (London: Penguin, 1991).
4 Could the occult be the last line of defense against neo-liberal globalization? With the amounts of money being made from occulture, perhaps not.

heritage in the twenty-first century: repatriation of cultural artifacts, indigenous people's rights, property law, the tourism industry, curriculum revision, sustainable conservation, and virtual preservation. By contrasting and deconstructing the relationships between the natural and the artificial, the rural and the urban, the scientific and the supernatural, the folk horror revival encourages crucial questioning of the cultural, moral, metaphysical, and social consequences of twenty-first-century existence: what it means to be a human being in the Digital Age and where we are heading post-singularity.

Folk Horror Film Recommendations

Kwaidan (1964). Nominated for an Academy Award for Best Foreign Language Film, Masaki Kobayashi's anthology film *Kwaidan* (*Ghost Stories*) is one of the most beautiful yet unsettling folk horror films ever produced. Based on Japanese folklore collected by writer Lafcadio Hearn, each component narrative of *Kwaidan* reflects the seasonal mood of the story's setting. Eschewing actual natural environments for majestically painted stage backgrounds, *Kwaidan* balances the expressionistic and the impressionistic as nature projects onto and is projected onto by the characters of the film. Silence and traditional Japanese music alternate to reflect the movements of nature and the realizations of the characters. One of the stories, 'The Woman of the Snow', concerns a woodcutter who unknowingly marries a Yuki-onna (a snow spirit), which will have icily ominous repercussions for him and his family. In 1968, Daiei Films released their own cinematic version of this story, *The Snow Woman*, directed by Tokuzo Tanka, which is also a folk horror classic.

The Ancines Woods (*The Forest of the Wolf*) (1971). A 'real life' werewolf is front and center in Pedro Olea's 1971 film, *The Ancines Woods*. An adaptation of a novel by Carlos Martínez-Barbeito, *The Ancines Woods* is based on the savage crimes of nineteenth-century serial killer Manuel

Blanco Romasanta, the 'Werewolf of Allariz'. Looking as if it was actually filmed 200 years ago, *The Ancines Woods* takes place in a rural village in Northern Spain that is plagued by savage murders. Is it a werewolf or a lust killer? As an example of Spanish folk horror, *The Ancines Woods* embraces the unfortunate stereotype that rural inhabitants are animalistic, vulgar, and depraved, suggesting that the killer's urges emerged from the superstitions and brutality of his backwoods upbringing just as much as from congenital psychosis. The murderer's bloodlust is enhanced by the freedom of nature (no murders occur in the towns where he peddles his wares), an unrestricted space to release his repressed anger and violent sexual desires. His connection to the primal is expressed by the killer's obsessive need to thrust his hands into the forest soil, a fetishistic, delusional communion of the inner beast and the savage powers of nature. *The Ancines Woods* uses the thick forests of the area to enhance the foreboding mood, an atmosphere of trepidation where the woods can swallow one up into their primeval labyrinth, never to be seen again. Deep in the wilderness, our blackest desires and repressed passions are released and projected onto nature. The wolf is our shadow self: bloodthirsty, fierce, and liberated from the restraints of civilization. *The Ancine Woods* feels so authentic that you won't be able to innocently stroll through the forest ever again.

Venom (*The Legend of Spider Forest*) (1971). Peter Sykes directed two of the stranger Hammer films, *Demons of the Mind* (1972) and *To the Devil a Daughter* (1976), but those can't compete with his folk horror/sci-fi/spy/mystery concoction *Venom*. In a rural German village ensconced in the Black Forest, a former Nazi scientist is continuing his experiments with chemical weapons and a nerve poison derived from spider venom, using his alluring daughter and the legend of an enticing yet murderous Spider Goddess as a cover for his nefarious plans to resurrect the Third Reich. There's also sadomasochism, superstitious villagers, and stolen art treasures. The plot is a glorious mess, but Sykes creates a hauntingly dreamlike atmosphere for the Bavarian countryside.

The Legend of Hillbilly John (1972). The US's greatest folk horror author Manly Wade Wellman incorporated authentic folklore and superstition from southern Appalachia and North Carolina as well as inserting his own rural legends (the malevolent Shonokins) into his wondrous tales. During the Great Depression, Wellman served as Assistant Director of the Works Progress Administration's New York Folklore Project, as well as befriending folk musician Obray Ramsey, who would have a profound effect on Wellman's writing. Directed by TV horror pioneer John Newland, *The Legend of Hillbilly John* is an adaptation of two of Wellman's 'John the Balladeer' stories: 'O Ugly Bird' and 'The Desrick on Yandro'. Silver John is a wandering troubadour who helps protect the mountain folk from supernatural evil through his folksy wisdom, quick wit, and silver-stringed guitar. This episodic film mirrors John's peripatetic journey through the deep Appalachian valleys as he moseys through battles with witches, warlocks, a giant thunderbird, a West African trickster god, and ol' Scratch himself. John's songs both comment on the dramatic situation and fill in exposition for regional and occult background. In 1994, bluegrass artist Joe Bethancourt released an album of his interpretations of Silver John's ballads entitled *Who Fears the Devil?* and electronic project Out of Orion has released four CDs based on the John the Balladeer tales as well.

A Warning to the Curious (1972). The trope of sacrifice, that the land itself demands tribute for the cycle of life to keep turning, renewing, and replenishing the connections between human beings and their environment, is a crucial concept in folk horror. The gods of nature and the spirits of place must not only be celebrated, but also humbly placated lest their awesome powers turn on vulnerable, fragile humans. Unable to deal with chance and accident, many folk communities require the psychological comfort of a metaphysical quid pro quo with the unknown, and so crops, blood, and lives must be exchanged for solace, bounty, and the appearance of control, predictability, and stability. This folkloric invocation of protection, consecration, and memorializing the dead through sacrifice is at the heart of M R James' fearsomely eerie story 'A Warning to the Curious', and its superbly haunting 1972 adaptation as part of the BBC's annual *Ghost Story for Christmas* series of television films. In search of one of the legendary Anglo-Saxon crowns buried along the coastline of England as a supernatural defense system to ward off invaders, recently redundant Paxton seeks to unearth this treasure in an effort to prove to himself that he has not lost his status and significance in the face of the Great Depression. In order to prevent just such thefts, the Ager family has been charged with the responsibility of protecting the crowns and, by proxy, England itself. This obligation transcends time and even mortality, as Paxton finds to his horror. The undead William Ager stalks Paxton and his stolen prize, and even after Paxton tries to make amends for his violation of this supernatural covenant, he must pay for disrupting the ancient relationship between genius loci and the British folk. Director Lawrence Gordon Clark is at the height of his cinematic mastery in *A Warning to the Curious*, utilizing the moody north Norfolk coastline and its stark woodlands to create one of the most authentically atmospheric horror films ever made. The dual sacrifices of the watchman and the transgressor suggest that vigilance, atonement, and punishment are inherently parts of the contract that communities (local or national) make with the mysterious. The crown is not evil nor, necessarily, is its guardian (the Agers have selflessly sacrificed their freedom for this pact); it is Paxton's selfish need for individualistic, exceptionalist self-aggrandizement that threatens the sacred order of a country and its people. Paxton's desecrated corpse is marked by the very soil he sought to betray.

Poor Pretty Eddie (1975). A hillbilly Southern Gothic, *Poor Pretty Eddie* focuses on a black singer, Liz Wetherly, who ends up stranded in a forgotten town in the backwoods of Georgia. This isolated community is lorded over by a wannabe Elvis named Eddie (shades of Jesco White), who is almost worshipped by the strange townsfolk. Things turn ugly for Wetherly when Eddie decides she's going to make him famous, culminating in a bizarre down-home wedding and bloody revenge. The cast includes Shelley Winters, Slim Pickens, and Ted Cassidy, so you know you're going to be in for some folksy melodramatic weirdness. Eddie's obsession with wanting to be a celebrity at all costs and the validation, materialism, and power that goes along with it displays a folk community corrupted by mass media, commercialism, and the fame industry. Eddie's domain exists outside but parallel to mainstream American culture, a grotesquely 'wholesome' decadence that suggests what the US would have looked like in the 1970s had the Confederacy won the Civil War. The dark racial undercurrents and sexual violence tear away the façade of Southern hospitality in this (very) loose adaptation of Jean Genet's *The Balcony.*

The Wind That Walks (1981). Although New Jersey is not usually noted for its folk horror credentials, a 1981 public television-produced short film called *The Wind That Walks* perfectly captures the clash between two opposing belief systems: science and natural mysticism. The film concerns two scientists searching for the New Jersey Devil who actually discover the secret of the cryptid in the lonely, desolate Pine Barrens. Reminiscent of Nigel Kneale's *The Abominable Snowman of the Himalayas* as well as the works of Algernon Blackwood, the uncanny atmosphere and intelligence of *The Wind That Walks* may be an inspiration for found footage film *The Last Broadcast.*

The Queen of Black Magic (1981). Many folk ballads use the theme of the jilted lover to justify the acts of violent revenge that are visited on the jilter. Lilik Sudjio's *The Queen of Black Magic* takes this concept a step further and has the wronged female protagonist not only get back at the gigolo who dumped her, but also at the whole village for throwing her off a cliff in the false assumption that she is a witch. Luckily, she is saved by a warlock who schools her in the occult and she soon gets her demonic vengeance, as the ignorant townsfolk have created the very thing they thought they were destroying. Exploding entrails, self-decapitations, floating severed heads, and attacks by bees and worms are all shown in their gory wonder. What really elevates this Indonesian film into the top ranks of folk horror are the extensive scenes portraying the rites and rituals that act as initiations into the indigenous practice of witchcraft and give *The Queen of Black Magic* a brief feeling of mystical authenticity in the chaos of absurdity.

Children of the Corn (1984). Creating American folk horror can be a dicey proposition when you have over 200 years of slavery and the near-extermination of indigenous people in your nation's collective karma. Certainly, the US has the vast landscape, the legends, and the lore, but more importantly the feelings of isolation and zealotry that have been connected to the very first European settler communities. As H P Lovecraft noted, 'Here is material for a really profound study in group-neuroticism; for certainly, no one can deny the existence of a profoundly morbid streak in the Puritan imagination'.[5] Fritz Kiersch's version of Stephen King's short story has all these signifiers of folk horror, but also adds the disturbing aspect of creepy murderous children who sacrifice adults to their inhuman god, He Who Walks Behind the Rows, to the formula. The endless, monotonous cornfields and huge skies engulfing the town of Gatlin, Nebraska, let one's mind go on forever with nothing to stop the madness. The combination of Christian imagery reconstructed through 'pagan' worship (inverting the usual trope) provides a familiar yet unsettling tone. A key folk horror theme is the clash between modern exceptionalist individualism and pre-industrial Arcadian collectivism, and *Children of the Corn* displays the problems with both modes of life. Although the main characters make many of the clichéd mistakes protagonists make in horror cinema, the overwhelming sense of remoteness and inversion more than make up for the stupidity of the heroes. Malachai and Isaac are two of the most repellent characters to ever appear in a Stephen King-inspired film.

5 H P Lovecraft, *The Annotated Lovecraft* (New York: Dell, 1997).

The Serpent and the Rainbow (1988). Wes Craven's loose adaptation (maybe 'inspired by' is more accurate) of botanist/anthropologist Wade Davis's heart-stopping search for 'zombie powder' focuses on the influence of voodoo on the citizens of Haiti. Partially filmed on location in Haiti, Craven connects supernatural power and political control in the real-life figures of the Tonton Macoutes, who used arcane fears as one of their weapons to terrorize Haitians. *The Serpent and the Rainbow* delves into villages where bokors (vodou sorcerers) and houngans (vodou priests) contact the loas (vodou gods), who bestow upon them occult powers to control not only the body and mind, but also the soul. While Craven's imagery and mood feel faithful, unfortunately the script by Richard Maxwell is typical Hollywood in its misunderstanding of folk mysticism and its practitioners. More William Seabrook than Zora Neale Hurston, *The Serpent and the Rainbow* plays up nightmarish terrors and demented obsessions rather than the complex living body of beliefs and practices that are a fundamental part of life for the people of Haiti. Craven's film crosses Freddy Krueger with Maya Deren.

Insumasu o ouu Kage (1992). Chiaki J Konaka's weirdly sensual TV adaptation of 'The Shadow Over Innsmouth' emphasizes folk horror's interest in heredity and returning to one's beginnings as family secrets, self-discovery, guilt, and biological imperatives all create a stifling atmosphere, Lovecraft style, that, nevertheless, is impossible to resist. The strange rituals on the beach performed in the 'Boat of Resurrection' perfectly symbolize the attraction and repulsion that draws the protagonist home, which also serves as a commentary on the abandonment of the rural for the economic opportunities of the urban (Cthulhu meets *Akenfield*?). The latent hereditary connection between the protagonist and the ichthyological environment of the accursed town in the source text is explicit and straightforward in this adaptation, and yet the social aspects of the struggle between hometown loyalty and the attractions of the city are not ignored. The dreamlike environment of isolated shorelines and primal rites on a torch-lit beach recall Algernon's Blackwood's blissfully frightening melding with an oceanic god in 'The Sea Fit'. There's also an interesting cover of The Rolling Stones' Paint It Black on the soundtrack.

Dagon (2001). Horror master Stuart Gordon (director of the paradigm shifting *Re-Animator*) adapts horror mega icon H P Lovecraft in a film focusing on the hideous inhabitants of the sinister, isolated town of Imboca. *Dagon* is probably the closest we will get to the fabled Stuart Gordon/Brian Yuzna/Bernie Wrightson cinematic version of Lovecraft's masterpiece 'The Shadow Over Innsmouth'. Both Lovecraft's cosmic horror and folk horror share some philosophical points, particularly the overturning of the notion that free will is what guides human destiny: humans have no agency in the unalterable, uncaring mechanisms of nature, biology, and instinct. It is a necessary self-delusion to believe we live in a human-centric universe and that the cycles of nature have any concern for our species. *Dagon*'s atmosphere is damp, wet, slimy, grotesque, and kinky, mirroring the half fish/half human denizens of the village and the Cthulhu-like deity they serve. The folk horror tropes of sex, fertility, and sacrifice climax in an incestuous revelation and an attempted auto-da-fé that signals the end of one kind of life and the birth of another, under the sea.

True Detective: Season One (2014). The first brilliant season of Nic Pizzolatto's anthology series manages to mix the nihilistic philosophy of Thomas Ligotti, the occult symbolism of Robert W Chambers, and the thick Southern atmosphere of Harry Crews into a folk horror gumbo. In a case spanning seventeen years, two homicide detectives investigate ritual murders in the backwoods parishes of Louisiana, discovering an occult significance to the sacrifices that goes back generations and up the heights of political power. The use of the bayous, waterways, and levees summons a spooky, isolated feeling that is not without its beauty: earthy communities decorated with fetishistic root works called 'Devil's Nests' and hypnotic spiral motifs. The slowly creeping kudzu gradually retaking abandoned architecture suggests that no matter how far we get from our natural beginnings, humans will never escape their connection to the soil. It's too bad that Pizzolatto pulled back from having a truly cosmically pessimistic ending to the series, settling instead for buddy cop pleasantries.

Wekufe: The Origin of Evil (2016). Although it's only sixty-eight minutes long, Javier Attridge's brilliant *Wekufe: The Origin of Evil* manages to touch on colonialism, industrialization, the survival of indigenous cultures, the polymorphic nature of myth, environmental exploitation, racism, tourism, the collusion of government and corporations, and the hypocrisy of Christianity while still being a menacingly terrifying film rather than a meta-hipster-woke borefest. A couple (a journalism student; an aspiring filmmaker) travel to Chiloe, an island off the coast of southern Chile, to investigate the legend of the Trauco, an incubus-like creature with a violently voracious libido. Belief in this sexual monster is used to explain the high frequency of rapes, incest, unexplained pregnancies, and non-marital children in the community. Mainland officials scoff at the stories of the locals, yet the islanders know there is something evil in their midst, a corruption that comes from without rather than from within. Attridge immerses the viewer in the Patagonian environment, invoking a damaged habitat and a damaged people stalked by venture capitalists and the Brujeria, an Afro-Latin witch cult also referenced in works by Bruce Chatwin and Alan Moore. *Wekufe* is an extremely self-aware film, identifying specific tropes from folk horror (*The Wicker Man*), found footage (*The Blair Witch Project*) and documentary films (the false objective perspective), but it never descends into parody or mimicry. In the film, myth is presented as a way to perpetuate, conceal, and explain away real human barbarities as supernatural occurrences that happen without mortal agency or blame. Attridge also does horror fans a huge favor by revealing the heretofore secret Chilean influences on Poe, Lovecraft, and Melville! With films like *Wekufe: The Ori-*

gin of Evil, Issa Lopez's *Vuelven*, Sol Moreno and J Oskura Nájera's *Diablo Rojo PTY*, Cristobol Leon and Joaquin Cocina's *La Casa Lobo*, and Rodrigo Aragão's *The Black Forest*, Latin America/South America may be a serious contender in unseating the UK as ground zero for folk horror.

The Black Forest (2018). Serious horror fans should know the name Rodrigo Aragão. Over the last ten years, this writer/director has been creating his own Brazilian folk horror mythos filled to overflowing with the low budget, ultra-gory, anarchic comedic energy of the early films of Sam Raimi, Peter Jackson, and Shinya Tsukamoto filtered through a South American picaresque sensibility. Starting with 2008's *Mangue Negro*, all of Aragão's works are connected through a recurring grimoire called *The Black Book of Cipriano*, based on the real *Book of St. Cyprian* used in Brazilian macumba rituals. *Mar Negro* (2013) is his first masterpiece, telling the story of a small coastal village where fishermen catch a strange creature that bites one of them. This bite introduces a parasitic virus into their community. which not only turns the infected into zombie cannibals but unleashes occult powers and Lovecraftian monsters. Aragão's films use horror and folklore to satirize prejudice, politics, economics, machismo, sex, and class hierarchy in his home country.

The Black Forest represents a tonal shift to a more serious approach as Aragão mines the deep seam of Brazilian witchcraft and macumba through exploring the folk horror theme of the supremacy and corresponding fear of the feminine. Focusing on a rustic parish in the Amazon, *The Black Forest* is like a sub-astral, South American twist on Jaromil Jireš's surrealistic coming-of-age film *Valerie and Her Week of Wonders*. We witness a young woman's initiation into the world of adulthood and wisdom, which involves promises that are broken, hopes dashed, and the corrupting presence of the black arts. Fate weighs heavily over all the characters, a web of pre-determined influences that is inescapable and damning. Feeling like it emerged from the bottomless soil of thousands of years of agonies and ecstasies (perhaps the only earthier film than this is Juan Diego Escobar Alzate's stunning *Luz: The Flower of Evil*), Aragão's tale goes back farther than just the rural/urban dichotomy and illuminates the primal unconscious. Influenced equally by Gabriel García Márquez and Coffin Joe, *The Black Forest* oscillates between the natural poetry of its environs and the ferocity of unleashed desires, hatreds, and fears as folk magic bridges the gap between pastoral Eden and worldly Hell.

> "Don't you understand that if your crops fail this year, next year you're going to have to have another blood sacrifice? And next year, no one less than the king of Summerisle himself will do. If the crops fail, Summerisle, next year your people will kill you on May Day."
> —Sgt Neil Howie (RIP)

Interview: The Rowan Amber Mill

STEPHEN STANNARD'S WORK encompasses many musical genres, but the bedrock of his artistry is folk music in a diversity of forms, expressed to perfection through his musical project The Rowan Amber Mill. Stannard's connection to the rural landscape and environment is not only aesthetic, but also familial, and that closeness informs his art as well as his weltanschauung. Much of Stannard's work (whether with The Rowan Amber Mill or his collaborative projects Rowan : Morrison and Meadowsilver), delves into the idea of animism, the notion that there are souls and spirituality in natural phenomena that inspire human creativity that then reflects back on how human beings perceive, conceive, and live with nature that inspires more creativity, and the cycle continues. Taking in English history, M R James, strange children's shows, obscure horror cinema, seasonal imagery, and the songs sung by the workers in the fields, Stephen Stannard's oeuvre can be symbolized by the Roman god Janus: one face looks back and another looks forward, what was and what is to come. The Rowan Amber Mill's *Through*

Dark Polished Glass, a stunningly diverse trip through the historical and occult byways of Old England and Stephen's first solo release under his own name, *High and Dry* were both released in 2022 to well-earned critical acclaim. The next stage of his 'Woodland Folkadelica' is in full force on The Rowan Amber Mill's sonic merging of folk horror and hauntological 'lost' films *The Haunted Future Silence Bequeathed* (the accompanying visual and textual materials for this album are worthy of standalone release). Stephen's work can be found at millersounds.co.uk

William Burns: What are your key TV/film/music memories that you think helped form your artistic identity?

Stephen Stannard: TV was ridiculously important to me in my youngest years, the unbridled joy of watching programs like *Camberwick Green*, *Bagpuss*, *Pipkins*, et al. What struck me very much later was that these children's TV programs (and many others around that same time) had at their core the idea of people (or often puppets/creatures) helping each other along and also generally being very happy with life. I always really enjoyed those wonderfully simple songs. At that time (the mid 1970s) there was a lot of folk song and folk tales incorporated into children's TV shows (no doubt due to the coming of age of the folk boom generation before). I think the coalescence of those ideas allied to the folk song idiom probably, subconsciously, connected the neural pathways and led me toward the pursuit of happiness via the creation of folk songs. The other major influence had to be the work of the BBC Radiophonic Workshop on both radio and TV. They were making sounds that sounded, literally, out of this world and I had absolutely no idea how such noises were made. I can remember three pieces that really struck me at the time were the *Doctor Who* theme (particularly the end credits with the swirly visual feedback vortex), *The Tomorrow People* theme, and the theme tune to *Joe and the Sheep Rustlers*. So, musically, they have shaped my interest in the creation of new folk songs and my interest in synth music.

WB: Your work is very connected to landscape, particularly the environment of East Devon. How does geography inform your music?

SS: I would say that I am as connected to the idea of landscape and environment as I am disconnected from the idea of mainstream culture, media, and 'society'. No doubt stemming from a rural upbringing which included lots of time spent in woodland and farmland (the extended family being employed almost exclusively as timber fellers and farm labourers), so that connection to the land runs right to the core. The idea (which is as old as time itself) of either expressing love of the landscape in song, or using an agrarian metaphor to reflect my thoughts on aspects of the human condition, seems a very natural one.

WB: Do you have an interest in the occult and the supernatural? If so, how do these interests inform your aesthetic?

SS: I'm an atheist, so I have little interest in the occult and supernatural per se. What I do find of interest is the psychology of supernatural beliefs, and to what extent, in this 'age of enlightenment', the modern resurgence in supernatural beliefs is the result of a lack of trust many feel with regard to organized religion, politics, and print media. What I do find endlessly fascinating and inspiring is how the supernatural (especially aspects of paganism) is portrayed in art. Again, that kind of 'back to the fields' paganism looms large in many of my favorite folk songs such as John Barleycorn, or in the supernatural ideas in the works of Alan Garner, or representations of the 'old religion' out of time i.e. *The Wicker Man*. What I find incredibly inspiring is the process of these multiple refractions from times of yore where trees, rocks, places, etc. were portrayed as human spirits or with human qualities, then later woven into folk tales, songs, and fairy stories, which then begat novels and drama, which then refract back into song, and it continues on.

WB: How does The Rowan Amber Mill 'work'? What are your artistic/musical goals?

SS: Whether The Rowan Amber Mill does 'work' is a matter of frequent debate with myself. The process of writing usually stems from a theme or story arc that I have been playing around with in my head for a significant length of time (likely to be years rather than months); at the same time I think what kind of musical approach I fancy or think would fit that project. I usually start with the music, and then noodle along on acoustic guitar or keyboard until I have something I am happy with musically. I will then start writing the lyrics and tweaking the basic arrangement, feel, and tempo to fit in with the lyrics. By the end of that writing process I will have that song sufficiently familiar in my head that I can record basic drums and then the bass. I will then add guitar and/or piano and temporary guide vocals. At that stage I can have a think about finessing the drums and bass to add to or complement the feel of the song. I will then add any further instrumentation, be it orchestral elements or synth parts. I will then record the vocals (either mine or someone else's). At that stage I will then live with it for a few weeks, before returning to the song to thin out the arrangement and begin mixing it.

My artistic goals are always the same: to push myself to produce better work given the constraints of my abilities; to produce work with no consideration with regard to the saleability or commerciality of that work and to disregard the levels of interest in any particular release; and to continue working exclusively on things that I am enthused about, rather than what I think people will want to hear. With that freedom, of course, comes the negative aspect that I usually often hop from genre to genre, as I react to the previous project, so I may go from a string-laden album of arrangements of traditional folk songs to a soundtrack of songs that surfs on a bed of heavy analogue synth pop and psych rock. I know that this is a pretty unhelpful challenge to those who follow my work, and also makes the idea of promoting the releases, if not virtually impossible, at the very least unworkable in practice.

WB: What are your musical influences and how do you incorporate them into your work?

SS: I do not like the idea of incorporating any musical influences in my music, and I tend to shy away from listening to things that are close to the genres I am working in. However, I would say that listening to music I love probably seeps through unconsciously in the songwriting but I wonder how much of that is discernible (I would hope not too much). I suspect in some ways I have been influenced in my songwriting by singer-songwriters such as Neil Young, Leonard Cohen, Townes Van Zandt, Martin Carthy, Nick Drake, Simon and Garfunkel, etc., through to Billy Bragg, Stephen Duffy, Cat Power, Agnes Obel, Elliott Smith, Kevin Tihista, etc. Some bands that may have exerted an unconscious influence would be bands like Fairport Convention, Bait, The Eighteenth Day of May, Circulus, The Owl Service, and Midlake — all of which have made me think (in my enjoyment of their music) about how wonderfully diverse music can be. I would say in terms of discernible influences in my own music, the work of the Radiophonic Workshop is probably the most direct and I would cite Paddy Kingsland especially.

WB: Your early band Miller reminds me of aspects of work by The Mekons in its focus on an Anglicized version of Americana. What was it about American country music that inspired you?

SS: I didn't appreciate country music as a kid, and that was probably down to Sunday mornings being the time my parents would play their limited range of vinyl, which was very much geared towards the sappy and saccharine end of country and western: Billie Joe Spears, Crystal Gale, et al. Country music, especially the singer-songwriter tradition, obviously shares much with the folk tradition as 'music of the people', so it seemed natural that I would gravitate towards the less saccharine end of country music at some point. In the late 1990s *Uncut* magazine cover-mounted a CD selection of alternative country songs under the name *Sounds of the New West*. This compilation sent me on a labyrinthine journey of discovery through Americana, through Townes Van Zandt, Woody Guthrie, The Byrds, Calexico, The Handsome Family, Wilco, Patty Griffin, Iron and Wine, etc. and that really got me hooked. I think probably all those influences melded with the fact that I was playing a lot of slide guitar and banjo at the time, and that probably gave our music a sort of country tinge.

WB: How did you decide to start The Rowan Amber Mill? Is the name a reference to Robin Hardy's *The Wicker Man*? It's interesting that you have a side project called Rowan : Morrison, which also seems to be a *Wicker Man* reference and a bit of serendipity.

SS: I was raised in an area full of (by then disused and crumbling) windmills. I have always enjoyed the idea of the place of the miller historically being a lynchpin to the production of our 'daily bread' and the possibility of his using his position of power as an influence. Amber seemed to fit the purpose too, as a beautiful element derived directly from fossilized tree resin. So, we had Amber Mill. The Rowan bit came from a group discussion and Rowan seemed to fit as we were big fans of *The Wicker Man*, also it was a berry-bearing tree, and the name of a cat belonging to Donna (our percussionist at the time). It all seemed to fit. *The Wicker Man* was a big influence on me (both the film and its soundtrack). The first song I ever recorded for release (with the band Miller) was Find Heart (Salvation), which was inspired by the procession scene where Sgt Howie is lured to the clifftop, so it has that constant driving bodhran beat allied to some organ and recorder. Much later, when I joined forces with Angeline Morrison, it seemed to be feted that we should call the duo Rowan : Morrison (thankfully saving us the stress and acrimony of having to come up with a band name).

WB: How did you approach your early work contained on *Folk Devils and Moral Panics* and *Midsummer*?

SS: I'd left Miller because we'd lost our way, and the other main songwriter and myself just couldn't agree on anything which meant we weren't writing anything new. So, I left the band and, free from the constraints of style and accommodating personnel, I was able to afford myself the freedom of writing and recording songs to please only myself and to concentrate on the weird folk direction I had been gravitating toward. I recorded a number of demos and, being relatively pleased with them, I began to get a band together including Terry Stacey (the drummer from Miller) and Kim Guy who I found via Myspace (the much-missed Myspace, I should say). We began rehearsing with the idea of getting some weird folk-friendly gigs (a ridiculous idea because at the time you were only ever going to get those gig opportunities in the big cities — certainly not in Devon and Cornwall, where the folk scene was strictly trad folk only). *Folk Devils* was pretty much my demos with a little bit of additional drumming from Terry and additional vocals and recorder from Kim. We used it as a quasi-demo (only sending out to a few people — not releasing it 'properly' until later and only as a download). We were concurrently recording *Midsummers* and, though we were using *Folk Devils* as a bit of a template, we were re-recording tracks with different arrangements and adding new songs from our repertoire, and basically trying to achieve more of a band sound. We released *Midsummers* and started to find some kindred spirits in the weird folk community. Sharon Eastwood joined — another singer and recorder player (you can never have too many) — before heading off in a slightly baroque direction with the Heartwood album. Things were falling apart a bit at that stage with illness, the unsustainability of trying to be a gigging band without a significant level of interest in our music, and with the reality of imminent fatherhood I put The Rowan Amber Mill and music on hold whilst raising my daughter and working from home.

WB: *The Book of the Lost* is an intriguing album. How did this collaboration with Emily Jones come about?

SS: I was friends with Emily from Myspace and exchanged messages frequently with her, long before we got around to making any music. When we did, it was Emily's suggestion that we should work on some soundtracks to imaginary films and she came up with the title *The Book of the Lost*. We wrote and recorded our individual songs and dialogues separately about four individual imaginary films, but we needed a conceit to draw the strands together. Emily had the idea of *The Book of the Lost* being an anthology TV series showing obscure horror films (that luckily no one had ever heard of) and we came up with a plethora of fictional films together with plots, cast, and incidental artwork, and I put together a video showing *The Book of the Lost* opening titles. We released it and it seemed to find an appreciative audience, so much so that we didn't bother to do a follow-up!

WB: The span of your 'imaginary soundtrack' *Disciples of the Scorpion* is really impressive. Is soundtrack work something you are interested in? What are some of your favorite soundtracks?

SS: When *The Book of the Lost* was finished, I did some songwriting and when we reconvened I was keen to do an album for *Ghosts on Mopeds*. Emily (quite rightly) thought it would have been impossible to distance it sufficiently from *Psychomania* that it would have been satirizing. Instead, *Disciples of the Scorpion* (originally *Children of the Scorpion*) was intended as the follow-up to *The Book of the Lost*. We both came up with a very basic concept, that of a 1960s story of a DJ and his psychotropic influence over his audience. Unfortunately, as we kept developing ideas separately we couldn't agree on a consistent direction for the plot and the idea drifted and Emily decided she didn't want to continue with the project. I kept developing the plot and writing and recording songs over a number of years, and was keen for it to be a true soundtrack in its variety of styles. I hope it all dovetailed together to form something that works. I doubt I would have the patience or the chops to soundtrack a complete film, although I did work on a couple of three-minute short films for a film course a few years back and it was very enjoyable and rewarding. Some of my favorite films have such good soundtracks that I find myself returning to time and time again. Some of my favorites are the weird folk vibes of *The Wicker Man*, the *Quadrophenia* film soundtrack by The Who, and the pastoral beauty of the soundtrack to the Ken Loach film *Kes*.

WB: Meadowsilver is your collaboration with Gayle Brogan and one of the leading figures in the folk horror revival, Grey Malkin. How did this project come about?

SS: Another collaboration that has its roots in Myspace where Grey and myself became aware of each other's music from The Hare and the Moon and The Rowan Amber Mill respectively. We did have the intention to work together previously but we couldn't find the right singer to get involved. Then Grey suggested Gayle Brogan and she proved to be an absolutely perfect addition. Most times, collaboration in something creative is a difficult and fraught pursuit, but Meadowsilver is the complete opposite, it feels free and easy and completely without stress and ego, it is a very liberating experience and I think that comes across in the music. Both Grey and Gayle are always in demand with their musical collaborations, but I hope that when time allows we are able to work together in the future.

WB: Do you find the folk horror label helpful to your work and its reception?

SS: I wouldn't say it is particularly helpful overall. Everyone has their own opinion about what folk horror is musically, often this can lean heavily on darker horror and rely on sound effects and grainy atmospheric pads. That is not what I tend to do. My own music tends towards the use of melody and orchestral sounds to convey an uneasy pastoral atmosphere. The folk horror label hopefully attracts a wider listenership to my music, but it probably disappoints many listeners whose tastes lay elsewhere.

WB: How did your contributions to A Year in the Country come about?

SS: I was asked to do it by Stephen Prince. I had been in the doldrums a bit with aborted musical projects allied with precious little time for music-making. So when he asked me to contribute to some compilations along with some amazing artists I was very inspired. The Year in the Country compilations are wonderful and very well put together. I would have loved to contribute more to the compilations and to other series released by other labels, but I find myself stuck in the position of not wanting to commit to writing a specific piece to fit a concept as, until it is done, I have no idea whether I am happy enough with the piece or if it fits the concept envisaged by the curator.

WB: Your Rowan : Morrison project in collaboration with Angeline Morrison has resulted in some of your most evocative music. How is Rowan : Morrison different to The Rowan Amber Mill?

SS: I think musically it shares a fair bit of DNA with The Rowan Amber Mill. I tend to approach the Rowan : Morrison projects with a more acoustic vibe in mind. Where it really differs is that Angeline is one of the most extraordinarily talented singer-songwriter arrangers around. She also brings her wonderful range of stylistic subtleties to the projects we undertake.

WB: One of my favorites of your releases is the *Lost in Seaburgh* album with Angeline Morrison. Why a tribute to M R James?

SS: The biggest inspirations for *Lost in Seaburgh* were the TV adaptations of *Whistle and I'll Come to You* and the 1970s *Ghost Story for Christmas* adaptations of M R James' work. These adaptations build upon the rather scant foundations of his original ghost stories. So, really it was the enjoyment of those stories and adaptations that just made it seem like an inspiring direction to head toward.

WB: I believe that no horror writer is better at suggesting, alluding, and hinting than M R James. How important is mood and atmosphere to your aesthetic?

SS: I do find the writing of M R James and his somewhat formulaic approach to the stories of great interest. He tended to leave lots of space and subtlety for the recipient to dream up their own imagery and dread. I tend to write songs with a visual or narrative(s) in mind, so subtly conveying a mood, atmosphere, or image is integral to that. Of course, whether the listener picks up on that same narrative, atmosphere, imagery, or is transported elsewhere is a different matter, and of equal validity.

WB: Your work in Rowan : Morrison is tied to seasonal imagery. What is it about the changing of natural environments that is of interest to the work of this project?

SS: I suspect that being tied to the landscape and environment is intrinsically linked to the changing of the seasons and the march of time itself, allied to the themes of growth, loss, and rebirth. You could view our album *In the Sunshine We Rode the Horses* both as a calendar of the year, as a metaphor for the stages of life, and also a timeline for the apocalyptic harm we have wrought to this planet. We have also recorded lots of specifically winter-themed songs, be they carols, wassails, traditional tunes, Christmas songs, etc. and I think this is probably a mixture of us trying to control (in song) the bleakness of winter allied to the thought that, if we can see through the winter, then we will be able to see life, light, and growth slowly return with the spring.

WB: I think your Making Tea for Robots project is fantastic and probably your most 'hauntological'. What was your approach to *Follows Shortly*?

SS: I was desperate to record an album of synthesizer songs and wanted to make some tunes to evoke the wonderful theme tunes and library music of the TV 'Programs for Schools' of the late 1970s and early 1980s. So, I would have a type of generic educational program in mind (i.e. a history, technology, or economics program) and then put a twist on it as to how (with the benefit of hindsight) the information may not have been entirely accurate. Then I'd put together a theme tune that (hopefully) could be mistaken for a real theme tune from those times using analogue synths (or soft synths) available at the time (i.e. Mini Moog, Prophet 5).

WB: Do you feel any connection to the hauntological genre and its philosophy?

SS: I'm pretty sure elements of my work must share similar elements to those in the hauntological scene. But, to be honest, I do my best to steer clear of it as I want to stay as remote as possible from any influence.

WB: Releases on your MillerSounds label usually involve a variety of media and visual artifacts included with the physical albums. Why? Do you prefer a certain medium for your music?

SS: I really like the CD format purely on listening terms. The compression of MP3s removes far too much of the color and depth of a song, so when you spend a long time working on a song (especially during the mixing process), you really want the end product to sound the very best that it can. Most often the album as a whole is telling a story, the addition of artifacts (be it posters, art prints, etc.) helps expand or underscore the narrative behind the album.

WB: Do you feel there are unifying themes that run through your work?

SS: The overall unifying themes running through my work are probably attempts to explain certain specific elements of the human condition. For instance, I often place the settings/subjects of my songs in the distant past, to enable me to make a comment on the dissatisfaction I have with the mess we are currently living through i.e. how we appear psychologically unable to prevent repeating the mistakes of the past, or the lack of value society places on the worth of individuals, or the abuse of power, how we allow ourselves to be divided. These are the kind of themes I tend to weave stories around, albeit they may be dressed in clothes of times long gone.

WB: What would your dream project/collaboration be?

SS: I am always very open to collaborations, but I tend not to be the one who suggests collaborations (I'm a bit too shy to take such a bold move). There are quite a number of people within the scene whose work I adore and who I think I would collaborate well with to make an interesting and fulfilling project.

WB: How important is performing live to your creativity?

SS: Performing live hasn't been important to my creativity. I rarely perform live, and I do feel like I am missing out on it. Conversely, much of my music is well suited to live performance, but it is not easy finding places where that live performance can be expressed in the right way.

As I am so wedded to the notion of place, the ideal setting would be in a woodland setting, or an open air festival, or failing that a stage where a projection could give a decent hint of a woodland setting. Performing live is a very large commitment of time that takes away from the process of making new music, so to justify that commitment of time and resources you really need to have the ability to book a decent amount of gigs in a short period of time. So, while that remains a largely unrealistic proposition, I tend to shy away from live performance unless it is a one-off gig that I desperately want to play.

WB: In a globalized world of increasing technological and virtual lifestyles, why is it important to keep folk traditions alive?

SS: The folk tradition is important in a couple of respects. Firstly, many of the stories and songs express experiences and, dare I say, lessons from the past. They may be wrapped up in archaic language or in settings unfamiliar to modern times, but these are reflections of people who have led lives more emotionally similar to the ones we lead today than we may realize. It might also be that at some point, we actually start learning from the mistakes of the past. I also think it is just as important to be creating new traditions and to continue moving traditions on to reflect the times we live in. Another important aspect of folk music, the music of the people, is in these times where society has never felt so disparate and solitary, those traditions and songs do have the ability to help unite people and build communities, which will surely be an important step in healing some of the many conflicts society faces in these most turbulent of times.

WB: What is the future for The Rowan Amber Mill?

SS: The immediate future of The Rowan Amber Mill is an album of songs I have written (and begun recording) centered around aspects of the English Civil War (a period which has so many parallels with the last dozen or so years). After that is finished, I have another batch of songs ready with no particular theme, but with more of a stripped-down, singer-songwriter feel to them. I also have an album of songs that will blend banjo with prog rock synthesizer, which actually works much better than it sounds on paper.

The Rowan Amber Mill (and Related) Discography

The Rowan Amber Mill

Folk Devils and Moral Panics (2008)
Midsummers (2009)
Heartwood (2010)
The Book of the Lost (with Emily Jones) (2013)
Silent Night Songs For a Cold Winter's Evening (with Angeline Morrison) (2014)
Harvest The Ears (Cuts From The Folk Horror Archive —Vol. 1) (2018)
Harrowed by the Stones (Cuts From The Folk Horror Archive — Vol. 2) (2020)
Golden Strings to Tether the Sun (2020)
Among the Gorse to Settle Scores (2020)
Disciples of the Scorpion (2021)
They Worked the Fields (2021)
Through Dark Polished Glass (2022)
The Haunted Future Silence Bequeathed (2023)
The Wolves Are Running in the Wildwood (2023)
Evocation Projection Harmony Solidarity (2024)

Meadowsilver

Meadowsilver (2019)
The Coronation of the Herring Queen (2019)
Singles (2019)
II (2022)

Rowan : Morrison

Bury the Forests (2018)
In the Sunshine We Rode the Horses (2019)
Fields of Frost (2019)
Lost in Seaburgh (2020)
Bride of the Wintertide (2021)

Making Tea for Robots

Follows Shortly (2018)

Stephen Stannard

High and Dry (2022)
Between Dust and Desire (2023)

Interview: Angeline Morrison

SANDY DENNY, SHIRLEY Collins, Allison Krauss, Vashti Bunyan, Alison O'Donnell. All distinguished members of the pantheon of illustrious folk music voices. In order to be elevated into this rarefied air, a singer must project fragile, ethereal empyrean sound but, at the same time, express a potent, commanding goddess-like power, representing the moon ascending over the sun. The voice must be timeless and celestial yet exposed and vulnerable, accessing the sadness and yearning as well as the glory and vibrancy that's at the heart of the human predicament. A singer who should be enthroned in this divine aggregation is Angeline Morrison. A truly eclectic artist, Angeline is at home in musical genres as disparate as soul, rockabilly, Italian pop, French ye-ye, UK beat, bossa nova, and jazz. But it is in folk music where Angeline transcends style and delves into the sublime. Her reverence for nature, the spiritual, and rural traditions inform all aspects of her art, especially when collaborating with The Rowan Amber Mill. Rowan : Morrison have created some of the finest folk horror-inspired releases yet, conjuring seasonal imagery and haunting encounters with the unknown. It is this hauntological evocation of beauty and tragedy, of suffering and spirituality, of the ghosts of the past and the hope for the future through her magical voice, that unites Angeline with the greatest folk music interpreters. Morrison's personal, aesthetic, and historical interests come full circle on her newest release, *The Sorrow Songs: Folk Songs of Black British Experience*, a collection of songs exploring the African diaspora and the continuing struggle to give voice to the black narrative in England and which has been justly praised by *The Guardian* and *The Quietus*. Whatever she sings comes from deep within her soul. Angeline's releases can be found at https://angelinemorrisonmusic.bandcamp.com/

William Burns: What are your key TV/film/music memories that you think helped form your artistic identity?

Angeline Morrison: Probably folk horror soundtracks. I was a macabre child and always loved anything creepy…

WB: Your work is very connected to landscape, particularly the environment of Cornwall. How does geography inform your music?

AM: Landscape and nature are absolutely essential to my creative process, and because of this they are always present in my work. I have all my best ideas when I am out in nature, it shapes me continually. The landscape of Cornwall is famous for its beauty — seas, cliffs, beaches, fields, woodland — but also the land of Cornwall was very aggressively hollowed out by the mining industry, and you can see traces of this all over the county. It all feeds into my work.

WB: I noticed that your work often focuses on the power and majesty of the natural world, specifically clouds, the sun, and the sky. Do you have an interest in the occult, paganism, or the supernatural? If so, how do these interests inform your aesthetic?

AM: Yes, I have an interest in all of those things, and in the immaterial in general. It's quite hard to pinpoint exactly how this informs my aesthetic, other than to say that it seems to seep in through the cracks of everything I make.

WB: What are your artistic/musical goals?

AM: I just want to make beautiful things.

WB: What are your musical influences and how do you incorporate them into your work?

AM: My musical influences are so varied, I'm not even sure I could list them all! Sometimes I consciously work them into music I'm writing. For example, I might start with a particular intention to make a song that sounds like a lost recording from a certain era. At other times, they creep up from somewhere deep inside me, and surprise me.

Growing up we listened to a lot of Jamaican music, and a lot of soul. My mum was absolutely obsessed with Sam Cooke, so he was a huge influence. As one of few artists at the time who also composed his own material and set up his own publishing company, Sam Cooke was so much more than just this gloriously golden voice... My dad's pop records from the sixties are also an inspiration, as a child I was always looking for Oldies stations on the radio so I could hear more of these sounds. It sort of felt like I already knew them, in some way.

WB: You have recorded in very eclectic styles of music. Do you have a favorite genre?

AM: As someone who loves, lives, and understands the world through music, I do find it quite hard to favor particular genres over one another. In my work you will hear the interweaving of all the genres that have been most formative or had the most profound effects on me. Some of these aren't genres at all but fragments of music, or motifs. The ones that settled deepest into the storehouse of my unconscious are the ones that have the strongest influence.

WB: How did The Ambassadors of Sorrow come together?

AM: I put The Ambassadors of Sorrow together as a band, in order to bring to life a particular set of songs I had written. The line-ups have changed a great deal, but I've always been lucky enough to work with some excellent musicians. At the moment it's a solo project... But to go back to the beginning, all these songs were pouring out of me, and it soon became very clear that this was a 'family' of songs. These songs belonged together, each was a sort of familial variation on a theme. The songs were all inspired by a soundscape and visual landscape of early to mid 1960s popular music, particularly the UK Beat scene, and also the more dramatic musical moments found in Italian pop music of that era. I didn't have the funds available to work with an orchestra, but on most of those songs there's an orchestral accompaniment in my head. Or at the very least, a string quartet...

WB: The Ambassadors of Sorrow album *Easterly* is very interesting, almost like funk folk with its rock 'n' roll rhythms. How did you approach recording this album?

AM: Thank you! I'm glad you can hear the folk as well as the rock 'n' roll, and the tiny threads of funk. This album was recorded quite quickly, within a week. The engineering and production was the work of Jess Carter, who also played drums on the album, a multi-talented human if ever there was one. He completely understood my vision for the sound and the feel of the songs, and this came together on Easterly.

WB: I loved The Ambassadors of Sorrow album *There is No Ending*. It sounds like rockabilly and the 1950s country-inspired pop of The Everly Brothers and Ricky Nelson but with a feminine touch. What were the inspirations for this album?

AM: Once again, thank you! Billy Fury's album *The Sound of Fury* (1960) is a major influence in so many ways. I became quite obsessed with Billy Fury. His life is so interesting, and there was just something so remarkable about him, a sort of aura. That album was recorded within twenty-four hours, which was quite common at the time. It's a work of genius and captures that immediacy and aliveness that you'd expect to hear if the clocks are chasing you. I wanted to see if I could capture a similar feel, both in terms of the sonic style of the music of Billy Fury and his contemporaries — that exciting transitional moment where rock 'n' roll morphs into the Beat sound, so beautifully expressed by early Beatles recordings — and I also wanted to see if we could capture that 'lightning in a bottle' feel that is all over *The Sound of Fury*.

In terms of my other inspirations, I think you can hear my love of Françoise Hardy's early to mid 1960s recordings on this album, and my lifelong love of the traditional music of the UK and Ireland is imprinted on everything I have ever recorded. Even if other people can't hear it, it's always there for me…

WB: Your most recent songs on Bandcamp are in the vein of traditional British folk. I'm especially interested in the song He Comes In The Night. How did this song come about? Any reason for the use of this style for your most recent compositions?

AM: It was really time for my trad folk influences to take center stage in my musical creativity. I have always sung traditional song, danced traditional dance, and loved folk customs. I wanted to honour this and devote myself musically to these songs that have danced around in my head and imagination since I first heard Shirley Collins on the radio as a child. That is a voice you never forget, and it had a profound effect on me. After I heard her, I began to seek out more music like this, continually building on the new knowledge and listening I gained.

In terms of the song He Comes In The Night, it was actually inspired by a real story of a haunting. I was researching and reading about hauntings in general and this extraordinary story came up, which took place in the late twentieth century in the UK. I won't name the people involved (even though the story is in the public domain), because one of the then-teenagers, now an adult, wished to put it all behind her. But that was the inspiration. I was fascinated by this story. I began to embellish it and create my own fictional narrative. In my story, the protagonist is not haunted by this visiting ghost, but instead is in love with it. The spirit's arrivals are something that the protagonist really needs in their life, and they are always looking for confirmation and signs. It could also be about mourning the loss of a loved one, who comes back to you in dreams that feel so very real that, upon waking, the realization of separation is too much to bear. Real sorrow and real grief weigh heavily at these times…

WB: What was your approach for your album *Are You Ready Cat?*

AM: With *Are You Ready Cat?* I wanted to make a sort of cloth woven of my love of French 1960s pop music, popular jazz, and bossa-influenced pop of the same era, and also, as always, folk and traditional music. I wanted to make something that had some sweet, lighthearted moments, as well as the melancholy and sorrow that is always present somewhere in my music…

WB: The two demos you posted for *The Sorrow Songs: Folk Songs of Black British Experience* are fascinating in how you are able to take tragedy and transform it into beauty.

AM: That is a lovely thing to say, thank you! Some humans seem to have a deep capacity for sorrow, they are able to examine it because they have an affinity for it. I seem to be one of those… In the case of *The Sorrow Songs: Folk Songs of Black British Experience*, this ability has really helped me. The seed of the idea for this album came to me many years ago, but it has taken a while to incubate and push through the soil. In the wake of George Floyd's murder, the world opened its eyes to many things. It became possible to discuss race, and be heard in ways I had never felt heard before. I'm one of a very small number of black folk singers and folk musicians in the UK (in the USA it seems you have a much more diverse folk scene). This has never stopped me from immersing myself in the scene, and generally folk enthusiasts are a very welcoming group of people. But being the only black person in a folk club, or at a folk festival, etc., well, it has an effect on you, and that effect is cumulative… So, I was reading W E B du Bois' *The Souls of Black Folk* (1903) in the aftermath of George Floyd's murder. *The Souls of Black Folk* is a very musical text: du Bois references music a great deal, and uses music to make many of his observations. It's a wonderful and moving book, and the chapter, 'Of The Sorrow Songs', moved me particularly, which is devoted to a study of Spirituals as a body of folk song by, about, and for enslaved Africans and their descendants in America. I immediately began to wonder why we didn't have a UK equivalent of the Spiritual. Here in the UK there is a historic black presence that there's a surprising amount of misinformation about. Black people have been present in these islands since at least Roman times, and of course we were absolutely integral to the growth and flourishing of the UK, the British Empire, European imperialism at large, and so on… So the idea that black voices are not represented in the surviving traditional songs we have made no sense.

There are existing songs that reference black people, but most of these are not songs I would want to sing. Also, it's clear from the lyrics that they were not written by black people, about their interior lives or experiences. I decided to research our historic black UK population and compose songs with the intention of honouring these ancestors, and representing their lives.

I cannot imagine that such songs never existed. First, humans are song-making creatures and make music wherever they go. Second, many of the UK's historic black population were singers and musicians. So I feel that it's simply that the songs did not survive. Maybe they just weren't collected, or recorded, or people just stopped singing them… I hope that my collection of songs will be taken up by the folk community, and that people will want to sing them. The wonderful Eliza Carthy will be producing this album, so I am super excited about that. I've made two demos temporarily available on my Bandcamp, as many people have asked where they could hear the songs.

WB: The Rowan : Morrison project with Stephen Stannard has resulted in some of your most evocative music. How did this collaboration start?

AM: It's always a joy to work with Stephen, whose musical genius, extraordinarily expansive imagination, and brilliant eye for detail really shape the whole sound and look of Rowan : Morrison. Our mutual friend, the folk singer and composer Emily Jones (daughter of sixties folk legend Al Jones), is actually the reason we began to work together. If you don't know Emily's beautiful work, I highly recommend you check it out.

WB: The Rowan : Morrison album *In the Sunshine We Rode the Horses* is tied to seasonal imagery. What is it about the changing of natural environments that is of interest?

AM: The changing of the seasons is, for me, a powerful metaphor for the transience of human life. We are part of a constant cycle of death and rebirth, and nothing in its current form will last forever.

WB: Why is the British countryside such a muse for your works?

AM: I have a very deep, very close, relationship with the countryside. It feels like my true home. When I am out in nature, anything is bearable. Nature washes you clean of all your troubles, and can nourish and soothe body and mind and soul…

WB: One of my favorites of your releases is the *Lost in Seaburgh* album. Why a tribute to M R James?

AM:There is something so timeless about his ghost stories. It has been traditional in the UK for an M R James ghost story to be dramatized at Christmastime (the BBC broadcast *A Ghost Story for Christmas* each year between 1971 and 1978, and five of these stories were M R James adaptations). He was also an intriguing person, and we wanted to honour him.

WB: The latest Rowan : Morrison album *Bride of the Wintertide* completes a triptych with *Silent Night Songs For a Cold Winter's Evening* and *Fields of Frost*, which explore songs that resonate with Yuletide and the winter solstice. Besides the obvious thematic connections, how do you view these three releases? Do you hear an evolution in terms of the performances or was the idea to have a cohesive uniformity to them in terms of the music and your vocals?

AM: *Bride of the Wintertide* does indeed complete this triptych. For both Stephen (aka The Rowan Amber Mill) and myself, the wintertime is a particularly magical and significant time of year. The winter solstice, Christmas, New Year, the turning of the year, turning within in the dark of winter to tend to the soul... Most cultures around the world have some form of festival of light that takes place in the darker winter months, and there is something about that that makes wintertime a time where you can feel a connection with your fellow humans, past, present, and future. We both felt that the previous albums had so much of our love, care, and attention poured into them, that we wanted to really shine a light on them and make them more visible. At the same time, there was more of the magic of wintertime that we wanted to explore in musical form... So the idea to create *Bride of the Wintertide* was born, which hopefully allows for both of these things to take place.

WB: Do you find the folk horror label helpful to your work?

AM: I personally really like it, but then I have always been a lover of horror, though of a highly specific type. I love the Hammer House of Horror films and TV shows, and any UK-made horror of the 1960s, seventies, or eighties. These films and TV shows tend to have really compelling soundtracks, and folk music (or musical motifs that suggest folk music) are often used. So, I like to watch these to comfort myself when the world feels cold… But to answer your question, I think other people who love similar things will find the music using this label, so it's all good.

WB: Do you feel there are unifying themes that run through your work?

AM: Yes, I do; there are many themes that run through all my work and could be said to unify it. These themes all make sense to me, even if they might not to other people… Nature, the land, sorrow, deep emotions, the inner life and the imagination, the changing of seasons, literature, the supernatural… There are too many to name, but that's a good start.

WB: What would your dream project/collaboration be?

AM: Working with Eliza Carthy as producer on *The Sorrow Songs: Folk Songs of Black British Experience* is a dream come true, so I'm happily focused on that for now.

WB: How important is performing live to your creativity?

AM: Well, I'm a shy and introverted person, so I'm not one of those musicians who only feels alive when they're on stage… Having said that, it is very important to connect with other people, and music is a powerful way to make those connections. Also, when I play songs live, I can get an idea of which ones work and which ones don't. So while I'm not always totally at ease performing live, it is a very important thing to do.

WB: In a globalized world of increasing technological and virtual lifestyles, why is it important to keep folk traditions alive?

AM: I think your question says it all really… Folk traditions connect us with nature, with the land, with other humans, with a shared past, and with ourselves in ways that I think virtual connections just can't achieve. I'm all for increasing technological advances, by the way; I just feel that they don't connect us with a shared mythos or Jungian collective unconscious in the ways that folk traditions can.

WB: What is in the future for Angeline Morrison?

AM: There is all this music crowding the inside of my head, I'm making more and more each day and it's all piling up. So hopefully my future will include loads of time and resources that will make it possible for me to record and release all this music…

Angeline Morrison Discography

Angeline Morrison

Are You Ready Cat? (2013)
The Feeling Sublime EP (2013)
Silent Night Songs For A Cold Winter's Evening (with The Rowan Amber Mill) (2014)
Hours of Sunlight (2020)
Clouds Never Move (2020)
The Sorrow Songs: Folk Songs of Black British Experience Demos (2021)
He Comes in the Night (2021)
Bright Blessings (2021)
Circular Waltz (2021)
The Brown Girl and Other Folk Songs (2022)
The Sorrow Songs: Folk Songs of Black British Experience (2022)
It's Not Fine (2023)
Ophelia (2024)

Rowan : Morrison

Bury the Forests (2018)
In the Sunshine We Rode the Horses (2019)
Fields of Frost (2019)
Lost in Seaburgh (2020)
Bride of the Wintertide (2021)

The Ambassadors Of Sorrow

Thunder In The Skies (2004)
Loathsome Food (2005)
Easterly (2009)
There Is No Ending (2011)

The Mighty Sceptres

All Hail The Mighty Sceptres! (2014)
Siren Call (2014)
Shy As A Butterfly / Nothing Seems To Work Right (2016)

We Are Muffy

The Charcoal Pool (2018)

Emily & Angeline (with Emily Jones)

EP1: The Blue One (2015)

An A–Z (well, Y) of folk horror music

A

The Advisory Circle: *As the Crow Flies* (2011)

Aghast: *Hexerei Im Zwielicht Der Finsternis* (1995)

The Albion Band: *Rise Up Like The Sun* (1978)

Albion Country Band: *Battle Of The Field* (1976)

John Allison: *Witches and War-Whoops: Early New England Ballads* (1962)

Amarynthia: *Walk the Wytchwoods* (2021), *Sisters* (2022)

And Also The Trees: *The Millpond Years* (1988), *Farewell To The Shade* (1989), *Green Is The Sea* (1992)

Aphrodite's Child: *End of the World* (1968), *666* (1972)

Apoptose: *Nordand* (2000), *Bannwald* (2010)

Arborea: *Wayfaring Summer* (2006), *House of Sticks* (2008), *Fortress Of The Sun* (2013)

Dave and Toni Arthur: *The Lark In The Morning* (1969), *Hearken To The Witches Rune* (1971)

Ashtoreth and Grey Malkin: *Pilgrim* (2019), *Hermit* (2019), *Heretic* (2021)

Autumn Creatures: *Funeral Gardens* (2018)

B

Les Baxter: *Cry of the Banshee* (1980)

The Belbury Poly: *Farmer's Angle* (2004), *The Willows* (2004), *The Owl's Map* (2006), *From An Ancient Star* (2009), *The Belbury Tales* (2012), *The Gone Away* (2020)

Matt Berry: *Witchhazel* (2011), *Kill the Wolf* (2013)

Joe Bethancourt: *Who Fears The Devil? (The Songs of Silver John)* (1994)

Bendith: *Bendith* (2016)

Blood Ceremony: *The Eldritch Dark* (2013), *Lord of Misrule* (2016), *Lolly Willows* (2019)

Jake Blount: *Spider Tales* (2020)

The Body and Big|Brave: *Leaving None But Small Birds* (2021)

Dock Boggs: *Country Blues: Complete Early Recordings (1927–29)* (2004)

The Bothy Band: *Old Hag You Have Killed Me* (1976), *Out of The Wind Into The Sun* (1977)

Anne Briggs: *The Hazards of Love* (1964), *Anne Briggs* (1971), *The Time Has Come* (1971), *Sing A Song for You* (1973)

Desmond Briscoe and Glynis Jones: *The Stone Tape* (2019)

Broadcast: *Mother Is The Milky Way* (2009)

Broadcast and The Focus Group: *Investigate Witch Cults Of The Radio Age* (2009)

A Broken Consort: *Crow Autumn* (2010)

Brytho: Numen: *Beating the Bounds (Folk Horror)* (2020), *'Wordless Winter Ways': The Visions of Dr Calder Halt* (2020), *No Parish but Albion: The Vagabond Trust* (2021), *The Companie of the Hidden Crone: Archival Recordings (1970–2021)* (2021), *The Wessex Mistery Transmissions* (2022), *British Cunning Broadcasts* (2022)

Vashti Bunyan: *Just Another Diamond Day* (1970)

Burd Ellen: *A Tarot of the Green Wood* (2022)

Kate Bush: *The Dreaming* (1982), *Hounds of Love* (1985)

C

Cabinet of Curiosities: *Searchlight Needles* (2008), *Blue Highways* (2010)

Caedmon: *Caedmon* (1968)

David Cain and Robert Duncan: *The Seasons* (1969)

John Cameron: *Psychomania* (2003)

Martin Carthy and Dave Swarbrick: *Prince Heathen* (1969)

Nick Cave: *Murder Ballads* (1996)

Cernunnes Rising: *Urban Druid* (2013)

Charles Vaughan: *Documenting the Decay* (2011), *Haunted Woodland Volume 3* (2012), *Pylon Reveries* (2017)

Children of Alice: *Children of Alice* (2017)

Circulus: *The Lick on The Tip of An Envelope Yet to Be Sent* (2005), *Clocks Are Like People* (2006), *Thought Becomes Reality* (2009), *Birth* (2018)

C.O.B.: *Spirit of Love* (1970), *Moyshe McStiff And the Tartan Lancers of The Sacred Heart* (1972)

Coil: *Moon's Milk (In Four Phases)* (2002)
Diana Collier: *Ode to Riddley Walker* (2020)
Shirley Collins: *The Power Of The True Love Knot* (1968), *Amaranth* (1976), *Lodestar* (2016)
Shirley Collins and The Albion Country Band: *No Roses* (1971)
Shirley and Dolly Collins: *Love, Death & The Lady* (1967)
Comus: *First Utterance* (1971)
Dorthia Cottrell: *Death Folk Country* (2023)
Current 93: *Earth Covers Earth* (1988), *Swastikas for Noddy* (1988), *All the Pretty Horses* (1996)

D

Dark Leaves: *Grey Stone in the Wood* (2018), *Laid Under Leaf, Under Branches* (2022)
Richard Dawson: *Peasant* (2017)
George Deacon and Marion Ross: *Sweet William's Ghost* (1973)
Dead Can Dance: *Aion* (1990), *Into the Labyrinth* (1993)
Dead Melodies: *Legends of the Wood* (2017)
The Declining Winter: *Haunt The Upper Hallways* (2009)
The Devil and the Universe: *Haunted Summer* (2014), *Folk Horror* (2017)
Keith Dewhurst and The Albion Band: *Lark Rise to Candleford* (1980)
Donovan: *For Little Ones* (1967), *HMS Donovan* (1971)
Doran: *Doran* (2021)
drcarlsonalbion: *La Strega and the Cunning Man in the Smoke* (2012)
Dr. Strangely Strange: *Kip of the Senses* (1969), *Heavy Petting* (1970)
The Druids: *Burnt Offering* (1970), *Pastime with Good Company* (1972)
Judy Dyble: *Gathering The Threads (Fifty Years Of Stuff)* (2015)

E

The Eccentronic Research Council: *1612 Underture* (2012)
Empyrium: *Where at Night the Wood Grouse Plays* (1999), *Weiland* (2002)
English Heretic: *The Sacred Geography Of British Cinema: Scene One* (2005), *The*

Underworld Service (2014), *Wish You Were Heretic* (2017)

Espers: *Espers* (2004), *The Weed Tree* (2005), *II* (2006)

Embertides: *Between Trees and Starlike* (2020)

Exuma: *Exuma* (1970), *Snake* (1972)

F

Fairport Convention: *What We Did on Our Holidays* (1969), *Liege and Lief* (1969), *Angel Delight* (1971), *Rising for the Moon* (1975)

John Faulkner and Sandra Kerr: *The Music for Bagpuss* (2018)

Faun: *Zaubersprüche* (2001), *Licht* (2003), *Renaissance* (2005)

Faun Fables: *Mother Twilight* (2001), *Early Song* (2004), *Light of a Vaster Dark* (2010)

Paul Ferris: *Witchfinder General* (2013)

Field Lines Cartographer: *The Ferric Landscape* (2020), *The Spectral Isle* (2020)

Archie Fisher: *The Man With A Rhyme* (1976)

Luboš Fišer; *Valerie And Her Week Of Wonders* (2006)

The Floating World: *The Wood Beyond the World* (2013)

The Focus Group: *We Are All Pan's People* (2007)

Folklore Tapes: *The Art of Magic* (2018), *Cornucopia — A Compendium of Practical Occultism* (2020), *Folklore Tape Library Catalogue Cassette Vol. I (2011–2016)* (2016)

Forest: *Forest* (1969), *Full Circle* (1970)

Forktail: *Forktail* (2018), *We Are the Ghosts* (2019)

Mark Fry: *Dreaming With Alice* (1972)

Furia: *The Fates* (1986)

The Future Kings Of England: *Who Is This Who Is Coming* (2011)

G

Gazelle Twin and NYX: *Deep England* (2021)

Don Gere: *Werewolves on Wheels* (2011)

Paul Giovanni and Magnet: *The Wicker Man* (Trunk Records version, 1998), *The Wicker Man* (Silva Screen version, 2002)

Gravenhurst: *Internal Travels* (2002), *Flashlight Seasons* (2003), *The Western Lands* (2007)

Greanvine: *Witch Songs* (2013), *Hanged with Gold So Red* (2021)

Green Lung: *Woodland Rites* (2019), *Black Harvest* (2021), *This Heathen Land* (2023)

Gwydion: *Sings Songs for The Old Religion* (1975)

H

The Hare and the Moon: *The Hare and the Moon* (2009), *The Grey Malkin* (2010), *Wood Witch* (2015)

Harvestman: *Lashing the Rye* (2005), *Music For Megaliths* (2017)

Hawthonn: *Red Goddess (of this men shall know nothing)* (2018), *Earth Mirror* (2021)

Head South By Weaving and Alison O'Donnell: *The Execution Of Frederick Baker* (2012)

The Heartwood Institute: *Astercote* (2015), *Secret Rites* (2018), *Witchcraft Murders* (2021), *Land of the Lakes* (2021)

Hedningarna: *Fire* (1996)

Hermione Harvestman: *Ghosts (Four Stories by M.R. James)* (2013), *May Eve* (2014), *A Harvest of Souls: Requiem for Dancers (Unseen)* (2016)

Hexvessel: *Dawnbearer* (2011), *No Holier Temple* (2012), *Iron Marsh* (2013), *Kindred* (2020)

The Hologram People: *Sacred Ritual To Unlock The Mountain Portal* (2021)

Hood: *Rustic Houses, Forlorn Valleys* (1998), *The Cycle of Days and Seasons* (1999)

Justin Hopper and Sharron Kraus: *Swift Wings* (2022)

Justin Hopper and Sharron Kraus with The Belbury Poly: *Chanctonbury Rings* (2019)

Ian Humberstone: *Black Dog Traditions of England* (2016), *Paths To The Foss* (2016)

Ian Humberstone/David Chatton Barker: *Devon Folklore Tapes Volume I: Two Witches* (2014)

Hunt & Turner: *Magic Landscape* (1972)

Ashley Hutchings: *Rattlebone and Ploughjack* (1976)

I

In Gowan Ring: *The Glinting Spade* (2002), *Hazel Steps Through A Weathered Home* (2009), *The Serpent And The Dove* (2015)

The Implicit Order: *Supernatural Folk Tales* (2011), *Halloween* (2011)

Incredible String Band: *The 5,000 Spirits or The Layers of an Onion* (1967), *The Hangman's Beautiful Daughter* (1968), *Wee Tam and the Big Huge* (1968)

Inkubus Sukkubus: *Beltaine* (1990), *Belladonna & Aconite* (1993), *Wytches* (1994), *The Goat* (2011), *The Way of The Witch* (2021)

J

Blind Willie Johnson: *The Complete Blind Willie Johnson* (1993)

Bob Johnson and Pete Knight: *The King Of Elfland's Daughter* (1977)

Emily Jones and The Rowan Amber Mill: *The Book of the Lost* (2014)

K

Paddy Kingsland and the BBC Radiophonic Workshop: *The Changes* (2018), *Doctor Who: The Visitation* (2020)

Mark Korven: *The Witch* (2016)

Sharron Kraus: *Beautiful Twisted* (2002), *Right Wantonly A-Mumming* (2007), *Pilgrim Chants and Pastoral Trails* (2013), *Joy's Reflection in Sorrow* (2018)

R.D. Kirdiv and S.V. Skirling: *Devon Folklore Tapes Vol. VII — Two Ruins* (2018)

Bobby Krlic: *Midsommar* (2019)

L

Lingua Ignota: *Sinner Get Ready* (2021)

A.L. Lloyd, Anne Briggs, Frankie Armstrong with Alf Edwards and Dave Swarbrick: *The Bird in The Bush (Traditional Erotic Songs)* (1966)

Lost Harbours: *Hymns and Ghosts* (2012), *Into the Failing Light* (2014), *In the Direction of the Sun* (2015)

Lord Summerisle: *Postum* (2015)

Loudest Whisper: *The Children Of Lir* (1974), *Loudest Whisper* (1981), *Maiden Of Sorrow* (1994)

M

Magna Carta: *Seasons* (1970)

Maiden Hair ov England: *Ancient Borders* (2021), *Trewanmead* (2021), *The Adder Witch* (2023)

Malicorne: *Malicorne* (1974), *Malicorne* (1975), *Almanach* (1976), *The Extraordinary Tour of France by Adélard Rousseau, known as Nivernais the key to hearts, Companion carpenter of duty* (1978), *Le Bestiaire* (1979)
Malinky: *Last Leaves* (2000)
Mamiffer: *The World Unseen* (2016)
Clint Mansell: *In the Earth* (2021)
Mathesar: *Quarrymass* (2018)
The McCalmans: *Burn the Witch* (1978)
James McKeown: *Sublime Knight Effect* (2013)
Sam McLoughlin and David Chatton Baker: *Tales of the Monstone* (2020)
Brona McVittie: *The Man in the Mountain* (2020)
Meadowsilver: *Meadowsilver* (2019), *II* (2022)
Mellow Candle: *Swaddling Songs* (1972), *The Virgin Prophet* (1994)
The Memory Band: *Oh My Days* (2011), *On the Chalk (Our Navigation of the Line of the Downs)* (2013), *A Fair Field* (2016)
Midwinter: *The Waters Of Sweet Sorrow* (1993)
Missionary Work: *The Ash Tree* (2021)
MMMD: *Hagazussa* (2018)
Angeline Morrison: *The Brown Girl and Other Folk Songs* (2022)
The Mortlake Bookclub: *Exquisite Corpse* (2016), *Requiem for Uriel* (2019)
Mandy Morton and Spriguns: *Magic Lady* (1978)
Mr. Fox: *The Gipsy* (1971)
My Autumn Empire: *Dreams of Death and Other Favourites* (2015)
Myriad Valley: *Eternal Space of the Mind* (2023)

N

Natural Snow Buildings: *The Snowbringer Cult* (2008), *Night Coercion into the Company of Witches* (2012), *Daughter of Darkness* (2013), *Aldebaran* (2016)
Kemper Norton: *Season One* (2008), *Carn* (2013), *Toll* (2016)

O

Alison O'Donnell: *Hey Hey Hippy Witch* (2009), *Climb Sheer The Fields Of Peace* (2017), *Exotic Masks And Sensible Shoes* (2019)

OGRE: *The Field Recordist's Guide to: Summoning Lesser Demons* (2017), *Ballard* (2018), *Gates of Nessus* (2020)
The Order of the 12: *Lore of the Land* (2022)
Out of Orion: *The Tales of John the Balladeer* (2013)
The Owl Service: *The View from A Hill* (2010), *Garland Sessions* (2012), *Swearing on the Horns* (2021), *Music For Film & Television* (2023)

P

Bob Pegg: *Ancient Maps* (1975)
The Pendlefolk: *The Pendlefolk* (1970)
Pentagram Home Video: *Walpurgisnacht* (2017), *Lost On The Red Hill* (2017), *Lost On The Seven Hills: A Ghost Story By Evrim Ersoy & Pentagram Home Video* (2018), *Walpurgisnacht II* (2018)
Pentangle: *Basket of Light* (1969), *Cruel Sister* (1970), *Solomon's Seal* (1972)
Popol Vuh: *In den Gärten Pharaos* (1971), *Aguirre* (1975), *Nosferatu* (2004)
Stephen Prince: *The Corn Mother: Night Wraiths* (2020), *The Shildam Hall Tapes: The Falling Reverse* (2021)
Vincent Price: *Witchcraft-Magic: An Adventure in Demonology* (1969), *A Coven of Witches' Tales* (1973), *Lord Dunsany* (1982)
Purson: *The Circle & The Blue Door* (2013), *In the Meantime* (2014)

Q

Quiet Clapping: *The Abbey Of The Black Hag* (2021)

R

Radiophonic Workshop: *Burials in Several Earths* (2017)
Manja Ristic: *The Black Isle* (2019), *Songs of the North* (2021)
Howard Roberts: *Lord Shango* (1975)
The Rowan Amber Mill: *Harvest The Ears (Cuts From The Folk Horror Archive — Vol. 1)* (2018), *Harrowed by the Stones (Cuts From The Folk Horror Archive — Vol. 2)* (2020)
Rowan : Morrison: *In the Sunshine We Rode the Horses* (2019), *Fields of Frost* (2019), *Lost in Seaburgh* (2020), *Bride of the Wintertide* (2021)
The Ruin: *Sinister Country Vol. 1: The Underworld and Wilderness*

(2018), *Beyond the Forest (Travels in Nightland)* (2018), *Forest Ritual* (2020)

S

Sidney Sager and The Ambrosian Singers: *Children of The Stones* (2022)

Buffy Sainte-Marie: *Fire and Fleet and Candlelight* (1967), *Illuminations* (1969)

Jeremiah Sand: *Amulet of the Weeping Maze* (2019), *Lift It Down* (2020)

Savanna: *Collected Madness* (1973)

Seatman and Powell: *Broken Folk* (2018)

Sedna Chronicles: *Sedna Chronicles* (2022)

Sorrow: *Under The Yew Possessed* (1993), *Sleep Now Forever* (1999), *Let There Be Thorns* (2001)

The Spectral Light: *Secrets to the Sea* (2021)

Splinterskin: *Wayward Souls* (2009)

Spriguns: *Revel Weird and Wild* (1976), *Time Will Pass* (1977)

Spriguns of Tolgus: *Jack with a Feather* (1975)

Sproatly Smith: *The Yew and the Hare* (2009), *The Minstrel's Grave* (2011), *Carols from Herefordshire* (2011), *A Trip of Hares* (2020)

Steeleye Span: *Hark! The Village Wait* (1970), *Please to See the King* (1971), *Now We Are Six* (1974)

The Stone Tapes: *Avebury* (2016)

The Strawbs: *From the Witchwood* (1971), *Ghosts* (1974)

Stone Angel: *Stone Angel* (1975)

Stone Breath: *Songs Of Moonlight And Rain* (1997), *Lanterna Lucis Viriditatis* (2000), *Cryptids* (2016), *Witch Tree Prophets* (2017)

Sunforest: *Sound of Sunforest* (1970)

T

Tenhi: *Folk Aesthetic 1996–2006* (2007)

Third Ear Band: *Alchemy* (1969), *Music From Macbeth* (1972), *Magic Music* (1997 version)

Tissø Lake: *The Hollow Wood And Wondrous Cold* (2006)

Toadstone: *Toadstone* (2018)

Traffic: *John Barleycorn Must Die* (1970)

Trappist Afterland and Grey Malkin: *II* (2020)

Trees: *On the Shore* (1970), *The Garden of Jane Delawney* (1970)

Trembling Bells: *The Sovereign Self* (2015), *Dungeness* (2018)

The Trysting Tree: *Midnight House (And Other Tales)* (2009)

Fletcher Tucker: *Cold Spring* (2017)

Tunng: *Mother's Daughter And Other Songs* (2005), *Comments Of The Inner Chorus* (2006), *Turbines* (2013)

U

United Bible Studies: *Stations Of The Sun, Transits Of The Moon* (2003), *The Solar Observatory* (2005), *The Shore That Fears the Sea* (2006), *Black Colcannon* (2007), *The Star of The Sea Moves Today to Its Rising* (2017)

Adrian Utley and Will Gregory: *Arcadia* (2018)

V

Vanishing Faces: *Foretold* (2020), *Apparition* (2021)

Various: *Anthology of American Folk Music* (1952)

Various: *Ballads of Seduction, Fertility, and Ritual Slaughter* (2023)

Various: *Before the Day Is Done — The Story of Folk Heritage Records 1968–1975* (2022)

Various: *Dark Hollers: Old Love Songs and Ballads* (2005)

Various: *Dust on The Nettles: A Journey Through the British Underground Folk Scene 1967–72* (2021)

Various: *Gather in The Mushrooms (The British Acid Folk Underground 1968–1974)* (2004)

Various: *Ghostly Whistlings: A Tribute to M.R. James* (2017)

Various: *Harry Smith's Anthology Of American Folk Music, Volume Four* (2000)

Various (Dark Britannica series): *John Barleycorn Reborn* (2007), *We Bring You A King With A Head Of Gold* (2010), *Hail Be You Sovereigns, Lief And Dear* (2012)

Various: *Of All the Trees That Are In The Woods: Historical Musick For The Rituals of Yuletide* (2020)

Various: *Songs Of Witchcraft & Magic* (2019)

Various: *Sumer Is Icumen'n In* (2020)

Various: *Willows Songs* (2009)

Various: *Witchcraft and Black Magic in the United Kingdom* (2019)

The Vernon Elliott Ensemble: *Ivor The Engine & Pogles Wood* (2007)

Voice of the People: *Vol. 3: O'er His Grave the Grass Grew Green* (1998)

Voice of the Seven Woods: *Voice of the Seven Woods* (2007), *The Withering of the Boughs* (2007)

W

Wardruna: *Skald* (2018)

The Watersons: *Frost and Fire: A Calendar of Ritual and Magical Songs* (1965)

Wavelength: *Folk Magic* (2016)

Sam Waymon: *Ganja & Hess* (2018)

Jane Weaver: *The Fallen By Watch Bird* (2010), *The Watchbird Alluminate* (2011)

Widow's Weeds: *Revenant* (2021)

Marc Wilkinson: *Blood on Satan's Claw* (2007)

Jim Williams: *Woodlands Dark and Days Bewitched* (2021)

Jim Williams, Martin Pavey, and Blanck Mass: *A Field in England* (2013)

Robin Williamson: *Music for the Mabinogi* (1983)

Willow Tea: *Home* (2022)

The Wizard of Wardle: *The Queen of the Well* (2018)

Wooden Tape: *Music from Another Place* (2023)

Wyrdstonez: *Cuffern* (2009), *Potemkin Village Fayre* (2015)

Y

A Year in the Country (Various Artists): *The Restless Field* (2017), *Audio Albion* (2018), *The Quietened Mechanisms* (2018), *The Quietened Village* (2019), *The Quietened Journey* (2019), *The Layering* (2020)

Chapter 3

The Illusionary Precipice: Found Footage and Nostalgia

The Found Roots of the Found Footage Film

> 'Film is 24 lies per second at the service of truth, or at the service of the attempt to find the truth.'
> —Michael Haneke, *24 Realities per Second*

ALTHOUGH IT WOULD probably bring a sneer to the majority of twenty-first-century horror fan's faces, the found footage sub-genre represented a bold, innovative initiative for horror cinema in 1999. Flying in the face of safe Hollywood franchise horror, the found footage film and its brother, the fake documentary (I refuse to use the term mockumentary for any film unless it is directed by Marty Dibergi), represented a seismic shift in the aesthetics of fantastique films more so than in content and story. By presenting these narratives as raw, unedited slabs of reality, calling attention to choppy camerawork, violating all the accepted rules of filmmaking and having the characters break the fourth wall between image and audience, the found footage film sought to achieve a technical and emotional authenticity that mainstream horror movies (and even the majority of independent horror flicks) had long since abandoned. Like Tony Montana, found footage films lie to tell the truth, forcing viewers to critique the validity and credibility of what we see, what we believe to be real, and what we are told is real. Like many aspects of twenty-first-century media, the found footage genre promises us certainty, but all we get is probability.

This obsession with real vs mediated experiences was a direct reflection of the influence and growth of the internet, digital filmmaking, and early social media, not only on what people watched but also on how they watched. In a fascinating inversion of encountering, absorbing, and evaluating media, the amateurism, mistakes, and clumsy execution of found footage films were held up as genuine, a reaction to the increasingly slick yet predictable perfectionism and homogenization of mainstream media (this may also explain the enormous popularity of another huge influence on found footage horror: reality TV, specifically the show *Cops*). The more professional the acting, directing, editing, and effects were, the less authentic cinema, and especially horror cinema, seemed to be. The found footage genre is a natural by-product of a society in which cameras, recording, and surveillance are an ubiquitous aspect of everyday life; everyone seems to be filming and being filmed constantly. Cameras are everywhere, in our phones, tablets, and computers, capturing not so much reality as creating perspectives that have become realities for some people. It's almost as if people won't believe something is real unless it is filmed or photographed and viewed through a screen, as Alex so insightfully noted in *A Clockwork Orange*. Decadent poet Charles Baudelaire, writing about the then-new technology in his *The Salon of 1859*, believed that capturing things on photographic film was 'shocking and cruel'; one wonders how that Decadent would feel viewing some of the utterly inhuman videos posted on YouTube for a laugh.

Although one of the main complaints about found footage films is the 'unbelievability' that characters would keep filming even in the event of dire circumstances, one has only to watch, read about, or experience events where onlookers stuck their phones up to record an accident, crime, or tragedy rather than actually help the victims, to show that the predisposition to assist and intervene has been erased by the selfish need to prove one was there when something happened. The moments of closest verisimilitude in the vast majority of found footage films usually occur at the beginning of the film, when we are introduced to a borderline sociopath who will sacrifice all and everybody in order to capture 'reality' on her/his camera: the viewer is forced to sit through establishing scenes that present the 'director' through the testing out of various POV camera techniques and the practice filming of her/his inane doomed friends, suggesting that the characters' fictional lives are just as mundane, boring, self-involved, and meaningless as our own.

The found aspect of the genre is particularly fascinating, as though it's a regular occurrence to stumble upon or discover film stock or cameras that have been left behind by missing filmmakers, documenting their own demise. Yet this strange phenomenon does have its literary precedents in horror, as supposedly 'real' narratives that have outlived their authors and are haphazardly discovered are used to achieve a feeling of the genuine in such immortal tales as Poe's 'Ms. in a Bottle' and Lovecraft's 'The Call of Cthulhu'. Perhaps the most important cinematic antecedent of the found footage genre is Ruggero Deodato's infamous *Cannibal Holocaust* (1980), a meditation on how filmmaking can corrupt and exploit as the consequences of confusing the staged and the actual reach brutal depths. The documentarians, the broadcasting network that ponders airing the exploitative footage, and even the viewer watching *Cannibal Holocaust*, are all indicted in the media crime of sacrificing compassion and ethics for sensationalism and spectacle. In an early version of viral marketing, Deodato even had his actors sign contracts that forbade them from appearing in any media for one year, perpetuating the illusion that they had all perished in the jungles of South America. This attempt at verisimilitude actually backfired on the director as not only was Deodato charged with obscenity, but a Milan court also accused him of murdering his actors and actresses. It wasn't until the actors appeared on television refuting the charges and Deodato showed the court how the grisly deaths were actualized through special effects, that the beleaguered director was let off the hook.

The found footage genre also owes an enormous debt to the personal home video taping mania that ran rampant as soon as affordable camcorders became available in the late 1980s through to the nineties. During this era, one could not go to a birthday party, graduation, wedding, or on vacation, without someone documenting these 'events' for embarrassing posterity. This need to record even the most mundane minutiae of everyday life opened up a particularly rich vein of the found footage film, the accidental recording of strange phenomena sub-genre, initiated by the unnervingly veracious alien abduction SOV film *The McPherson Tape* (1989). Even the antiquated, nostalgically innocuous medium of Super-8 films, stashed and forgotten in attics and basements all over the US, have been used to suggest 'real' authenticity and terror hiding in plain sight. Rewatching past celebrations, vacations, and other important moments of one's life through the lens of home movies presents an opportunity to not only freeze these events and people in time, but also allow non-filmmakers the ability to create their own visual narratives of suburban splendor and filial solidarity.

Scott Derrickson's *Sinister* (2012) and its 2015 sequel are largely by-the-numbers horror family melodramas, but what elevate the films are the disturbing home movies depicting the murders of family members in morbidly creative ways. The protagonists of the films find the reels of Super-8 movies in their homes and, through the viewing of them, unleash a demonic entity. The Super-8 snuff movies are the most compelling elements of the films, offering a grainy, washed-out retro aesthetic with brutal hangings, drownings, burnings, stabbings, and mutilations (much more convincing than the infamous *Guinea Pig* films that were stupidly mistaken for 'real' snuff movies by rocket scientist Charlie Sheen). Home movies have traditionally been a medium of wholesomeness, happiness, fun, and good memories. To use them to document grisly familicides is a shocking yet eminently watchable experience similar to the frisson of viewing the Zapruder film. Finding such horrific mementos in such a mundane place like a crawlspace begs the question of what other disturbing documents may be lurking at garage sales or in secondhand stores waiting to be discovered. The films are labelled in innocent, clichéd ways ('Pool Party', 'BBQ', 'Sleepy Time') that further add to their creepiness; even more haunting is the brilliant use of eerie music collages featuring Ulver, Aghast, Boards of Canada, Sunn O))), and Boris that soundtrack our viewing of the murder movies. Though nothing else rises to the heights of radiant morbidity that the found footage elements exhibit, *Sinister*'s obsession with watching, freezing moments in time, and capturing the past for future viewing explores what moments deserve to be found and immortalized and what moments deserve to be forgotten and remain lost.

Because of their insistence on constructing 'realism' and revealing what goes on behind the camera as films are made, found footage films and fake documentaries often highlight the production values and economic realities of creating an independent film that foregrounds aesthetic and subjective 'realism' over fabrication, which, in part, has led viewers to question their expectations of what a movie is. Does a film have to have high production values, a perfectly constructed script, and trained actors to be a successful film? The 1992 proto-found footage film *Man Bites Dog* is all the more visceral and harrowing without the usual cinematic niceties as filmmaker and killer begin to uncomfortably merge. Even the birth of the shot-on-video, warts and all, amateur porn phenomenon could be seen as a reaction against the professionalization and homogenization of the sex industry, its aesthetics, and its performers. Because of its emphasis on the rough and the raw, found footage films can be the perfect project for first-time filmmakers, as their errors and inexperience can actually be assets in creating an atmosphere of believability as the filmmakers in the films themselves are often portrayed as amateurs. Art imitates life imitates art and all are swallowed up in the spectacle. But from where and from whom did this contentious genre flow?

Ghost of an Idea

> 'I did try from the outset to subvert the concept of media 'reality' and infallibility. I used what I hoped was a visible warning sign (a fake documentary style), and I did express my subjective feelings in my work (regarding the consequences of nuclear war in *The War Game*, the conformist effects of popular culture in *Privilege*, the treatment of protesters in *Punishment Park*, the personal sentiments expressed in *Edvard Munch*, etc.).' —Peter Watkins, 'The Global Media Crisis'

Made by one of the most underrated (and important) filmmakers in cinema history, Peter Watkins' fake pseudo documentaries have been some of the most controversial films ever made. Combining political subjects and innovative cinematic techniques, Watkins' artistic vision is among the most uncompromising in any of the arts. Commissioned by the BBC to make a film about Britain's readiness to protect its citizens from a nuclear attack, Watkins created perhaps the most depressing, grim, and hopeless meditation on the insanity of nuclear proliferation: *The War Game*. Filmed in a stark matter-of-fact documentary style, *The War Game* juxtaposes scenes of unflinching misery and horror with interviews with ordinary citizens, government officials, nuclear physicists, politicians, and clergymen who are all shown to be ignorant, deluded, or propagandists. As WWIII is touched off over east/west conflicts in Vietnam and Berlin, the small English town of Rochester is hit by an errant nuclear missile, which sets off blast waves, fire storms, and massive destruction on an unimagined scale. Citizens are burned alive, blinded, maimed, vaporized, and irradiated in the immediate aftermath of the explosion and, as society collapses around the impotent responses of the British government, starvation, looting, martial law, and executions soon follow.

Watkins' amazingly 'real' scenes of the hypothetical attack show that there is no adequate way to protect people from the horrors of nuclear war; the government is lying to its constituents, giving them a false sense of security as a way to control and manipulate citizens. None of the political, social, economic, religious, or scientific institutions offer any protection, solace, answers, or criticisms, there is no voice of reason or dissent. None of these institutions offer any checks or balances to the madness as they all collude to maintain their power and domination over the masses. There's an eerie calmness to the speakers that is absurd and terrifying as they talk unemotionally on the topic of human annihilation; some of the speakers even sound hopeful that a nuclear war will prove their assertions correct. Watkins' speculations on the physical effects of a nuclear attack are devastatingly stomach-churning as they are, but it is his unflinching depiction of the psychological and emotional wounds of the survivors, both young and old, that are truly unbearable. Close-ups of shell-shocked, dead-eyed, hopeless men, women, and children plumb the abyss of despair. Even though these scenes are fictional, there is a truth here that transcends film. Watkins has the alchemical mastery to turn fictional supposition into reality and factual commentary into fantasist propaganda. The BBC, shocked at what Watkins produced, refused to air *The War Game* in 1965, finally allowing it to be screened to the British public in 1985. Ironically, *The War Game* would win the Academy Award for Best Documentary in 1966. Even after fifty-seven years, *The War Game* offers none of the nostalgia of other British cultural products of its time: there are no screaming teenyboppers, no 'Angry Young Men', and no high fashion with Jean Shrimpton. *The War Game* goes beyond kitchen sink drama into buckets-of-wedding-rings despair. Watkins' utilization of the fake documentary style would become part of his cinematic aesthetic, as seen by his brilliant critique of pop cultural commodification and friendly fascism in *Privilege* (1967) and in perhaps his most daring film, *Punishment Park* (1971).

Unbelievably, Universal Studios would help release and distribute Watkins' return to the fake documentary genre: the prescient Beatles-meets-Nazism critique of the authoritarian pop culture industry in 1967's *Privilege* (no doubt the execs at Universal thought they had another *Hard Day's Night* or *Help!* on their hands). Perhaps cutting too close to the bone for the dawning hippie era, *Privilege* did poorly at the box office. Watkins then made a film in Sweden called *The Gladiators* (which, along with Nigel Kneale's *The Year of the Sex Olympics*, predicted extreme reality TV competitions), but it would be his next film that would pretty much end Watkins' career in the mainstream: 1971's pseudo-documentary *Punishment Park*. The premise of *Punishment Park* is a what-if scenario where President Nixon announces a state of emergency in the early 1970s, declaring martial law and authorizing law enforcement to detain so-called revolutionaries as risks to national security without probable cause or warrants. Anti-war protestors, civil rights activists, feminists, conscientious objectors, communists, and leftist agitators are all arrested and face judicial tribunals made up of community members, union bureaucrats, and local politicians who decide the fate of the arrested. The convicted (and everyone accused is found guilty, of course) are offered a choice: serve a twenty-year sentence in a federal prison or go to Punishment Park, a fifty-three-mile section of California desert. If the prisoners can make it across the desert with no food or water within three days, reaching an American flag at the edge of the desert, they can go free. The hitch is that the prisoners will be hunted down by police, National Guardsmen, and military in training. If they elude their captors and reach their goal, the prisoners are free. If they are caught they are sent to prison to serve their twenty-year sentence. If they are killed during the grueling experience, oh well. They were subversive criminals anyway. The film tells parallel stories: one group has been convicted and is sent out into Punishment Park, while a second group is brought before a tribunal for their hearing. A European documentary crew interviews the prisoners, police, and National Guardsmen as well as filming the events that befall both groups of prisoners.

Using handheld 16mm cameras and a mix of both professional and nonprofessional actors (a technique also used in director Floyd Mutrux's pioneering docufiction film, 1971's *Dusty and Sweets McGee*, a raw, episodic look at the bleakly banal lives of LA addicts, dealers, and hustlers), *Punishment Park* accurately conjures up very real experiences of anxiety, paranoia, anger, frustration, and terror. Actors were allowed total freedom to extemporize and push confrontations to the edge and over. The frenetic camera movement, quick editing, and aggressive improvisation heighten the tension and authenticity to an unbearable level. The sound design for *Punishment Park* is a constant barrage of gunshots, screaming, shouting, jet planes roaring, and chaotic noise, which is in sharp contrast to the deafening silence of *The War Game*; in both situations, though, no one listens and no one is heard. Supposedly, a group of actors became so engrossed in their fake predicament that they started really fighting back against their 'pursuers' by throwing stones, which resulted in some actual gunfire (using blanks). No one was hurt, but the horrified reactions of the film crew were genuine and kept in the film. The question of where journalistic objectivity ends and humanitarian action begins is one that has only increased as time has gone on, especially now that cell phone technology can make anyone a documentarian. Should one hide behind the camera even as horrible events unfold in front of us? Is documentation more important than participation? The society of spectacle has become the society of surveillance as passive watching is no longer enough: one must submissively surveil, record, and create more footage to be consumed.

Watkins' focus on resistance, power, violence, and oppression was a direct answer to the then-current events that were rocking the United States, such as the riots at the Democratic National Convention in Chicago, the Chicago 7 trial, the Kent State shootings, and the FBI's illegal covert surveillance and attacks on political and social activists. Communication, or lack thereof, is the key to understanding Watkins' purpose, as the inability to be heard and an unwillingness to listen doom all combatants in Punishment Park. Each of the defendants represents a freedom guaranteed by the Bill of Rights and the Constitution, which is flagrantly ignored by the tribunal. The end of *Punishment Park* is inevitable, as Watkins posits that no one can escape institutional control in a police state (especially when there is no communication or meaningful listening between institutions and constituents), and his fake documentary makes this conclusion all the more genuine and infuriating. *Punishment Park* is no celebration of the seventies counterculture: it's a prescient memorial for all those who fought against the loss of personal and civic freedoms and a warning for those who would have the courage to do so in the future. Watkins' audacious use of cinema verité and documentary aesthetics to critique not only political and social institutions, but also the repressive use of media and film (which he has dubbed the 'Monoform') weaponized by these dominate, coercive forces, would later become a cultural phenomenon (exactly the kind of homogenized mass consumption he railed against in *Privilege*) through the simple tale of three filmmakers hunting down a folk legend.

> 'It's not quite reality. It's like a totally filtered reality. It's like you can pretend everything's not quite the way it is.' —*The Blair Witch Project*

One of the most debated films ever made, yet the controversy had nothing to do with its content, *The Blair Witch Project*'s aesthetics and marketing had audiences suffering from motion sickness as well as questioning the authenticity of information in the digital age. Written and directed by Daniel Myrick and Eduardo Sánchez, *The Blair Witch Project* was presented as film footage shot by three amateur documentarians deep in the woods of Burketsville, Maryland, where they were investigating the local legend of the Blair Witch. The filmmakers supposedly disappeared, leaving behind their cameras and film that were discovered in the forest a year later, resulting in the unedited footage documenting what happened to them. Made on a miniscule $60,000 budget, *The Blair Witch Project* made $250,000,000 worldwide, starting a certifiable phenomenon as well as becoming the most successful independent film of all time, dethroning John Carpenter's epochal *Halloween,* but later being dethroned by one of its own progeny, *Paranormal Activity*, in 2007.

A significant factor in *Blair Witch*'s massive success was its promotional campaign that listed the filmmakers (actually actors) as missing, utilizing fake police reports, flyers, and a website to help find them. Identified as the first mass market viral promotional campaign, the question of the genuineness of the film and the fate of its doomed filmmakers was debated, deconstructed, and criticized online and in traditional media as word of mouth and the question of fact or fiction reinforced the phenomenon. Perhaps the most brilliant bit of promotion was the television special, *Curse of the Blair Witch*, broadcast before the film's release and basically a fake documentary about a fake documentary. The film itself played on all the documentary tropes that viewers have come to identify as authentic: handheld cameras, talking head interviews, violation of the thirty-degree rule, rough editing, and a lack of finesse. Interestingly, as the documentarians become lost, despondent, sleep deprived, paranoid, and terrorized, their reactions become the actual subject of the film and are the true barometers of how authentic people believed the footage to be. The ubiquitousness of video cameras in American culture also gave the film credence in terms of cutting between the 'real' movie camera (as utilized in mainstream cinema and television) and the more personal, low resolution digital camera that is used to film the filmmakers themselves. It is the hand-held 'shaky cam' that provides a much more genuine and emotionally factual accounting of the filmmakers' experiences than professionally shot footage ever could. This notion of how one films, and what type of instrument one uses to film, as creating and questioning objective realism and subjective irrationality, would become a core element of many found footage films. The inability of technology, and specifically cameras and recording devices, to capture the totality of any experience, either human or paranormal (shades of *Blowup* and *The Stone Tape*), producing more doubt, confusion, and uncertainty rather than definitive answers is a key trope in the found footage genre.

Although the film has been the victim of parody overload (especially Heather's tearful apology to the parents of her doomed collaborators, and yet the earnestness of her sorrow and guilt makes her confession all the more 'real'), the film has some truly frightening imagery and scenes: the rock cairns, the ominous stick symbols, 'Coffin Rock', the filmmakers' possessions covered in slime, the bloody fetish filled with teeth, hair, and entrails, sounds of twigs breaking, children laughing, and screams in the darkness. The climax at the abandoned house, its walls covered with arcane symbols and children's bloody handprints, Mike standing stone-still in the corner and not responding to Heather's pleading, is one of the most terrifying endings in horror cinema. The film has become a nostalgic cultural touchstone for the 1990s (even though it was released in the last year of that decade) and a demarcation point for genre historians and critics who see the technological, aesthetic, and marketing strategies utilized by the film as the starting point for horror films in the Digital Age. *The Blair Witch Project* would span two sequels: Joe Berlinger's *Book of Shadows: Blair Witch 2* (2000), a misunderstood anti-found footage film, and the more traditional yet still entertaining *Blair Witch* (2016), but it is the original progenitor that not only changed horror culture but also filmmaking.

'The truth comes down to this one frame.' –*The Last Broadcast*

In the horror film equivalent of the chicken or the egg, the question of what came first, *The Blair Witch Project* or Stefan Avalos and Lance Weiler's *The Last Broadcast*, has raged ever since both films debuted in 1999. Though *The Last Broadcast* had been made a year before *The Blair Witch Project*, it seems that both films developed simultaneously without one being an influence on the other. *The Last Broadcast* focuses on a documentary being made by David Leigh who is investigating the 'Fact or Fiction?' murders. The victims of these murders are a pair of public access TV personalities who were killed under mysterious circumstances in the New Jersey Pine Barrens. In an attempt to keep their paranormal show from being cancelled, the hosts decide to do a live broadcast in the field, searching for the legendary Jersey Devil. Recruiting a sound man and a psychic for their devil hunt, all four go into the woods but only the psychic comes out. The survivor is blamed for the murders, which he denies. At his trial, the footage shot for the show in the Pine Barrens is used as evidence to convict him. Leigh investigates the murders as the premise of his documentary, and when he receives a mysterious box containing a damaged video reel with unseen footage from the night of the killings, the real perpetrator is revealed.

While *The Blair Witch Project* borrowed from other horror documentary recreations such as *The Legend of Boggy Creek* (1972) and the television series *In Search of…* (1977–1982), *The Last Broadcast* looks to more avant-garde films such as Michelangelo Antonioni's *Blowup* and Orson Welles' *F for Fake* to question whether objectivity is possible. Can a camera actually capture truth or is film twenty-four lies per second? Are all documentaries subjective and biased? The first digitally shot and edited film to ever be released, *The Last Broadcast* gains much authenticity with its grainy, low tech, low resolution shots of the ominous Pine Barrens, and the narrator's droning, monotonous, unprofessional voiceover also gives the film credence as an amateur's obsessive search for answers that reveals much more about the filmmaker than his subject. As the obsession with documenting and capturing 'real life' has grown exponentially since the release of both *The Last Broadcast* and *The Blair Witch Project*, the question of reality and the authenticity of representations of reality have become even more problematic. As cineastes have known for a long time, documentaries are not objective recordings but subjective artistic products, a medium through which choice, bias, interpretation, and point-of-view are all manufactured and manipulated through camera placement, editing, sound, subject matter, and the inclusion of participants. Fracturing the façades of the real, the genuine, the neutral, and the true as captured, presented, and absorbed through any recording device (including the human brain) and disseminating technology, is at the heart of the found footage genre. The nostalgia of belief in what we see, hear, read, and watch as being accurate, impartial, and factual is what feeds not only the interest in the genre, but also the tools that make the genre so fascinating and (potentially) a rich source of critical commentary and questioning in the post-singularity 'Metaverse' of the twenty-first century.

'All that is lost shall be found.' —Alfred Noyes, *The Paradox*

Perhaps it's the wistfulness talking, but the found footage movement had the same potential to be a punk-like, Brechtian DIY revolution that the SOV horror boom had in the 1980s, or maybe a better comparison would be with the concurrent indie lo-fi musical crusade of the early nineties. Like many initially innovative artistic forms, the entertainment industry pounced on the ability to make cheap, crap films with lousy special effects, and plot shortcuts that bypass deep characterization or intricate narratives. Very quickly the formula for found footage films was patented, with POV shots, malfunctioning equipment, boring extraneous footage, annoying characters, and a ridiculous need to keep filming even in the most absurdly dangerous situations being the most obvious ingredients. The found footage film's very assets have become ways to justify the lack of talent, imagination, creativity, originality and, most of all, actual terror that seems part and parcel of commercialized twenty-first-century horror. The low budgets yet enormous profits of films such as *The Blair Witch Project*, *Cloverfield*, and *Paranormal Activity* were just too tempting to resist. Yet, like punk rock, there are still some signs of life in the genre, some films and filmmakers that have made their mark on the horror genre and popular culture. Films such as the *REC* series, *Fury of the Demon*, *The Poughkeepsie Tapes*, *Frankenstein's Army*, *The WNUF Halloween Special*, *As Above, So Below*, *The Borderlands*, *Noroi: The Curse*, *The Outwaters*, and *Skinamarink* have proven that not all found footage films deserve the same groans that escape from horror fans when they see the Gravitas Ventures, Platinum Dunes, or Uncork'd Entertainment logo at the beginning of a film. Although of varying quality, entries in the *V/H/S* anthology series utilize blurry analogue resolution, crude acting, and inept edits to recall the awe of bringing filmmaking within the reach of anyone who could afford a VCR, a camcorder, and a blank tape. Degraded quality and static lines, once the signs of un-watchability, are now beloved nostalgic tropes, even for those who were only a gleam in the eyes of two teenagers in 1987 watching a rented copy of *Video Violence*.

Are found footage films and fake documentaries an attempt to re-historicize our digital age or at least bring history down to an individualized level? An attack on 'official', monolithic ways of recording, broadcasting, and disseminating news and information in a post-truth society? The found footage horror film is important not only as a product of its times, but also as a critique of those times and the virtual world we are living in and will continue to live in. Hopefully, the genre will not be lost to the vagaries of our disposable culture or the fading generational memories of horror buffs. The revolutionary concepts of the found footage film may be just waiting to be found by the next wave of horror filmmakers who are willing to look past the nostalgia and tropes and dig into the radical potentials this kind of film offers. The sub-genre of analogue horror offers a startling combination of glitchy viral videos, internet lore, and the art brut attack of SOV horror manifesting as cryptic online uploads and YouTube series such as *Local 58 WCLV-TV* and *The Smile Tapes*. Ironically, future filmmakers may have to look even farther back through the found footage era, past the glut of imitative product in the last twenty years, to earlier innovators like Peter Watkins, Floyd Mutrux, Paul Morrissey, Jean Luc Godard, and James McBride, not to slavishly emulate but to build on their still innovative concepts of how we conceive, perceive, and live in a society mediated by media. As the Wu-Tang Clan sagely noted, sometimes you have to look back to move forward, and we still haven't caught up with the implications of these pioneers' ideas and the consequences of their cinema as exemplars of what these techniques can bring to the next wave of docu-fiction/found footage film.

It's Like She Never Left: Blair Witch

WHEN *THE BLAIR Witch Project* crept up on audiences in 1999, no one could have guessed the massively successful phenomenon it would create for all us pre-millennial-blues-suffering horror fanatics. Not only was it the first sustained full-length found footage film, *The Blair Witch Project* was also the first film to connect its 'recovered' aesthetics with its viral marketing campaign that promoted the movie as a real event concerning real people. It purported to be raw footage with no edits, special effects, or post-filming manipulations, documenting the events that informed the film and enhancing its verisimilitude, which was quite brilliant in its understanding of what is necessary for viewers to recognize 'authenticity'. Of course, *The Blair Witch Project* would be cited as the heir to the found footage genre that has reproduced like a pack of hyper-amorous tribbles. Over the last decade, there have been more duds than triumphs as horror fans have had to suffer through countless shaky camera shots, digital glitches, and boring, extemporaneous footage that seeks to prove the recording is 'real'. The earliest films in the genre used these techniques quite well but over time these methods all seem like shortcuts to establishing characters, building suspense, creating atmosphere, and developing a compelling story. *The Blair Witch Project* did not fall out of the sky fully formed; it used the imagery of Karl Edward Wagner's terrifying short story 'Sticks', the phony cinema verité approach of *Cannibal Holocaust*, and the legends of seventeenth-century Maryland witch Moll Dyer to brew up a startlingly horrifying experience. The same can't be said for its sequel, 2000's *Book of Shadows: Blair Witch 2*, which went in the opposite direction from the first film by drawing attention to the fallacies of the hype, focusing on the artificiality of the myths and how belief in a mass delusion can result in hysteria. Director Joe Berlinger was even accused of purposefully sabotaging the emerging franchise by pushing disbelief well past acceptable levels of suspension.

Sixteen years later, director Adam Wingard (who has previously made the films *You're Next* and *The Guest*, and contributed short movies to the *V/H/S* and *V/H/S 2* anthology films) returned to the town of Burkittsville for *Blair Witch*, a direct sequel to the first movie. The film focuses on James Donahue who, with friends in tow, ventures into the Black Hills Forest to search for his sister Heather, one of the doomed filmmakers from the first film. After seeing a mysterious video on YouTube that may contain a glimpse of his missing sister, James and his crew pack up their film equipment and high-tech gadgets (including a drone) in order to solve the mystery of the disappearances. *Blair Witch* is similar to the 2013 remake/reimagining/reboot of *Evil Dead* in that it takes several key iconic concepts and unsettling images from the first film and expands on them in a fanatically graphic way: revisiting and intensifying the stick fetishes, the witch house, the foreboding woods, and the temporal/spatial distortions that made *The Blair Witch Project* so memorable. The notion that the supernatural cannot be accurately recorded, that the occult is an experience that goes beyond the mechanisms of logic and reason, and the hubristic belief that humans can use science and technology to conquer and tame forces that are beyond our ken, is at the heart of the Blair Witch franchise.

The characters in *Blair Witch* are actually tolerable, much more so than those in the *Paranormal Activity* series, who are so annoying that you can't wait for the demon/poltergeist/whatever to shut them up. (Why do characters in found footage films have to be so unpleasant? Is it a critique of how directors and writers look at their own audiences?) There's even a nod to the second Blair Witch film in the characterization of two Blair Witch obsessives who join James's search. Although it seems like it will fall into the same patterns of genre banality (the final five minutes of formulaic defeat and the abandoned/broken camera that is still filming), the last twenty minutes of *Blair*

Witch are a full-on assault on minds, bodies, and souls of the remaining characters. Although not as groundbreaking as its progenitor, *Blair Witch* is eerily entertaining, and, at times, truly frightening, and adds significantly to the Blair Witch mythos. Wingard's film is no nineties nostalgia trip back to the haunted woods of Burkittsville; it integrates new technologies and contemporary views of digital filming to enhance the primal horror found in the first film.

The last few years have seen some ferocious contributions to the witchcraft film category (*The Lords of Salem*, *The Witch*, *Witching & Bitching*, *Brand New Cherry Flavor*, *The Black Forest*, *Hagazussa*, *You Won't Be Alone*) and, while it may not have 'got the fear' like some of these other exceptional witchcraft films, Adam Wingard's *Blair Witch* is a worthy addition to both this underrated occult genre and to the often attacked found footage film style as well. *Blair Witch* recalls but also reaches ahead in its utilization of the continuing legend of the Blair Witch. Wingard's talents have vaulted him into the big time, helming 2021's highly entertaining kaiju battle royale *Godzilla vs. Kong*. Perhaps a Blair Witch-Godzilla-King Kong crossover is not outside the realms of possibility? Hey, if Toho once imagined films like *Godzilla vs. Wolfman* and *Godzilla vs. Ghost of Godzilla*, maybe there's still hope that an occult Godzilla film could one day grace our screens. A horror/tokusatsu fan has to dream…

Chapter 4

The Longing of the Permanently Lost: Franchise Nostalgia

> 'The true paradises are the paradises we have lost.'
> —Marcel Proust, *In Search of Lost Time*

FRANCHISES: nostalgia made concrete, material, and commodifiable. The bankability of franchises has kept nostalgia a valuable component of the culture industry: tried and true products that have built-in audiences and open wallets. Consumers can buy with confidence when they see the Bat Symbol or the numbers 007. Familiar characters, plots, universes, and catchphrases provide customers not only with security but also reminiscences of past glories and hope for the re-experiencing of feelings that were invoked in earlier adventures and simpler times. Franchises can create a kind of brand loyalty, which also helps with the ubiquitous merchandising that is a key element in the movie series nostalgia phenomenon. Just as it's hard to catch the Force in a bottle, franchises often offer viewers diminishing returns: the same ideas are run into the ground as sequels and retcons can water down the innovations of the initial films that generated the franchise in the first place (just look at the sequel/reboot hell that *The Texas Chain Saw Massacre* series is caught in). Is this the fate of all franchises, living off nostalgia, former achievements, and the recycling of memories, situations, and emotions? While franchises can be seen as equivalent to the familiarity and reassurance of old friends and bygone shared experiences, the key question is, can franchises balance nostalgia and inventiveness? Keep some foundational aspects but expand, extend, or revolutionize these beloved tropes? Of course, entertainment conglomerates aren't exactly excited to see one of their old reliable workhorses encouraged to throw off the reins and run wild and free, yet sometimes it may be necessary to teach an old Cujo new tricks. Outside of the culture industry, fandom can also be an impediment to the evolution of a franchise, as nostalgic fans can become grand inquisitors who will burn a movie, TV, or book series at the stake for not adhering to the gospel. Perhaps a more creative approach to franchises would be to treat them like mythology. Myths have returning characters, plots, and conflicts, but they don't abide by strict canonical rules. Their sense of continuity is often vague, irrational, contradictory, and absurd, with multiple narratives and differing accounts co-existing in the same corpus. Despite this lack of cohesion, myths are still powerful expressions of personal, social, environmental, and supernatural insights that resonate today. This chapter looks at examples of franchises and sequels that have played fast and loose with nostalgia and canon and are all the better for it.

Game Over Humanity: Alien: Covenant

THE *ALIEN* FRANCHISE is one of the most divisive in fandom. Most people would agree that the original 1979 film and its 1986 sequel represent high points in the science fiction, horror, and action film genres. *Alien 3*, the first feature film directed by David Fincher (*Se7en*, *Fight Club*, *The Social Network*, *Gone Girl*) had significant problems during its creation with studio interference marring an otherwise interesting take on the *Alien* concept. The *Alien* series would see a significant drop off with 1997's ludicrous (and not in a good way) *Alien Resurrection*, 2004's fun but inconsequential *Alien vs. Predator*, and 2007's lifeless and predictable *Alien vs. Predator: Requiem*. None of these sequels added much to the fascinatingly mysterious mythos of the first two films. It seemed as if the once proud *Alien* franchise had met an ignoble end, relying on the brilliance of the first film and the thrills of the second to keep its cultural cachet alive amongst its diehard fans. It took original *Alien* director Ridley Scott to face hug some life back into the series. Scott decided to go the prequel route and explore the story behind the enigmatic, crashed spaceship with the vaginal ingress, the awe-inspiring 'space jockey', the frighteningly sublime Giger biomechanical hieroglyphs on the walls inside the ship, and the origins of the xenomorphs themselves: all bewildering questions that the crew of the Nostromo, as well as *Alien* fans, have puzzled over for many years. Scott's first *Alien* prequel, *Prometheus* (2012), excited some viewers and bored others who wanted definitive answers to these questions, but instead got philosophical and metaphysical ruminations and queries. Those viewers who knew Scott's other visionary sci-fi epic, *Blade Runner*, should not have been surprised by his more intellectual take on the material, especially when it comes to issues of creation and creators' responsibilities to their creations. Deconstructing the 'noble' and 'selfless' motivations of science and technocratic innovation, as symbolized by the Engineers and the Weyland Yutani Corporation, is intrinsic to almost all the films in the *Alien* series, including *Prometheus*.

This critique of accountability and intention is continued in Scott's sequel to *Prometheus*, *Alien: Covenant*. *Alien: Covenant* begins with a group of colonists on a journey to a remote planet. Awakened by damage to their ship, the crew pick up a radio transmission from an unknown planet. Investigating the source of the transmission, some of the crew descend to the planet, where they discover a crashed Engineer spaceship, an abandoned city, and the android

David, who is the lone survivor of the original Prometheus mission. David has been busy in the last ten years, experimenting with the Engineer's sinister 'black goo', constructing and genetically modifying different forms of those acid-blooded creatures we all know and love. Interestingly, although the first *Alien* is acknowledged as 'Lovecraftian' (usually by people who have a superficial grasp of the author's work), it is *Prometheus* and *Alien: Covenant* that are much more in line with the cosmic fatalism, recklessness of scientific curiosity, and diminishing of human superiority found in the author's works. *Alien: Covenant* isn't a great movie, but it's not a terrible one either. Many of the plot points have already been used in other *Alien* films to much better effect. The excitement of seeing multiple types of xenomorphs is tempered by the extensive CGI effects that can't compare with the shockingly innovative practical effects work showcased in *Alien* and *Aliens*. The characters are likeable, but not especially memorable. It's nice that Katherine Waterston, Billy Crudup, Demián Bichir, and Danny McBride are not your typical action heroes, but they lack the commanding presence of a Sigourney Weaver, a Michael Biehn, or even a Noomi Rapace.

The truly fascinating aspect of *Alien: Covenant* is Michael Fassbender's amazing performances as both Walter and David, identical looking robots who have very different moral compasses. It is to Fassbender's considerable credit that David is much more frightening than any xenomorph in *Alien: Covenant*. His logical, calculating, Machiavellian evil actually makes the aliens superfluous in their own movie. As android Ash (David's great great great 'grandson') commented in the original *Alien* when explaining his fascination with the xenomorph, "I admire its purity. A survivor, unclouded by conscience, remorse, or delusions of morality". David is revealed to be the true Prometheus, stealing from the Engineers the power to create and destroy life, as the anger, jealousy, and rejection that David felt towards his own creator Peter Weyland will now be wrought on all sentient 'natural' beings. The covenant between creator and created has been broken, with no doves, olive branches, or rainbows in sight. David's ruthless will to power is the true threat; the xenomorphs are only the tools of his megalomaniacal revenge. One of the greatest scenes in the entire *Alien* franchise is David's triumphant accessing of the sleeping colonists and human embryos on The Covenant starship soundtracked by the glorious strains of Wagner's Entry Of The Gods Into Valhalla from *Das Rheingold*, signaling the victory of the superior automaton over his masters. It is this character that actually gives *Alien* fans some hope for this franchise, as the *Alien* origin story and the morally questionable inventor David have become much more interesting than the aliens themselves. Long live the new flesh.

"You're kinda like a young me. Deadites ruined your life and you're hot as hell": Ash vs. Evil Dead

ANTICIPATION. Expectation. Disappointment. These three sensations are the most common feelings in any form of fandom, especially as decades roll by and fans wait patiently (or impatiently) for the next instalment, the next chapter, the next missive from a beloved series or artist. When the silence is broken and the delay ends, the prodigal hype threatens to ruin the experience. Some works are able to overcome the hype, conquer the jaded, and fulfill fan's hopes (like Brian Wilson's legendary lost album *Smile*); some works are swallowed up by their own overwhelming burden of history and their fans' projections of their own wants, desires, and nostalgia onto the phenomenon (the *Star Wars* prequels and the continuations, perhaps?). One such long promised work has been the fourth film in the original *Evil Dead* series (not counting Fede Álvarez's masterful 2013 sequel/ reimagining and Lee Cronin's 2023 gloriously gore-drenched *Evil Dead Rise*) that would resume the misadventures of Ash. The reuniting of director Sam Raimi, actor Bruce Campbell, and producer Rob Tapert to continue the story of much put-upon hero Ash's war against the Deadites has been promised and teased for over twenty years. As the cult status of *The Evil Dead*, *Evil Dead 2*, and *Army of Darkness* (the greatest third film in any cinematic trilogy; so there, Ingmar Bergman and Michelangelo Antonioni) have grown exponentially, Raimi, Tapert, and Campbell have worked together on a variety of projects over the last two decades, but all anyone wanted to know was when *Evil Dead 4* would come out. Finally, after countless rumors and speculation seemed to doom the project from ever becoming reality, Raimi and co. threw their fans a curveball. Instead of a film, the cable channel Starz announced that the continuing adventures of our beloved Deadite fighter would be the subject of a new TV series, *Ash vs. Evil Dead.* The show would premiere on Halloween 2015 and the publicity machine went into overdrive. As the premiere date got closer, *Evil Dead* fans were cautiously optimistic but also had some apprehensions. Would the TV medium be able to do justice to The Three Stooges-meets-*The Exorcist* surrealistic, demonic fluid-spewing anarchy of the films? Could Sam Raimi bring back his manic directing style, a style that really hasn't been evidenced in the last twenty years? Did Bruce Campbell still have the idiotic arrogance and the ultra-cool, ultra-quotable heroics last seen in 1992?

All fears were put to rest by the first episode of *Ash vs. Evil Dead.* Combining everything that was so endearing and exciting about the *Evil Dead* trilogy, *Ash vs. Evil Dead* is a more than worthy successor to the franchise. The show begins with Ash suiting up for what appears to be a battle, but is really just his struggles with a girdle to get ready for a sleazy night on the town, all to the glorious strains of Deep Purple's Space Truckin'. Hanging out at a dive bar, Ash manages to charm some barfly into having sex with him in the bathroom, using his fake hand to enhance the experience. Ash lives in a trailer park in Michigan, works a low paying retail job (though not at S-Mart; maybe he was fired after the mayhem he caused in housewares), and has left his encounters with the Deadites behind him. Of course, this being Ash, he once again summons evil through his mishandling of *The Necronomicon* (using it to impress a woman during a dope smoking, poetry reading session) and the Deadites come back looking for revenge. Ash is joined in the show by his hero-worshipping sidekick Pablo (Ray Santiago) and a no-nonsense spunky co-worker named Kelly (Dana Delorenzo), but there are other characters who are also affected by the unleashing of the Evil Dead. Amanda Fisher (Jill Marie Jones) is a Michigan State trooper who is mistakenly blamed for her partner's death at the hands of a Deadite, and Ruby (Lucy Lawless) is an enigmatic woman who seems to have some connection to the Deadites and *The Necronomicon*. The acting, directing, action sequences, and special effects are all first rate and prove that time has only honed the skills of Sam Raimi. And yet the real test of this show was always going to be Bruce Campbell and his portrayal of Ash. Fortunately, Campbell's performance is right on the mark, transforming the brazen pomposity of his *Army of Darkness* persona into a pathetic, self-deluded middle-aged loser, drinking Moscow Mules, hitting on anything that moves, and shamelessly insulting everyone and everything. But when the chips are down, Ash steps up and proves that no one wields a chainsaw like he does (sorry, Leatherface).

Raimi, Campbell, and Tapert created a series that was faithful to the spirit of the films but also took the franchise's concepts in new directions. Not only does the show entertain like nobody's business, but it has also fleshed out and extended the Evil Dead mythos to include Ash's father Brock (who could only be portrayed by The Six Million Dollar Man himself, Lee Majors), Ash's daughter Brandy (Arielle Carver-O'Neill), and the murderous Ash Muppet, Ashy Slashy. The series also features the return of fan favorites like Cheryl Williams, Linda, Professor Knowby, and Henrietta (played by Ted Raimi, of course). The series ended on an eschatological all-out bonanza of Kandorian proportions, but it's a relief to know that Ash is still fighting Deadites in a Mad Max post-apocalyptic futuristic wasteland (shades of the infamous original 'Captain Supermarket cut' ending of *Army of Darkness*) with a cybernetic hand and a battle modified Delta 88. Bruce Campbell has stated that he has officially retired from the physically and sarcastically demanding role of Ash and so this TV series might be, like Odysseus returning to Ithaca, his last hurrah. (If the Ash saga is truly ended, can I suggest a series based on the greatest *Evil Dead*-inspired movie ever, Shinichi Fukazawa's *Bloody Muscle Body Builder in Hell*?) Equally frightening and hysterical, *Ash vs. Evil Dead* may be, if I can indulge in a little of Ashley Williams' patented hyperbole, the greatest horror TV show ever made.

Drunk on the Memory of Its Perfection: Blade Runner 2049

IN 1982, A movie premiered that would become one of the most influential films of the late twentieth and early twenty-first centuries. That film was Ridley Scott's *Blade Runner*, a loose adaptation of Philip K Dick's novel *Do Androids Dream of Electric Sleep? Blade Runner* takes place in the Los Angeles of 2019, where bio-engineered beings called replicants are used as slave labor. Harrison Ford plays Rick Deckard, the titular Blade Runner, a cop whose job is to hunt down fugitive replicants and 'retire' them. Scott's film was a box office disappointment and got mediocre reviews in 1982, but his vision of a dehumanized, bleak future, a sprawling, overcrowded polyglot cityscape where it rains all the time and the sun never shines (unless you live like the gods of Olympus above the clouds), a world on the brink of social, environmental, and technological fragmentation, has left an enormous mark on pretty much every dystopian science fiction film/TV show/ graphic novel/videogame that has come since. *Blade Runner*'s aesthetic and its philosophical questions of what constitutes being human have proven prophetic in terms of the current issues of genetically modified life, corrupt alliances between science and corporations, and artificial intelligence that confront our contemporary lives. If any film has most exemplified a weird longing for a future that never came to pass (thank goodness) it must be *Blade Runner.* Sequels to classic films are usually a losing proposition (partly because of the loss of the novelty factor of the first film and partly because of the effect of nostalgic hindsight) and so the announcement of *Blade Runner 2049*, a thirty-five-year belated continuation of the series, seemed like a longshot. Thankfully, Ridley Scott and original screenwriter Hampton Fancher are closely involved with the sequel and their collaboration with inventive director Denis Villeneuve (*Sicario, Arrival, Dune*) has produced an excellent continuation and timely update of the themes of the original film. The maturation of the original themes come to fruition in *Blade Runner 2049*, in which nostalgia for what humans were is peeled away to reveal a new more inclusive and liberating ontology.

In the thirty years since the events of the original, a new version of replicant has been created by the Wallace Corporation (replacing the Tyrell Corporation, inventors of the initial replicant technology); Wallace's creations are more servile than their predecessors and now work as Blade Runners, searching for and destroying any replicant that is not the newest model. One of the new breed of Blade Runner is K (Ryan Gosling in Kafka-esque mode), who is recruited to investigate the possible existence of a child produced biologically by two replicants. This 'miracle' child represents an extraordinary leap in the evolutionary chain, a new stage of existence that could threaten the dominance of homo sapiens and offer a revolutionary breakthrough to the institution that can control and exploit the child. K's quest for the child, a mission complicated by the LAPD, who want the child dead, and the Wallace Corporation, which wants the specimen to help speed up the production of replicants, is also a quest for his own identity and origins. K (and by extension all replicants) has to stop trying to live up to past definitions of what a human being is and embrace the new humanity as exemplified in the child. By yearning for an outmoded version of humanity and what it means to be human, K is an unwitting accomplice in his own subjugation and oppression.

Villeneuve's direction is a worthy successor to Scott's dazzling, trendsetting approaches to the original. Villeneuve recreates the look of the original *Blade Runner*, but also adds new color to the palette, especially in scenes occurring outside of Los Angeles. Whether it's the stark Edward Hopper-esque look of a lonely farm or the harsh orange miasma of a deserted, irradiated Las Vegas (with a cameo from Elvis!), Villeneuve's shots are brilliantly and strikingly realized. The only disappointment is with the use of CGI in Los Angeles, as the clean digitized imagery can't match the startlingly gritty, tactile pessimism of the original.

It would make sense that Ryan Gosling would play a replicant as he has made his living playing sociopathic characters with no affect (*Drive*, *Only God Forgives*, *The Place Beyond the Pines*), but his portrayal of K is truly moving, as a being that struggles with emotional connections and the consequences of being an alien in a society that treats him like a thing. Harrison Ford's return as Deckard is no nostalgia trip as Ford brings a mature perspective to both his hard-boiled exterior and to his world-weary, wounded inner pathos. Jared Leto gives his usual offbeat weirdo performance as the megalomaniacal technocrat Wallace, but it is Sylvia Hoeks as the replicant Luv who is truly frightening in her murderous, single-minded drive to fulfill her duty no matter what the cost. Although the score doesn't hit the hauntological heights of Vangelis's soundtrack for the original film, Hans Zimmer and Benjamin Wallfisch do an admirable job of producing waves of futuristic nostalgia throughout the film. (One has to wonder, though, what kind of music would have been created had American hip hop artist El-P, or the late and much missed Jóhann Jóhannsson, been able to score the film as originally suggested.) Where the film could have fatally faltered would be if it had sacrificed substance for style, but, luckily, the sequel manages to engage in the same interrogations of binaries that made the original *Blade Runner* so special: real vs artificial, organic vs manufactured, memory vs fantasy, choice vs biological imperative, past vs future, and now even male vs female. Both films suggest that no one is born human; we have to earn that title by our actions, our choices, and our ability to feel for other people. What we were is not as important as what we are and what we can be; the nostalgia for a humanity that no longer 'works' in a society that has passed the point of using human beings as its standard is both fascinating and frightening. The question in both films is not if the replicants have souls, but, rather, how do we know if we (the 'real' humans) have souls and what should we do with them if we have them?

One of the reasons the 1982 *Blade Runner* resonated so strongly in the sensitive minds that viewed it way back when was that it was a frighteningly realistic depiction of a postmodern, post-industrial society. Does *Blade Runner 2049* (along with its conceptual kin, David Cronenberg's brilliant *Crimes of the Future* and Julia Ducournau's *Titane*) give us an accurate glimpse of the posthuman age? *Blade Runner 2049* is not only a commendable addition to the *Blade Runner* mythos, but also proves that the science fiction genre is still the most innovative, creative, and cerebral type of film the cinematic medium can offer us.

Is It Future? Or is It Past?: Twin Peaks: The Return

IN THE SPRING of 1990, a strange mania spread over the United States. Normal people became obsessed with coffee, cherry pie, logs, and a dead woman wrapped in plastic. The reason for this craze was the television series *Twin Peaks*. Created by Mark Frost and visionary director David Lynch, *Twin Peaks* was a truly original take on the mystery genre. On the surface, the show was an investigation into the murder of homecoming queen Laura Palmer in the idyllic small town of Twin Peaks, WA, a place that seemed to be stuck in the wholesome

1950s. As the series progressed, that innocent façade cracked to reveal sordid sex, drugs, secrets, crime, and evil spirits eating away at the heart of America like a starving cancer. The series managed to be campy and horrifying, funny and tragic, screwball melodramatic and brutally realistic all at the same time. Lynch used the surreal nightmarish imagery of *Eraserhead* and *Blue Velvet* in a startlingly different way in *Twin Peaks*, and yet the eccentric characters and their peculiar peccadillos seemed all the more endearing because they didn't step all the way off the ledge as Lynch's characters often do. As happens to most pop culture phenomena, the American public gave up on the show when Lynch refused to reveal Laura Palmer's murderer in a timely fashion and, when the killer was unmasked in the middle of the second season, viewership had dropped off significantly. The show limped to the end of its second season with a fittingly enigmatic series finale directed by Lynch that didn't answer questions but provided much to speculate about.

Over the last twenty-five years, the cult following of *Twin Peaks* grew and the influence of the show began to be felt in the early 2000s television renaissance as a new generation of TV shows paid homage to the groundbreaking series, with everything from *True Detective* to *Gravity Falls* copping the *Twin Peaks* vibe. So, it was with much joy but also trepidation that fans greeted the news that *Twin Peaks* would return as an eighteen-part mini-series on Showtime in 2017. This would not be a dreaded reboot, but, rather, a continuation of the original series with as many of the original cast included as possible. Lynch and Frost reunited to write the new episodes, with Lynch directing the entire season. The first four episodes would be shown as two short movies in order to properly ground the series in the right atmosphere and continuity. And so, on May 21, 2017 the first two new episodes of *Twin Peaks: The Return* were aired, with the following two airing on May 28.

If any fan was worried that the new series would betray the quirky, dreamlike spirit of the original, these first four episodes put any worries to rest. *Twin Peaks:The Return* is in perfect harmony with its originator, even going further and deeper into what made the original series so magical.The initial episodes focus on Special Agent Dale Cooper (Kyle MacLachlan) as he tries to escape his imprisonment in the Black Lodge, surrounded by red velvet curtains, jagged pattern floors, a dancing little person, and a one-armed man. It is about time for Cooper to return to our reality, but his evil doppelgänger, powered by the demonic Bob, doesn't want to return to his dimension and has a sinister plan to stay here. Cooper's spectral reappearance and bad Coop's murderous machinations draw both the denizens of Twin Peaks and the FBI back into the narrative. *Twin Peaks:The Return* intertwines the psychological and the metaphysical as Lynch continues his innovative use of amnesia as a symbol of the fluidity of identity, the human psyche as a blank slate to be written over and erased numerous times in our lives with both angelic and satanic consequences. Lynch's idiosyncratic illusory directing has never been more powerful; his ability to make the mundane fantastic and equate the beautiful and grotesque are in full force. (Although how the podunk Roadhouse books acts like Nine Inch Nails, the Chromatics, and Sharon Van Etten is still a bigger mystery than who killed Laura Palmer ever was). Lynch has not lost a step in all these years and, ironically, the imagery and pacing of the new *Twin Peaks* is closest to his epochal first film *Eraserhead*, especially with its frightening sound design and hellacious machines.

Lynch's fascination with multiple identities, shifting personas, and amnesiac fugues is wonderfully unnerving in *Twin Peaks:The Return*, just as it is in his films *Lost Highway* and *Mulholland Drive*. But it is the return of the beloved characters of *Twin Peaks* such as the Log Lady, Ben Horne, Deputy Andy, Lucy, Deputy Hawk, Bobby Briggs, Gordon Cole, Leland Palmer, and Laura herself that is the real treat of the new series.These characters are like old friends, weird old friends, but old friends nevertheless.The new characters, such as Michael Cera's Marlon Brando-fixated Wally (Andy and Lucy's son) and Eamon Farren's Richard Horne (the spawn of a possible sexual assault of an incapacitated Audrey Horne by Agent Cooper's evil doppelgänger from the Black Lodge) prove that there is plenty of room for more oddballs in this town. Although some might be put off by its very deliberate pacing (which is a relief from most shows where at least 100 things have to happen in each episode), *Twin Peaks: The Return* is a triumphant extension of everything that was so endearing and mesmerizing about the original series. Even if one was totally au fait with Lynch's oeuvre, not even the most informed viewer could have predicted Episode 8, one of the most fascinating, surreal, phantasmagorical, and horrifying hours of television ever broadcast.

The Return Episode 8 starts off with Cooper's doppelgänger escaping from prison with his partner Ray Monroe. Soon, the two fugitives turn on each other, with Monroe gaining the upper hand. As he prepares to kill the evil Cooper, strange apparitions looking like lumberjacks (herein called 'the Woodsmen') emerge from the forest and proceed to rip into the body of Cooper's doppelgänger, revealing the spirit of BOB within. Terrified, Monroe tries to run but is encircled by floating spectres. Monroe manages to get to the car and drives away. Pretty normal for *Twin Peaks*, right? From here, the narrative elevates to heights never before seen on television.

The viewer is taken back in time to 1945, Alamogordo, New Mexico, where the first atomic bomb test has just occurred, and the Woodsmen are there, wandering through a devastated convenience store. The explosion has rent the dimensional veil and a strange being releases plasmatic fluid that contains orbs that resemble ovum, one of which looks like BOB. Crimson and gold energy from the bomb attempts to pierce the ovum, fertilizing the egg with infernal power. With the dimensional wall torn down we can see into another plane of existence: a woman sits on a monolith atop a cliff overlooking a purple ocean. The woman, who is dressed in a 1940s-era dress, sits next to a weird machine and listens to a record. The machine starts to buzz noisily and a man who resembles a younger version of the giant who appeared to Cooper in the first series after he was shot, enters the room. The man switches off the machine and then walks into a room that is an old movie theater. Film of the atomic bomb denotation, the convenience store, and the BOB egg is projected and the man floats as streaks and flashes shoot from his head and coalesce into a universe of stars. The woman walks into the theater and observes this spectacle. A gold sphere reaches out to her, the circle having Laura Palmer's face. After kissing the sphere, the woman releases the Laura globe, which travels through a tube, out of the ceiling, and towards Earth.

Meanwhile at the Alamogordo blast site, an egg hatches and a frog-insect creature emerges. A young couple walk past a gas station, find a lucky penny. and share an innocent kiss. A pair of the spectral Woodsmen stop another couple's car and one repeatedly asks the frightened people "Got a light?" He goes to a radio station where he again asks for a light. The Woodsman murders the receptionist and incapacitates the DJ. The Woodsman recites the words, "This is the water and this is the well. Drink full and descend. The horse is the white of the eyes and dark within." This bizarre recitation goes out over the airwaves, causing listeners to fall asleep. One of the listeners is the young woman who found the penny and kissed her date. The frog-insect creature climbs through her window and descends down her throat. The reciting Woodsman kills the DJ and leaves the radio station. He walks into the desert as a horse neighs in the night.

Twin Peaks: The Return is no conservative, play it safe exercise in nostalgia, pandering to fans, feeding us refried garmonbozia. Episode 8 finally reveals the origins of the Twin Peaks mythos, and it is just as enigmatic, poetic, and shocking as anything in either the series or the movie *Twin Peaks: Fire Walk With Me*. The formation process harkens back to *Eraserhead*'s Man in the Planet, the Lady in the Radiator, and Baby Spencer as an amalgamation of the cosmic, the anachronistic, the grotesque, and the sensual. Attraction, conception, gestation, and birth are linked in a ballet of seduction and violence, Eros and Thanatos. The consequences of creation and destruction, of sex and reproduction, rip through inner dimensions and outer galaxies spawning the angelic and the demonic, the innocent and the psychotic, bliss and terror. Lynch is the Roi surréaliste: combining the highest and lowest of human existence as well as satirizing and parodying the middle, where too many of us hide. The imagery for the episode tops anything that has come before in a Lynch film: grotty tactile decrepitude layered with abstract transcendent radiance. And in the center of this as above, so below maelstrom is the god-like genius of David Lynch who, with Episode 8, surely deserves to be spoken of in the same breath as Buñuel, Dali, Ernst, Magritte, and Carrington for doing something none of those ascended masters ever did: turn television into an artistic palette that exceeds all that has been done before in that hoary medium.

Chapter 5

An Ethereal Composition of Disjointed Memories: Nostalgia as Catalyst for the New

> 'What would we be without memory? We would not be capable of ordering even the simplest thoughts, the most sensitive heart would lose the ability to show affection, our existence would be a mere never-ending chain of meaningless moments, and there would not be the faintest trace of a past. How wretched this life of ours is! —so full of false conceits, so futile, that it is little more than the shadow of the chimeras loosed by memory.'
>
> —François-René de Chateaubriand, quoted in W G Sebald's *The Rings of Saturn*

THE CONSEQUENCES OF nostalgia are usually seen as retrograde rather than avant-garde: bringing up the rear of artistic movements rather than being at the vanguard. The culture industry is flooded with remakes, reboots, and homages that draw from older works and yet these pastiches are often denigrated (sometimes rightly so) for being too slavishly imitative of their progenitors. (How many synthwave artists have released ersatz John

Carpenter, Goblin, and Tangerine Dream tracks? Too many is the only acceptable answer.) Artistic simulacra have to walk a very fine line. References, quotations, and call backs can become tedious and often reflect creative laziness as it's easier to repeat a nostalgic trope than produce a new permutation. On the other hand, update and change too much and the nostalgic spell is killed. (Witness the new *Star Trek* films or when they revise a beloved ride at Disney World.) And yet, these retro creations can be fun and entertaining, recognizing and celebrating esoteric and obscure people, works, and movements that may otherwise be banished to the dustbin of history. Can nostalgia spur new ingenuity? Can a return become an advance? Do references and homages only look back or can they be turned inside out, revitalized, and recontextualized for the present? The notion of looking back to move forward into the future can offer a solid foundation for building the new, but it can also open the door for critical indictments and forced rehabilitation of past problematic works, artists, and ideas in order to bully art, artists, and appreciators to conform to current political, cultural, and social ideologies under the threat of being branded or erased. The seemingly benevolent and harmless experience of nostalgia can be used as a Trojan Horse to sneak in agendas that suppress rather than encourage creativity and free expression. Yet fans are fans, and it is their love of the past and the intense nostalgia that they feel for genres that first excited them that leads artists to create contemporary works that celebrate seasoned passions and inspirational moments, rather than diminish them with boring clones and flavorless reproductions. This chapter looks at works and artists that use nostalgia as an impetus, an incitement, a spark from which to not only revere the past but also to propagate new growth, sidewinding shoots, grown from the humus of both personal and cultural history.

An Ethereal Composition of Disjointed Memories

Why We Need to Keep Saying His Name

WHILE JORDAN PEELE and Nia DaCosta's *Candyman* has received critical and box office kudos, it's important to note that while 2021's *Candyman* is extremely relevant to what's going on in American society today, many of the same themes are also embedded in Bernard Rose's original *Candyman* film. Both films are based on horror icon Clive Barker's short story 'The Forbidden', which takes place in Barker's hometown of Liverpool, England and focuses on a university student named Helen. Helen is researching her thesis on the rhetoric of graffiti and ventures into a housing estate populated by poor working-class people to study the anonymous writings on the walls. Much of the graffiti mentions 'Candyman' and Helen begins to connect this mythical figure to a serious of violent attacks and murders plaguing the dilapidated complex. The fearful residents refuse to speak about the spectral killer and Helen's probing into the legend brings her face to face with Candyman. For the 1992 adaptation, director Bernard Rose kept the overall outline of the original story but moved the setting to the United States and added racial issues as well as additional social criticism to Barker's narrative. Rose chose Chicago (one of the most segregated cities in the US), specifically the public housing project of Cabrini-Green, as the backdrop to the creation, manifestation, and continuance of an urban legend. Cabrini-Green was one of the most notorious subsidized housing complexes in the US, with high rates of poverty, crime, gang violence, and drug abuse: an unofficial prison where the strongest inmates ran the yard. Much like what Stanley Kubrick did with Stephen King's novel *The Shining*, Rose elevates Barker's story into a critique of the connections between race, class, and trauma in the US, uncovering the unhealed historical and social wounds created through hundreds of years of oppression and silence. Candyman's transformation from human being to folk villain results from punishment for an interracial relationship that crossed not only racial but also class boundaries, denying any aspects of nostalgia for or dismissal of scary stories used to frighten children and provide thrills at slumber parties. Both Rose and DaCosta's versions of *Candyman* imagine urban myth in the same way psychologist Bruno Bettelheim interprets fairy tales: instructional stories that not only warn children of the dangers awaiting them in a predatory world, but also act as metaphorical introductions to ideological and social rules, regulations, and etiquette. (Even the name 'Candyman' recalls the temptation that lured in the abandoned Hansel and Gretel.) For Rose and DaCosta, the relationships between power, race, class, and gender are the crucial 'moral' to these urban horror tales.

The figure of Candyman has become part of the 'urban wyrd', an expression of the urbanized and gentrified horrors that lurk under paved streets, down dark alleys, stalk abandoned buildings, and haunt public parks. Candyman is a terrifying warning of the price one pays for transgression, crossing strict racial and class lines, especially if the transgressor is a member of a vilified, downtrodden group. Although Rose's film is titled after Candyman, the character of Helen Lyle is just as, if not more, important than the titular 'monster', as she becomes the vessel through which the story of a historical tragedy will endure, resonating with people who are still victimized and exploited. Although Helen is white and upper class, the fact that she is a woman who has been deceived, belittled, and subjugated by the men and patriarchal institutions in her life makes her a worthy successor for reminding current city dwellers of the pain and suffering that resulted from the injustices of Candyman's torture, mutilation, and murder. These agonizing incidents formed Candyman, and forge the legend of Helen too, and their stories will continue, resonating with people who have been, still are, and may be in the future persecuted and exploited. The figures of Candyman and Helen will continue to extend their unholy existences until the racial, social, and gender abuses that created them are brought to light and acknowledged by victims and victimizers. Perhaps some of Rose's more artistic and oblique connections of race, class, gender, and past traumas do not sting as sharply, precisely, or authentically as DaCosta's more direct confrontations with the horrors of institutionalized and historical oppression. Yet Rose's position as an 'outsider', an Englishman making a film in the United States about American racism and gentrification, gives his *Candyman* a more impartial, alien perspective on these issues, which only adds to the abstruseness of the original film. DaCosta ingenuously transforms the individual tragedy of Daniel Robitaille's punishment, death, and transfiguration into Candyman into a symbol for generations of black men murdered by racist perpetrators as portrayed by her male main character, Anthony McCoy. Much like racism itself, the Candyman legend moves virus-like through communities, spreading and reproducing itself through fear, violence, ignorance, and hatred. While the oppressors stay largely hidden behind upper-class academic propriety or in the past in Rose's *Candyman*, DaCosta's *Candyman* explicitly showcases direct exercises of race and class power as being the reason why Candyman still haunts the lives of the oppressed. Unfortunately, the sequels to Rose's *Candyman* have little to none of the ideological critique that Rose's and DaCosta's films do, and it remains to be seen if DeCosta and Peele will continue the saga of Daniel Robitaille, Helen Lyle, and now Anthony McCoy.

In 2011, Cabrini-Green was demolished by the Chicago Housing Authority. Perhaps the ghosts contained in that building of misery and degradation have at long last been freed, and yet the story of Candyman is still stubbornly with us, waiting to be finally exorcized for good. DaCosta's film ends with the direct order to "Tell everyone", a recognition of black oral traditions as an alternative to mainstream media channels, and the need to identify and document the traumas that are forgotten by official histories and serve the interests of powerful oppressors. Stories and memories fade with time, forgotten by individuals, communities, and nations. Erasure can absolve both personal and collective guilt and responsibility in the moment, but the ghosts of the past will eventually come back. Remembering can be extremely painful, but if we don't acknowledge the past we will be haunted by these personal and collective traumas. Just because something is forgotten doesn't mean it didn't exist. In identifying systemic racism, language matters, but it can't be the only thing that matters: words must be supported by reasoned, equitable, and compassionate behavior, as how we speak to each other needs to be directly connected to how we treat and interact with one another physically, emotionally, and ethically, right here, right now. Until that day, Candyman's name and the historical crimes committed against him will continue to possess us all.

Electric Wizard: Live at Webster Hall

> 'I'm into all that shit, anything like that. I'm into poppy, occult weird shit. I collect seventies porno with witchcraft in it. I collect weird movies, fucking goat heads, black fucking mass shit, really old, weird shit, statues of Pan and all from the Victorian times. I love that whole vibe. I love that era. I like what they were trying to evoke, the horror movies. It seemed like, right around '71, people went fucking heavy. It was cool to be fucking doom.' —Jus Oborn, interview, *Metal Maniacs*

THE LAST TIME doom metal/occult rock gods Electric Wizard toured the US was in 2002 (they did make a one-off appearance at Maryland Deathfest in 2012) and so the stars were right again for their return. Since then, the Wizard have released four albums of horror-inspired heaviness (2004's *We Live*, 2007's horror rock masterpiece *Witchcult Today*, 2010's *Black Masses*, and 2014's *Time to Die*, as well as three EPs), had multiple line-up changes (most significantly the addition of second guitarist Liz Buckingham), and have mentored several younger bands (Blood Ceremony, Satan's Satyrs, Witchsorrow, Uncle Acid & the

Deadbeats). Throughout this time, Electric Wizard singer/guitarist Jus Oborn has stayed true to his Euro-Cult/biker/satanic film obsessions, infusing his lyrics, sound, imagery, and cover art with references to Jean Rollin, Hammer films, Anton LaVey, Aleister Crowley, H P Lovecraft, Robert E Howard, Sergio Martino, *Psychomania*, *Werewolves on Wheels*, Alex Sanders, lurid sensationalistic paperbacks, and Italian fumetti comics like *Zora* and *Sukia*. Electric Wizard created what is considered one of the heaviest, sludgiest, slowest, most fuzzed-out stoner epics of all time with 2000's *Dopethrone*, but have changed over time into a more aggressively psychedelic hard rock band that conjure ritualistic sounds that mesmerize and exhilarate. Although they have been accused of living in the past through their deification of Black Sabbath and the *Man, Myth, and Magic* era of Old Weird Britain, Electric Wizard's sleazy dedication to the seventies underground would seem like an empty retro mélange if their music wasn't so immense and their passion so deep. The Wizard's aesthetic is a rejuvenation of those cultural touchstones rather than mere opportunistic pastiche. (This is heavy metal and so taking on the trappings of the dark side without really immersing oneself in it isn't unheard of.) The band not only celebrates what was once dismissed as trashy and degenerate, but also takes on all those past signifiers and acculturated associations to become the band we wished had been, but wasn't, but now is and shouldn't be in the twenty-first century Digital Age. Anachronistic? Maybe, but who cares when it's this much fun? Jus's true love for the horror culture of the past is no mere cash-in, but an aesthetically-informed resistance to the homogeneity, commodification, and shallow investment that pass for contemporary underground ethos, like when vapidly ignorant reality TV stars wear Ramones, CBGB, or MC5 T-shirts. It's ironic that for so many years, scuzzy erotic exploitation films were villainized, punk rock nihilism was excoriated, and VHS tape trading culture was neglected, yet now the culture industry, academia, and online careerists are feeding on it, looking for any sustenance to keep themselves relevant and monetized.

The Wizard's psychotronic grade-z ethos is best epitomized in their anti-straight world slogan/Luciferian hymn Legalise Drugs & Murder, which may not jive with contemporary social justice/cancel crazy ideologies, but fits the doom metal credo wholeheartedly. The legend of Electric Wizard has grown over the last decade, so much so that their announced concert at Webster Hall in New York City sold out in a day. It's not often that the devilish gang stops riding around the Seven Witches in Dorset and brings their evil hymns to the colonies. Anticipation was quite high as metalheads, hipsters, occult rock aficionados, Euro trash horror fans, and weirdos of all types filed into the Webster awaiting the arrival of the Wizard. Openers Satan's Satyrs played a solid set of punked-out hyper garage metal with bass player/singer Clayton Burgess looking like a young Ozzy, pummeling his bass to tracks from their ultra-cool albums *Die Screaming* and *Wild Beyond Belief*. Satan's Satyrs set the stage for a night of evil-infused music with horror-riffic paeans to Alucard, Creepy Teens, and Instruments of Hellfire.

After a break, the stage went dark and the sounds of thunder and wind filled the hall as Electric Wizard strolled onto the stage to wild cheering and the sparking of many lighters. As it is, so be it. The ritual commenced. Beginning with the title cut from *Witchcult Today* (the greatest occult rock album ever recorded), the Wizard locked into a diabolic groove that never let up. As the band powered through their set, visuals from Jess Franco's *Exorcism* and *The Rites of Frankenstein,* as well as Euro cult films *Crucible of Terror* and *The Devil's Wedding Night*, and a weird loop of a hippie chick tripping out with a skull, perfectly accentuated the sleazed out, ominous songs like Satanic Rites Of Drugula, Return Trip, Incense For The Damned, Dopethrone, and The Chosen Few. Oborn's guitar playing resembled a combination of Tony Iommi's blackest riffs and Ron Asheton waved his instrument around like a magickal weapon over a hypnotized crowd that could either only nod their heads to each track or attack each other in frenzied ecstasy. Liz Buckingham's rhythm guitar provided a fiendish drone echoing through each song that slayed all in her witchy Maxine Sanders way. Bass player Clayton Burgess (pulling double demonic duty tonight) and drummer Simon Poole conjured up an infernal throb, especially during the invocation of Black Mass. The show ended with the epic Funeralopolis, and as the Wizard exited the stage, the silence now oppressive, the spell was broken, the ceremony done, weed smoke dissipated like frankincense from the Black Pope's thurible, and the chosen few disappeared back into the darkness of the Gotham night. Who knows when Electric Wizard will return,[1] but the legend of this show will live on in the minds and ears of those who were lucky enough to witness this rare otherworldly sonic equinox.

The Abyss's Gaze: The Void

IN 2007, CANADIAN filmmakers Adam Brooks and Jeremy Gillespie founded Astron-6, an independent production company that specializes in affectionate parodies of eighties-style horror, sci-fi, and action films such as *Father's Day*, *Manborg*, and *The Editor*. These movies are paeans to the low budget, gore-filled, ultra bizarre flicks that were churned out to feed the ravenous VHS audience looking to rent anything and everything to keep their VCRs playing. Although the films are extreme satires of the eighties and the film genres themselves, Astron-6's cadre of super creative lunatics clearly love the movies they are skewing and celebrating, whether it is slasher psychos, stylish giallos, post-apocalyptic shockers, or your average direct-to-video exploitation blow-out. Astron-6's writing/directing team of Gillespie and Steven Kostanski (a much in demand makeup artist who has worked on the new version of *It*, *Suicide Squad*, and the brilliant television series *Hannibal*) have broken away from the comedic

1 The Wizard returned in 2019, kind of blowing up my apocalyptic metaphor.

mode of their past films and produced what may have been the best horror film of 2016: *The Void*.

The Void begins with small town police officer (Aaron Poole) about to end his shift when he finds a wounded man collapsed on a lonely country road. He rushes the man to an all-but-deserted isolated hospital, but soon after this noble rescue, two armed men take over the hospital and demand to kill the new patient. As if this standoff wasn't tense enough, outside the hospital hooded cult members have surrounded the building. Inside, some of the staff begin to metamorphose into grotesque, tentacled monsters. Characters transform, mutate, and give birth to more monstrosities, reflecting the key themes of patriarchal anxiety, maternal/paternal guilt, and the uncontrollability of offspring.

Although certainly not a parody, *The Void* is informed by homages to seventies/eighties/nineties horror, harkening back to the works of John Carpenter (*The Thing, Assault on Precinct 13, The Fog, Halloween II, Prince of Darkness*), Lucio Fulci (*The Beyond, House by the Cemetery*) and Michele Soavi (*The Church, The Sect*). Taking Carpenter's patented use of paranoia and the siege mentality and mixing this hysterical heightened awareness with the blood and body fluid-soaked glories of Italian horror cinema creates an atmosphere of utter terror and stomach-churning wonderment. Like the best of horror films, it's familiar yet unsettling: we have seen situations like this before but there's also something not quite right about it. Nostalgic reassurance is used against the viewer of *The Void* as those who recognize the tropes are in for a startlingly shocking reckoning. The crowdfunded special effects in *The Void* (all practical, no CGI) clearly owe much to Rob Bottin's astonishing designs in *The Thing*, but the creators of *The Void* rather perversely keep much of the monsters' designs in darkness, yet show the graphic injuries and disfigurations of the human victims in all their gross-out glory.

Also noteworthy is the score, which — although a compilation with tracks from Jeremy Gillespie, Brian Wiacek, Menalon, and Blitz/

/Berlin assisted by industrial/dark ambient innovator Brian 'Lustmord' Williams — hangs over the film like a cohesive darkness. If all there was to *The Void* was over-the-top carnage and nostalgic call backs, that would still be enough to justify a viewing, but the last thirty minutes of the film is where it transcends the horror genre and breaks through into the fantastique. Gillespie and Kostanski add heaped doses of Lovecraftian cosmicism, existential nihilism, and the metaphysical surreality of David Lynch, Alejandro Jodorowsky, and Dario Argento to *The Void*. Although familiar in much of its imagery and structure, *The Void* separates itself from other throwback nostalgia horror movies like *Fear Itself* or *Summer of 84* by aligning more with challenging twenty-first-century fantastique films such as *Beyond the Black Rainbow*, *Mandy*, *The Lords of Salem*, *Here Comes the Devil*, *The Outwaters*, and *In the Earth* as cinematic experiences that take viewers into another reality beyond the expected horror tropes and safe, comfortable genre acquaintance that puts audiences more at ease than disconcerted or anxious. Gillespie and Kostanski push these sensitivities past the expected points of reference, resulting in a film that imaginatively liberates itself from the tired clichés that often infect the genre. This willingness to be daring rather than conservative is demonstrated in the startling, but weirdly affirming, ending of *The Void*, which Lucio Fulci might describe as 'a not unhappy' dénouement. If you are satisfied with corporate horror like *It* or the execratory hipster remake of *Suspiria*, then don't bother with *The Void*. If you want your mind turned inside out, then *The Void* will open new vistas of the horrible and the sublime for the adventurous cinematic explorer.

Chapter 6

The Vice of the Aged: Do They Still Got It or Living Off Past Glories?

> 'In a certain sense the past is far more real, or at any rate more stable, more resilient than the present. The present slips and vanishes like sand between the fingers, acquiring material weight, only in its recollection.'
>
> —Andrei Tarkovsky, *Sculpting in Time*

AS OLDER GENERATIONS' memories grow dimmer and millennial/Gen Z interest in the past is shrinking by the hour, the amount and kinds of media that can house vast repositories of cultural artifacts, seemingly forever, has grown exponentially. Information technologies, cloud storage services, and streaming entertainment recollect for us: if you can't remember, just Google it. Entire catalogues of writing, film, music, and art spanning thousands of years are available to those who can afford a cell phone. (Of course, not everyone has the money nor the entrée, which can be interpreted as another repressive weapon in the global class struggle.) Even if one doesn't have the monetary resources to pay for downloads and streaming, there are ways both nefarious and virtuous to enter this Alamutian paradise. While this unprecedented access to invaluable cultural riches seems to be the greatest technological innovation in the history of the planet, it does beg the question of nostalgia's place in a world of instant answers and immediate satiation. There's always an element of doubt in nostalgia, the questioning of perception and memory that leads to a certain amount of filling in the blanks, that places nostalgia somewhere between reality and fantasy. There's a strangely comforting uncertainty to nostalgia that gives it a mysterious quality that can be quashed by facts. Finding out that the plot to a half-remembered horror movie from one's childhood deviates sharply from one's memory can be an extreme bummer. IMDb can kill one's dreams as quickly as the education system. There's also the threat that this accumulated cultural warehouse can be a smothering burden to fans unsure of what to consume and to artists who are creating under their own collective histories. How do artists with significant back catalogues approach their bodies of work, now forever enshrined and available? Are they in competition with their younger, more popular, selves? Are they haunted by their own works? 'Nostalgia act' is a pejorative label that identifies those musicians who live off past glories and have not released new or significant material in years. Churning out the same hits everyone expects and demands because audiences pay often exorbitant prices for tickets and insist on being entertained, most older artists can be unwilling to alienate the casual fan with deep pockets and hazy memories of certain songs that received airplay in their youth. This is not to say that these concerts can't be enormously entertaining, but they speak directly to yesterday and sentimentality rather than innovation and creative risk-taking. And yet, there are some mature artists still pushing their artistic boundaries and unwilling or unable to play it safe. The reviews in this chapter look at musicians with a combined musical history of over 140 years and over 150 releases and who are still negotiating the line between nostalgia and experimentation.

Goblin Live at the Music Hall of Williamsburg

THE SOUND OF Italian horror is just as important as its garishly beautiful visuals. Dario Argento's psychedelically gothic blood baths are justifiably celebrated as the epitome of Italian horror excess, but one wonders if his status would be as exalted if it were not for the crucial contributions of premier prog-rock collective Goblin and their all-out sonic assault. Goblin's legendary soundtracks for Argento's *Deep Red*, *Suspiria*, *Tenebrae*, *Phenomena*, and *Sleepless*, and their equally impressive work for George Romero, Luigi Cozzi, and Joe D'Amato, have cemented their formidable reputation in the hearts, minds, and ears of horror connoisseurs. The shifting line up of Goblin has seen various combinations, offshoots, and competing versions of the band play concerts and record, but Goblin has never been fully experienced live in the US until now. Second only to The Beatles' arrival on American shores, the Goblin tour (featuring original members Claudio Simonetti, Maurizio Guarini, and Massimo Morante and youngsters Bruno Previtali on bass and Titta Tani on drums, accompanied on some songs by a feral interpretive dancer) has induced a frenzy amongst horror music fans. For their sold-out show at the new bohemian capital of the world, Williamsburg, Brooklyn, the power of Goblin conquered the bearded New York audience. Openers Secret Chiefs 3 (led by Faith No More/Mr. Bungle's Trey Spruance) set the occult mood with an intense set that included a wall-shaking rendition of John Carpenter's deathless *Halloween* theme and a tribute to the master Ennio Morricone. Soon after, the mighty Goblin hit the stage, commencing an audio/visual overload dazzling through volume, virtuosity, and European cool. Seeing Simonetti come out wearing the silver mask from *Demons* set the tone immediately. The journey into Italian horror began with the ominous bass rumblings of Mad Puppet from *Deep Red* and progressed through selections from *Sleepless*, *Dawn of the Dead*, *Phenomena*, and *Tenebrae* (Simonetti's use of a vocoder was brilliant as their rendition of the theme was one of many amazing highlights) as well as tracks from their non-soundtrack albums *Roller* and *Back to Goblin*. Collaged images from Argento's and Romero's films were projected behind the musicians and elevated the experience to dizzying heights of maniacal perversity. The effect of hearing these compositions live for listeners who had only previously heard them through TVs or in theaters can't be accurately described, but the ecstatic responses from the audience should be evidence enough of the majesty of the event. The infamous theme from *Suspiria* was the zenith of this ritual, with every sigh, chime, and witchy sound gloriously reproduced and amplified to supernatural ecstasy. Goblin even did a rendition of Happy Birthday To You for Massimo and made it sound fresh and daring. Clearly, the band relished playing for the Brooklyn crowd, and the audience loved every minute.

Expectations seldom exceed reality, but Goblin's performance broke through into another dimension, thrusting the stunned audience into that wonderfully decadent giallo, Euro sleaze atmosphere. This was truly an event for all those obsessive horror fans who remembered the first time they watched their bootleg copy of the uncut *Tenebrae* or unwittingly rented a VHS copy of *Suspiria* and had their mind blown. The kind of fans who obsessively collect every different cut of Argento's oeuvre and have numerous copies of Goblin's catalogue in multiple media. While the members of Goblin must realize that it is the older, horror-related tracks that the crowd wanted to hear, it didn't seem to affect them one bit, cheerfully giving the audience what they wanted. This understanding also extended to the various goods hawked by the group, including a tour-only EP on blood red vinyl (again, they know what their fans want and are willing to pay for) sold at their merchandise table. Nostalgia on stage, projected on screens, and retailed as product might sound cynical, but so what? It was the perfect Euro-cult evening. Rumor has it that the great Italian horror composer Fabio Frizzi will be making his stateside live debut in the new year. Seeing Fulci's maestro summoning up the themes to *Zombi, The Beyond*, and *City of the Living Dead* in person could result in the ultimate Euro Trash Horror event. Then Italian horror music fans can die happy.

Addendum:
Fabio Frizzi, Live at the Music Hall of Williamsburg

WELL, IT LOOKS like Italian horror music fans died and happily went to hell, as on October 30, 2017, Fabio Frizzi came to the Music Hall in Williamsburg to entertain those who traveled through the seven gateways or just arrived by boat from Matul. The night before, Frizzi and his band played a live score, his 'Composer's Cut', for a showing of *The Beyond*, but it was on October 30 that the full depth and breadth of his musical oeuvre was showcased. Frizzi has long been a horror movie music icon, starting with his collaborations with Franco Bixio and Vincent Tempera through his famed scores for Lucio Fulci's greatest works, up to contemporary soundtracks for films such as *House of Forbidden Secrets* (2012) and *Puppet Master: The Littlest Reich* (2018), as well as his incidental music for Cadabra Records' audio adaptations of H P Lovecraft's 'The Festival' and Edgar Allan Poe's 'The Black Cat'. The venue provided folding chairs for the audience so one could sit and truly listen to, concentrate on, and appreciate Frizzi and his associates' performance. Opening with an unexpected cover of King Crimson's The Court Of The Crimson King, Frizzi and his crew acknowledged the prog rock foundation of many of Frizzi's scores. Frizzi's was backed by a seven-piece band including two electric guitarists, a bassist, a drummer, a keyboardist who doubled on flute and harmonica, and an outstanding female vocalist who hit her piercing shrieks all night long. Frizzi himself played a little keyboard, a little acoustic guitar, but, more importantly, conducted his ensemble like Paganini Horror himself. Astonishing versions of cuts from his soundtracks for *Zombi, The Beyond, City of the Living Dead, Manhattan Baby*, and *A Cat in the Brain* were melded with scenes from the films projected behind the band. This audio/visual experience was a rampaging tribute not only to Fulci but also to Frizzi's own creativity and virtuosity, reminding the audience how crucial his musical contributions have been to the enshrining of Fulci in the pantheon of horror director gods. The highlights of the concert were performances of music from *Sette Note In Nero* (surely one of the most sublime horror soundtracks ever recorded) and westerns *Silver Saddle* and *Four of the Apocalypse*. Frizzi took time out to address the audience, thanking them and expressing his appreciation for the love and support they have given him. After this heartfelt, beautiful connection with his fans, Frizzi then serenaded us with an encore from *The Beyond* and film clips of a tarantula removing a man's tongue. What better expression of endearment could any Italian horror fan receive? Frizzi's live show is a must-see experience for any horror fan, Euro or not, demonstrating that in merging sinister yet gorgeous sounds and frightening yet stunning visions, the Italians still have not been bettered. Much like Goblin's appearance the previous year, there was a similar nostalgic feel and a consumerist side to that nostalgia (I have never seen so many posters, CDs, and records sold at a merch table) but when considering that this was Frizzi's first tour of the US and the unmitigated joy that he exuded while playing for an adoring audience, perhaps it's better to call this a celebration rather than a memorial. Now if we could only get Carlo Maria Cordio and Pino Donaggio to come to Brooklyn…

Nick Cave and Warren Ellis at the Kings Theater

THE TITLE 'LEGEND' is thrown around so much these days that I am expecting soon to read about Pete Davidson's 'legendary' tattoos. A legend is someone who will leave behind a legacy of greatness, of glory, and of achievement that goes beyond the known expectations of human beings. Legends touch lives and lives to come through their chosen medium; they take risks, sacrificing aspects of themselves, driven to reach the heights of what it means to be exemplary and then exceed those boundaries into the unknown. A legend eclipses mundane reality and is remembered more as a myth than an actuality. Legends are creators of beauty and truth in a world that doesn't value or even understand the kinds of beauty and truth that legends impart to us. The enhanced sensibilities of a legend call others to experience life more fully, the highs and the lows, blazing forward with no compromise, no matter how suicidal or foolhardy it seems. Most legends aren't identified as such until they have shuffled off this mortal coil, often in obscurity, and if they are contemporaneously celebrated, it's for their past rather than their present works. For over forty years, Nick Cave has been steadily building his case for legendary status through his art and the way he lives his life. Singer, songwriter, poet, author, composer, and screenwriter, Cave has consistently brought an aesthetic and personal intensity to every one of his projects, throwing himself into his obsessions with death, loss, transcendence, and love. Beginning with the psychotic noise of The Birthday Party, Cave confronted audiences with unhinged characters, biblical tales of bloody vengeance, and sounds that could drag a listener to hell and back. When The Birthday Party gloriously crashed and burned, Cave started The Bad Seeds from the ashes and continued his journey into and through the heart of darkness, modernizing the Delta blues into a howling, stomping, frenzied embrace of existential angst, raw passion, and the search for salvation. Cave takes much inspiration from the Southern writer Flannery O'Connor, as both Cave and O'Connor specialize in brutal spiritual awakenings forced by coming face to face with the mysterious evils of existence: truth only revealed through extreme tests of faith. Cave's persona is both The Misfit and 'Minister' Hazel Motes, revealing the grotesque, ironic horrors of hypocrisy and false piety of holy roller conmen, superficial, self-righteous Christians, and hubristic secularists. Time mellows even notorious rebels and, along with collaborator Warren Ellis, Cave began to explore quieter, more introspective songs of tenderness and devotion while also expanding his oeuvre into soundtracks. Cave and Ellis scored several films such as *The Assassination of Jesse James by the Coward Robert Ford* (2007), *The Road* (2009), and *West of Memphis* (2012), showcasing the duo's sense of atmosphere and dramatic tension. Cave and Ellis took an extended pandemic-inflicted vacation from The Bad Seeds and created a new album *Carnage* in 2021, and it is in support of this album and the last Bad Seeds album *Ghosteen* (2019) that the two men are touring the post-plague United States in 2022.

Fittingly, then, on Flannery O'Connor's birthday, Cave and Ellis took to the stage at the Kings Theater in Brooklyn. Accompanying Cave and Ellis were three backing singers and a touring musician who played bass, drums, and a laptop that provided backing tracks. This stripped-down arrangement perfectly complemented the songs, almost entirely drawn from *Carnage* and *Ghosteen*. Opening with Spinning Song, the first track on *Ghosteen*, Cave continued his use of Elvis as a metaphor for kingly ascendancy, which started all the way back in 1985 with the raging Tupelo. Ellis, looking like a hillbilly Gandalf, played synthesizer and sawed at his violin like a mad fiddler as Wendi Rose and the backing singers provided exquisite harmonies to Cave's brooding baritone. T. Rex's Cosmic Dancer fit perfectly with the other joyous exultations, and yet the almost evangelical fervor was leavened with moments of destitution and deprivation in Shattered Ground, Carnage (which namechecks Ms O'Connor), and especially during the song Ghosteen, written in tribute to Cave's fifteen-year-old son Arthur who died in a tragic accident. Rather than wallow in self-pity or fixate on nostalgic memories of his son, Cave attempts to communicate with him through sound and connect the audience with the life spirit of a young man taken far too soon. The healing power of music elevated not only Cave and his musicians, but the entire crowd, as well as performances of Hand Of God, Lavender

Fields, Waiting For You, and God Is In The House that transformed the Kings Theater into The Church of Immaculate Sound: Cave's euphonious preaching held his devotees entirely in his grasp. The crowd demanded two sets of encores, and the first saw Cave return to the psychodramas of yesteryear with the feral Hollywood and the menacing Henry Lee, but the second encore left the audience with odes to adoration, connection, and hope as Cave and Ellis uplifted all with vigorous versions of Into My Arms, Jubilee Street, and the closing hymn-like Ghosteen Speaks. Next time he graces a stage near you (in any form), make every effort to experience him. Cave, although proud of his expansive body of work (and rightly so), has a relentless need to keep moving forward, stretching his creative abilities as far as he can without any concessions to anyone but himself and his muse. Not content to be fossilized in the post-punk/goth Hall of Fame, Nick Cave demands progressive excellence not only from himself but also from his listeners. Neither he nor we should be looking back, but always onward towards the next peak.

Chapter 7

The Enemy of Truth: Is Nostalgia Counter-Revolutionary?

> 'Nostalgia is masochism and masochism is something masochists love to share.' —Andrei Codrescu, *New Orleans, Mon Amour: Twenty Years of Writings from the City*

IS NOSTALGIA A harmless skip down memory lane? Can nostalgia be used like propaganda to mollify, entice, and seduce: encouraging us to turn off our critical thinking, stick our heads in the sand, and revel in a past that actually may have never been, a past gone mad? While conservative politicians have made nostalgia an intrinsic and explicit part of their political platform, the social consequences of nostalgia on culture and art can be sinisterly opaque. For much of the culture industry, nostalgia has become an appealing gimmick that sells products but lowers creative expectations. While franchises, sequels, reboots, remakes, and homages all utilize nostalgia to various degrees, it's the exploitation of the past and its cynical use of fandom's loyalties, that have weaponized nostalgia as a key aspect of the society of the spectacle. Certainly, cinema is not the only perpetrator using nostalgia to disguise the paucity of ideas and creativity in contemporary culture; the music industry's endless remixes, reworkings, covers, virtual duets, retreads, and composing by committee are perhaps even more nauseating than film and TV. While nostalgia can be inspirational, it can also be a levelling agent where all our individual histories are reduced to one totalizing past, constructed by ideology and sold to us through media. The past, present, and future become products that are interchangeable, bought, sold, rented, as memory becomes just another commercial. The form of nostalgia utilized by the culture industry is one that removes any political, social, or critical aspect to remembrance and the past: decontextualized and stripped of any sense of individuality or multiple subjectivities. The ghosts of the past have either been 'busted' or transformed into marketable commodities that are directed at audiences sentimentally attached to long-lived franchises and brands. This synergy of media, merchandising, and memories creates an idealism as well as an artificial longing: there was a perfect time, a perfect place, a perfect emotion that can be experienced again through consumerism: the equation of being with having with appearing. Pacified with product, lost in the reverie of a suspect yesterday, current situations and material history are neglected as the short moments of anesthetizing nostalgia dissipate into feelings of disappointment, despair, and alienation. Needing to numb these emotions, we buy more product to give us our nostalgic fix, which, of course, never really satisfies. The new digital bourgeoisie and their virtual culture produce nothing and consume everything: nostalgia feeding a predatory instinct for validation at any price from anyone for anything. The most interesting works that use nostalgia are the ones that not only soothe but also unsettle, as doubt and uncertainty are central aspects of desire, memory, and remembrance. The essays in this final chapter are accusatory, calling out those people and franchises that are infantilizing, manipulating, and cashing in on viewers and fans, using our own memories, connections, and passions against us.

Who Protects Us from the Superheroes?

> 'Suppose we want truth: why not rather untruth? and uncertainty? even ignorance? The problem of the value of truth came before us — or was it we who came before the problem? Who of us is Oedipus here? Who the Sphinx?'
> —Friedrich Nietzsche, *Beyond Good and Evil*

RECENTLY, IN A rare interview with entertainment news website *Deadline*, the greatest living comic book writer and professional curmudgeon Alan Moore savagely critiqued the spate of superhero movies that have become the dominant box office hits of the 2010s and 2020s. For those of you who don't know who he is, Alan Moore is one of the most creative and insightful authors of the late twentieth and early twenty-first century. Moore specifically chose the 'vulgar' medium of comic books to express his brilliance and ended up completely changing and reinventing the genre in terms of not only content but the format as well. Moore's justly celebrated runs on such comics as *Swamp Thing*, *V for Vendetta*, *Miracleman* (now published by the Marvel Entertainment/Disney yakuza), *From Hell*, *Promethea*, *The League of Extraordinary Gentlemen*, and *Providence* brought mature, thought-provoking, and challenging ideas and perspectives to a medium that had been dismissed as 'kid's stuff' for much of its history. It was Moore's award-winning deconstruction of superheroes and the mythologizing behind them in *Watchmen* that brought him to the attention of the non-comic reading public, but it also brought the attention of larger sections of the culture industry, specifically the wonderland of Hollywood. Film producers saw dollar signs in Rorschach's morphing mask, and so Moore became hot property in Tinseltown. Far from being flattered by this wooing, Moore questioned what rights he had to the characters he created for DC Comics, especially now that big money contracts were being tossed back and forth between teams of lawyers. Finding out that he essentially owned nothing and that he had no say over merchandising, reprinting, and licensing deals, nor was he guaranteed any say in potential screenplays for cinematic adaptations of his work, rubbed Moore the wrong way. He would be appropriately compensated if he just kept his mouth shut, played ball with the nice corporations, and said that anything they produced was the greatest thing since *Superman IV*. Moore couldn't sell his creative soul and walked away from millions of dollars.

Unfortunately, Moore's stand on artistic integrity had no impact on the churning out of films containing characters and stories he created: 2001's *From Hell*, 2003's *The League of Extraordinary Gentlemen*, 2005's *Constantine*, 2006's *V for Vendetta*, 2009's *Watchmen*. On principle, Moore has refused to work on any of these projects, has not taken a dime from them, nor has he watched any of the films. (Perhaps Moore should check out Damon Lindelof's *Watchmen* series for HBO, which manages to deepen and extend some of the themes of the original comic books in interesting ways but still can't touch the progenitor.) The fact that none of these films were blockbusters can be seen as double vindication for Moore: watering down his bold interpretations bored intelligent viewers, while the core original ideas that were the catalysts for the film versions confused and alienated viewers who wanted the smash/bang superficiality of the vast majority of prior comic book adaptations like the Superman and Batman series of films. While the superhero films and TV series of the 1970s–1990s were certainly popular, they did not set a new paradigm for the domination of the world's attention as the 2010s onslaught of Marvel's, and to a lesser extent DC's, 'cinematic universe' juggernauts have. Of course, this begs the question why now, why here? What has changed in our society to encourage such mass adulation of these types of film?

Moore vents particular spleen at the way these monolithic, totalitarian, entertainment institutions have blitzkrieged, dominated, and indoctrinated media and, by proxy, viewers' imaginations:

> They have blighted cinema, and also blighted culture to a degree. Several years ago, I said I thought it was a really worrying sign, that hundreds of thousands of adults were queuing up to see characters that were created 50 years ago to entertain 12-year-old boys. That seemed to speak to some kind of longing to escape from the complexities of the modern world, and go back to a nostalgic, remembered childhood. That seemed dangerous, it was infantilizing the population. This may be entirely coincidence but in 2016 when the American people elected a National Socialist satsuma and the UK voted to leave the European Union, six of the top 12 highest grossing films were superhero movies. Not to say that one causes the other but I think they're both symptoms of the same thing — a denial of reality and an urge for simplistic and sensational solutions.[1]

Is Moore claiming that although not every bourgeois Marvel Comic Universe fan could have become a Donald Trump or a Boris Johnson, that a particle of Trump and/or Johnson is lodged in every bourgeois MCU fan? At first, Moore's outlook seems to be an unfair, almost conspiratorial, critique, but think about fandom and their delusionally nostalgic, immature, and insanely violent responses to parts of the superhero movie regime: Ben Affleck got death threats after being cast as Batman, Twitter raged over Captain Marvel, Black Panther, and Wonder Woman, and *Avengers: Endgame* left some of its viewers in such fury and despair that they expressed it in almost a weaponized manner. Confusing consumer product branding for authentic political and social representation, fandom swoons over fictional characters who now take on the superficial characteristics of oppressed racial, religious, ethnic, gender, and sexual identities. Are these responses indicative only of fandom, or of larger forces and

1 Tom Grater, 'Alan Moore Gives Rare Interview: 'Watchmen' Creator Talks New Project 'The Show', How Superhero Movies Have "Blighted Culture" & Why He Wants Nothing To Do With Comics,' *Deadline* (October 9, 2020), https://deadline.com/2020/10/alan-moore-rare-interview-watchmen-creator-the-show-superhero-movies-blighted-culture-1234594526/ [Last accessed June 4, 2024]

movements in our society: people obsessed with self, living in the little world they have created where their every opinion is validated and celebrated? They are the victims of their own deep lack of common sense and genuine communal experience, which fuels the utter disrespect for the divergent views of others, the irrational stubborn insistence that is the badge of honor for the narcissistic exceptionalist. When children don't get what they want, when they feel left out and ignored, when they are reprimanded and have to face the consequences of their actions, they often respond irrationally. Some children will duck responsibility and put the blame on others. Some children will look for the quickest, easiest way to get what they want; other people's feelings be damned. Some children demand until they are blue in the face, will bully, insult, lie, and physically intimidate others, embodying the notion that might makes right on the playground, the internet, during online gaming, on social media, or even in the seats of power that rule over us all.

Superheroes were created for children because they represent childhood dreams, hopes, and aspirations, as well as the fears and terrors of a child in an adult world. Superhero films have become the ultimate dehumanizing spectacle: audiences are encouraged to be passive, childlike viewers who watch in awe as powerful god fetishes save the world, and the 'powerless' weak mass of human beings cowers and allows these superhuman 'adults' to act in our collective name: 'perhaps fascism was always just a weaponised nostalgia'.[2] In Moore's epochal *Miracleman*, the superpowered demagogues can't allow inferior human beings to be in control of their own planet, and so they seize power from them, creating a Shangri-La that allows for no real choice or agency for homo sapiens: we are the ants at the new gods' Olympian picnic to be stuck in an ant farm for our own good. Even in a utopia, there are still expendable inhabitants who exist at the bottom of the social and political hierarchy, far beneath

2 Alan Moore, 'Illuminations', *Illuminations* (New York: Bloomsbury, 2022).

their superior 'protectors'. There has never been a paradise that was not built on someone's bones.

As some dude in the Bible suggested, there comes a time to put away childish things and become an adult. Alan Moore tried to do this forty years ago by making comic books more complex, more insightful, more emotionally authentic, more adult, so we wouldn't have to give up comics as we got older. Moore's move from author to mage is just another step in his own personal development and maturation, a continuing, individualized journey that uses the science and art of causing change in conformity with will to fuel his lifelong evolution as both an artist and a human being. In contrast, the MCU demagogue is holding all of us hostage, keeping us dazed, homogenized, and hypnotized, in a state of permanent, arrested adolescence while emptying our wallets more thoroughly than any supervillain ever has. One can only hope that, inevitably, the fickleness of fandom and the short attention spans of audiences will turn on the monoform spectacle of superhero media, and it will perish at the hands of the very consumers it constructed. And yet for all of Moore's astute observations, maybe he's got it backwards. It's not the superhero film that is controlling our minds, bodies, and dreams; superhero films are just a reflection of an infantilized society which denies individual/group agency and responsibility, expecting a savior to make everything all better, to right the wrongs of our lives and our world, in the name of truth, justice, and the always American way.

Ever Get the Feeling You've Been Cheated? American Horror Story

THANKS TO COVID-19, Season 10 of FX's *American Horror Story* was postponed until Fall of 2021. Though the premiere date had not been officially stated, rumors and conjectures about the subject of the tenth season had already been all over social media and the internet. A few hints and teasers for this season's theme have leaked out, with a photo posted by series creator Ryan Murphy on Instagram seeming to allude to a nautical motif, with fans guessing at a deserted island, mermaids, sea monsters, a ghost ship, or a haunted beach as the horror tropes for the storyline. Not content to leave it be with the attention raised by these provocative hints, Murphy has now started a poll asking Twitter followers what type of stories they want to see in a 'double feature' format for the new season, adding another narrative to the mélange. To further titillate fans, there are reports that *AHS* recurring actress Kathy Bates will have 'crazy, erotic sex' with former child star and new addition to the *AHS* cast Macaulay Culkin, this season. Culkin commented, "This sounds like the role I was born to play." Murphy released the official season 10 poster emblazoned with the hackneyed image of a mouth with sharp teeth and red lips getting an *AHS* logo tattooed on its tongue, for those who still think tattoos and piercings are edgy. Finally, on August 25, 2021, *American Horror Story: Double Feature* premiered, with one storyline 'Red Tide' debuting in August, and 'Death Valley' premiering in September. I won't even dignify this series with a review but suffice to say that 'Death Valley' plumbs the nadir of stupidity and snaps the suspension of disbelief with a storyline that includes Dwight and Mamie Eisenhower, Amelia Earhart, Richard Nixon, John F Kennedy, Marilyn Monroe, Steve Jobs, Buzz Aldrin, Neil Armstrong, Lyndon B Johnson, Stanley Kubrick, Henry Kissinger, and a Thetan. I'm surprised Tupac and Biggie weren't drafted into this dog's breakfast as well.

As horror fans recover from this double dose of manna from hell, I think it important to consider the role of fandom in *American Horror Story*'s success. One could argue that *American Horror Story* shows no real love for the horror genre, offering just one more fandom scam, a swindle that appears to appeal to horror fans and yet denigrates as it attempts to entertain. *American Horror Story*'s stereotypical and pseudo-intellectual approaches to horror and its fans are masked by critics using such terms as 'campy', 'ironic', 'postmodern', 'homage', and 'tribute' in order to hide the fact that the emperor has no clothes. *American Horror Story* has become an unfunny parody, laughing at the marginal status of horror and its fandom, making fun of the history, concepts, and passion that enliven the genre and its followers. It is an approach to genre and its fans that follows in the path of J J Abrams' various projects, Justin Roiland and Dan Harmon's *Rick and Morty*, and even the much-loved *The Big Bang Theory*, as being ready-made merchandized products delivered right to fandom in the same way a bitter pill is rolled up in cheese to give to a dog. Producers, network executives, corporate bankers, advertising firms, and entertainment accountants are all aware of the undying loyalty, disposable income, and fierce investment that fandom brings to their brands.

Horror fans are now a prime target audience and marketing demographic meant to be milked the same way that all the other fandoms are. Horror and its fans were the outsiders, the neglected, the underdogs, even the despised for being interested in the transgressive, darker aspects of human experiences. Now we are merely consumer metrics. Thanks to Murphy's algorithmic approach to the genre and its fandom, we can truly appreciate the *Glee*-ification of horror, like when Murphy paid tribute to that horror classic *Moulin Rouge* in *American Horror Story: Freak Show* when Jessica Lange's character sang David Bowie's Life On Mars?, even though the song was released in 1971 and that season of *AHS* took place in the 1950s. (This is not to say that cross-blending different genres, aesthetics, and styles is not a valuable creative strategy to invigorate artistic works, but throwing stuff at a wall to see what sticks only worked for maybe Jackson Pollock.) And yes, Murphy was the creator of the series *Glee*, showing off his impeccable horror genre credentials and his ability to generate in-depth complex dramatic tension, proving that the solution to all serious teenage problems is to sing bad covers of songs that weren't that great to begin with. But Murphy did merchandise the hell out of *Glee*, which made him an artistic genius.

Part of what makes *American Horror Story* supposedly so 'original' is its willingness to parody not only the tropes of the horror genre, but also social and political issues. Even the show's own success was self-reflexively explored in the 'Roanoke' story arc. The assumption that the series invented or even perfected using horror to not only satirize topical subjects and cultural ideologies, but also lampoon the characteristics and expectations of horror films themselves, is laughable, but again shows how the ignorance of genre history can be used against the viewers of *AHS*. Switched-on horror fans stifled a yawn when 2019's *American Horror Story: 1984* attempted to make fun of the slasher film, when Amy Holden Jones's *The Slumber Party Massacre* (1982) already did it in a brilliant and more contemporaneous fashion. Murphy's apparent need to mock horror in such a way as to appear to be so far above the uncouth genre and its ignorant fans is an unfortunate continuation of the attitude of the vastly overrated, disdainful *Scream* franchise, the sneering progenitor of genre-condescending dreck like *AHS*.

If you are at all interested in viewing a truly original horror series made by a creator with artistic vision and an authentic love for the genre, I would suggest Alex de la Iglesias's *30 Coins*, a physically, mentally, and spiritually shocking meditation on the intersection of religion, power, and the supernatural that debuted on HBO in 2020–2021 and which has now returned for the 2023–2024 season. Alex de la Iglesias is a true master of horror, as evidenced by films like *Accion Mutante*, *Day of the Beast*, *Perdita Durango*, and *Witching & Bitching*, movies filled with dark humor, existential drama, social critique, metaphysical questioning, and gore-soaked terror. Blood is the central metaphor of de la Iglesias's works, a multifaceted symbol of life and death, transformation and heritage, savagery and sacrifice. His focus on how the sacred and the profane are really two sides of the same coin informs the beautiful but terrifying mythos of his new TV series, centered around the thirty pieces of silver Judas was paid to betray Christ. *30 Coins* asks the crucial question, how does one fight evil without becoming evil yourself? For de la Iglesias, it is the human capacity for the purity of love and selflessness that enables us all to keep going, even in the face of monstrous forces determined to destroy not only our hearts and minds, but also our souls.

And so, it appears that Ryan Murphy's genre franchise will continue to grow. FX recently announced a spin-off anthology series titled *American Horror Stories* (what an original, creative title…) that will feature self-contained episodes, as opposed to a season-long story arc. The newest season of *American Horror Story (NYC)* was a watered-down version of William Friedkin's brilliant and still controversial 1980 gay leather subculture-informed *Cruising* (as well as sardonically playing on the whole 'AIDS was manufactured' conspiracy theory); luckily, the TV series managed to iron out all those pesky psychological ambiguities and fragmenting gender identity issues that made the film so fascinating. (Perhaps I'm being too hard on *AHS* as there are rumors that the show's creators will not take the easy, sensationalist low road for the next season of *AHS: Delicate* and have recruited Renaissance woman Kim Kardashian for a role.) Murphy is also reaching his insidious tentacles into true crime and Hollywood Babylon exposés, turning genuine tragedy into exploitative, sensationalistic TV manure. (Just think what filmmakers like Panos Cosmatos, Julia Ducournau, Adrián García Bogliano, Peter Strickland, Jennifer Kent, and Rodrigo Aragão could do with the same resources, promotion, and opportunities.)

Perhaps the real horror story here is a globalized media conglomerate voraciously searching for new novelties to consume, deadly to anything that even smacks of originality and sincerity. Ryan Murphy will cheerfully keep shoveling the horror genre and its fans into the gaping maw of the culture industry, ready to reap all the financial and celebratory rewards of selling us out to his corporate masters.

Star Wars: The Last Jedi? Not Even Close

IN 1977, THE last great pop culture upheaval began. For some, that seismic change in culture was punk rock, but for us kids who were too young to appreciate the Sex Pistols and The Ramones, ours was a different revolution. The simple story of a farm boy who saves the galaxy, *Star Wars* transformed not only the movie industry but also what childhood meant to millions of children all over the world. The heroic struggle between good and evil, illustrated in archetypal, easy-to-grasp yet creatively exhilarating ways, was perfectly suited for a child's mentality, and yet did not trivialize or oversimplify the film's message. The Force was religion and philosophy; it gave meaning and significance to a world on the brink of nuclear annihilation. *Star Wars* was a new hope indeed. In 1980, anticipation was at fever pitch, not so much for the election between Carter and Reagan, but for the newest missive from the *Star Wars* universe: *The Empire Strikes Back*. Us *Star Wars* fans were three years older, wiser, a bit more sophisticated and jaded, but *The Empire Strikes Back* delivered in a big way. *Empire* was like a Greek tragedy as the House of Skywalker was torn asunder; our hero Luke faces a horrible self-truth, ending in the best father/son fight since Oedipus (Luke doesn't lose his sight, but does get a hand lopped off). We were also introduced to the coolest Star Wars character ever: the enigmatic Boba Fett. Here was the epitome of the creative power of *Star Wars*. After the greatness of *Empire*, it seemed inevitable that the next *Star Wars* film would disappoint. *Return of the Jedi* had its moments; the sequences with Jabba the Hutt are brilliant, Errol Flynn-old Hollywood swashbuckling action, but, of course, the hideous face of merchandising, a necessary evil that didn't affect the integrity of the first two films, gave us the cuddly Ewoks, a sales bonanza, but a slap in the face to those who took *Star Wars* seriously as art. In this film, we see the beginning of the franchise feeding upon itself with a repeat of the attack on the Death Star, a rousing, exhilarating climax to the first film, but boring and inferior in *Return*.

Then, appropriately, silence. The children of *Star Wars* grew up (or should have).

The second coming of *Star Wars* came, fittingly, right as the new millennium was dawning. Again, the expectations for the return of the saga of Skywalker could never be met. The prequel films displayed the hubris of the maestro George Lucas, and the harder pill to swallow for fans was the sobering realization that you can't go home again. Nostalgia is a poor substitute for a mature, evolving sense of art and of the self. Perhaps it was time to put away the action figures and Underroos and find something more meaningful, deeper, and intellectual. Most did not. If anything, many fans became more entrenched, more nostalgic, more demanding, narrower minded, and more insistent that *Star Wars* was the cultural foundation of the twentieth and twenty-first centuries, and those who worshipped and served this holy cornerstone strove to repeat the same faded glories of the original series over and over again, ad nauseam.

Enter J J Abrams. Fresh off his dumbing down of *Star Trek*, Abrams brought his Comic Con bravado and energy drink approach to filmmaking to the *Star Wars* franchise, churning out an extended retread of every *Star Wars* cliché called *The Force Awakens*. The film was met with near hysteria. *The Force Awakens* is the cinematic emperor with no clothes, the biggest example of such since *Pulp Fiction*. Disney's megalomaniacal campaign to connect *Star Wars* to every manufactured good, service, media, and institution known to humankind (a *Star Wars* themed electric razor? Really?) demands yearly product and dividends for its stockholders, and so, fresh off the assembly line, we are graced with *The Last Jedi*, the cinematic equivalent of Bantha fodder. First off, the title is total garbage as there will never be a 'last' anything in the *Star Wars* universe as this cash cow will be milked way past its prime. The script is filled with stillborn humor, lame catchphrases, and forced one-liners, just as eye-rollingly awkward as they are in the Marvel Universe atrocities. Writer/director Rian Johnson strings along huge lapses in logic and pays absolutely no attention to narrative sense: characters just appear when they need to appear, Princess Leia survives floating in the vacuum of space, characters' motivations change faster than the Millennium Falcon going at light speed. The villains are petulant and passé; the heroes are boring and predictable. Disjointed storytelling is no substitute for genuine suspense, and Johnson lazily shoehorns in past references and call backs to the other films to patch over plot holes big enough to fly a Star Destroyer through. The entire cast should get an award for most overwrought over-acting, wringing nonexistent drama from a hackneyed story. The clumsy attempts at social commentary are cloying and shallow; you'll find deeper insights in a *Fast and Furious* flick. The number of cutesy creatures in *The Last Jedi* has grown exponentially, and fans seem to embrace these vulgar paeans to consumerism, yet give the Ewoks a thumbs down.

Ironically, horror and sci-fi fans constantly scream about reboots and remakes, yet they go to these types of films in droves. The Abrams/Johnson *Star Wars* abomination is even worse than the prequels because at least the prequels tried to do different things with the brand (and Christopher Lee was in two out of the three films); though many fans believe they failed, these deviations were not born out of some cynical, Twitter-driven, false allegiance with fandom. The target audience for this film is either the most delusional *Star Wars* apologists or people who feel drinking copious amounts of cough syrup enhances the cinematic experience. With the Abrams/Disney *Star Wars* global spectacle, the production of the commodity known as the fan is now complete. Much like his beloved idol Steven Spielberg, Abrams seems to have no interest whatsoever in genuine artistry or authentic feeling, but rather indulges in easy, sentimental clichés and self-aggrandizement that offer nothing of real substance to the viewers of his films. This film is an opportunistic, superficial Jedi mind trick, hypnotizing viewers into believing that this movie is worthy of the name *Star Wars*. *The Last Jedi* is a parody of *Star Wars*, pandering to fandom's lowest, most base need for nostalgia and artistic conservativism. *The Last Jedi* is fish to trained seals; just keep clapping and you'll get your fill, but will you ever be truly satisfied?

The Empire Won: Star Wars: The Rise of Skywalker

> 'That's what terrifies you about them. It isn't their cruelty, it isn't even their shrewdness — it's their extraordinary naivete. Everything in their whole bloody world is a cliché, rests on a cliché, survives by a cliché. And they believe in clichés — there's no hope.' —Jean Rhys, *Good Morning, Midnight*

THE PHENOMENON OF déjà vu has long perplexed those who have experienced it. Coming from the French phrase meaning 'already seen', déjà vu is the feeling that one has previously encountered a current situation or event, a strong uncanny sense of recollection, the sensation that the present has happened before, over and over again. Usually classified as a psychological, biological, paranormal, or spiritual mood, déjà vu has become the overwhelmingly dominant undercurrent of twenty-first-century life. Transforming the art of film to the specialization of déjà vu is the insidious skill of cultural industrialist and ultimate Hollywood insider J J Abrams. Abrams has made a lucrative career in appearing to be the great savior of genre films, and yet his approach to writing and directing involves cutting out content, characterization, meaning, and depth, and inserting regurgitated plots, clichéd characters, questionable choices, and endless nostalgic allusions and references to better films. Abrams has an incredible ability to pick the low-hanging fruit of fandom but make it look like he's crafting something original, powerful, and enigmatic. His financial successes and supposed connections to fans have made most blind to his artistic failures, a monopolist of the fantastique in the society of spectacle as he colonizes and indoctrinates imagination as well as the hopes and expectations of his viewers.

Abrams' newest film and the culmination of one of, if not the most, popular film franchises in the history of cinema is *Star Wars: The Rise of Skywalker*. Abrams' hubristic attempt to 'correct' the choices Rian Johnson made in the previous film *Star Wars: The Last Jedi* (which is like blaming the collapse of a building with a faulty foundation on the worker who put in the windows) brings the saga of the House of Skywalker to its predictable end. *Star Wars: The Rise of Skywalker* follows the formula that Abrams initiated with *Star Wars: The Force Awakens*: copy the best parts of the original trilogy, throw a few bones to contemporary fans, introduce some yawn-inducing 'twists', make some shallow concessions to current social issues, and make a zillion dollars off merchandising. And so, the plot thins. Realizing that the petulant Kylo Ren could not measure up to the epic tragedy of Darth Vader, Abrams brings back the amazing Ian McDiarmid as Emperor Palpatine (how he comes back is never explained in the film) as the much-needed supervillain, and it is only in the scenes of the truly malevolent Sith Lord and the Giger-esque dead world of Exegol that any real thrills are conjured. Also returning is Lando Calrissian, displaying that age has done nothing to diminish Billy Dee Williams' charm and acting ability.

As for the trio of Rey, Finn, and Poe, the lack of any significant dramatic chemistry between them hampers any attempt to actually feel the highs and lows they experience. Their attempts at comedy and banter never rise above the good-natured bickering one can see on any episode of *Friends*. The finale of Kylo Ren's story arc is muddled and confusing as his conflicted psyche and angst still cannot make up for the genocide and patricide he has committed. Even his final act of sacrifice (aping his grandfather Darth Vader) is awkward and off-putting. The real shame is the waste of the character of Rey and the performance of Daisy Ridley. Abrams had a real opportunity to make the character resonant and mean something in terms of valor and transformation but decided to make her the Star Wars equivalent of the sweaty old school action hero. Rey realizes her potential as a truly enlightened character but instead of breaking free of the past and transcending the generic roles and classifications of the series, she chooses to repeat and extend them. It wouldn't be a 'final' Star Wars film without genealogical revelations and heroic demises, and we get both of them in *Star Wars: The Rise of Skywalker*. The deaths in the film seem cheap, clichéd, and exploitative. The one death that was actually shocking ends up being a total fake out, which, again, robs the film of any real pathos and proves what a manipulative con job this film is. Abrams seems to be reading from the Charles Dickens playbook as ol' J J just piles on ghosts, questionable origins, disputed inheritances, and last-minute twists of fate in an attempt to outdo 'A Christmas Carol', *Great Expectations*, and *David Copperfield*.

It is ironic that the Star Wars films are largely concerned with a small group of oppressed rag-tag idealistic rebels fighting a fascistic, totalitarian Empire that is seeking complete domination over all ways of life. Abrams, as one of the media overlords of the society of the spectacle, resembles the deceptive Senator-turned-Sith much more than he does Luke, Rey, Finn, or any of the intergalactic freedom fighters. For Abrams, film is simply a past reiterated, which creates a present that is controlled, dominated, and enslaved by economic power, totalitarian images, and the commodification of our authentic life into something that is as alienated, dead, and hopeless as Exegol. Like the character of Winston Smith in George Orwell's brilliant and still prescient novel *Nineteen Eighty-Four*, the recent Star Wars films rewrite old news items that have been contradicted by current developments in order for them to reflect contemporary ideology. Perhaps the Force will one day be realized as true genuine artistic creativity and help us live real, authentic lives rather than the third-rate clichés thrown up by the spectacle and the culture industry. May that Force be with us all.

P.S. Baby Yoda is awesome.

Cashing in On Memories: Toy Story 4

A REVIEW OF *Toy Story 4* seems superfluous. Everyone loves these films, critics fall over themselves to praise them, braying viewers (young and old) lap up every inane 'joke', audiences run to the theater blindly emptying their wallets and Apple Pay into the coffers of Disney/Pixar to the tune of $2.6 billion. And that's just box office receipts, not counting the endless merchandising that has blighted the world for the last twenty years. Here's the interchangeable review for all four films: the toys worry about not being played with and/or being replaced, the toys vie to please their owner, a new character is brainwashed into being a toy, the toys get in trouble and have to help each other solve a cute but frivolous problem, some cloying platitudes about growing up are spewed, and everything is A-OK in middle class suburbia. All to the maudlin songs of Randy Neumann. The plastic sentimentality of these films makes the Hallmark Channel look like Ibsen. These consumerist fantasies where products are actual living things have struck a chord not only with children (who tend to anthropomorphize inanimate objects anyway), but also with adults seeking to justify their commodified lives and revel in a fantasy world where products serve them and not the other way around.

The Toy Story juggernaut has not only conquered American viewers but has also spread its tentacles across the planet (Toy Story is the twenty-first highest-grossing franchise worldwide), infecting, engulfing, and reproducing in the imaginations of the masses like a neo-liberal, globalizing, materialistic virus. Toy Story's appeal to children is quite obvious, and its exploitation of kids' insatiable appetite for merchandise is no different than other ruthless marketing forces that create the very desires they claim to fulfill. What is more unsettling is the passive adulation that these children's films have invoked in adults and critics. The *Toy Story* movies have been nominated for Academy Awards, Golden Globe, and British Academy awards, and have some of the highest scores on review aggregate websites like Rotten Tomatoes and Metacritic: no other movie franchises have higher ratings. Perhaps it is the nostalgia that these films evoke that has captured the jaded hearts of grown-ups, returning them to simpler times where imagination and playtime were full-time jobs and could be indulged in without guilt or the feeling that one should be doing something more productive. And yet isn't nostalgia, by its very 'nature', a bit reactionary? Not only a personal longing for escape but the denial of current situations and forces, a way to revel in what once was and not face the present? Nostalgia is an important element in the creation of a kind of false consciousness, a need to believe that the sitcoms, movies, music, commercials, and popular culture of the past are accurate depictions of one's own personal history. Nostalgia presents itself not only as private delusions but also as social and political ones. The present is too complex, the future is too dark and scary, so let's go back to an idealized childhood and play with our toys both as individuals and as a society. We all know that products, buying, and accumulation make it all better.

It is not just on the big screen, but on screens of all sizes that Toy Story has achieved almost total colonization of the masses. Television shows, short films, direct-to-video specials, 'educational' software, and video games as well as print, music, and theme park attractions are all weapons in the franchise's spectacular domination of the culture industry. Disney/Pixar is basically a factory churning out unnecessary cultural products and environmental landfill that pacify, exploit, and inculcate its audiences. Has there been any Pixar film that has not been brutally merchandised and shoved down the throats of its audiences, audiences largely made up of exploitable children? As the ruling cultural behemoth of our times, the Pixar/Disney cabal has even thoughtfully provided the chance for all of us to buy a piece of Soul in 2010, revealing that any claims of their ruthless consumer campaigns as merely hollow materialism and spiritually dead machinations is just commie propaganda. Toy Story is a simple pleasure, easily digestible with a touch of bland moralizing and cheap mawkishness that renders its viewers docile and content. Toy Story has created a need only it can satisfy, and you will pay to be momentarily satiated until the next movie or Happy Meal promotion comes along. Authentic needs and experiences are stifled, forgotten, as we laugh at Buzz Lightyear's grandiose heroics or cry at Woody's goodbye to his owner. Disney/Pixar has produced, marketed, and sold us a disposable, consumable, image-based culture that has homogenized our imaginations, usurped everyday life, and watered down our emotions: a never-ending Opium War waged by the culture industry, but instead of using the narcotic extract of poppies, it is nostalgia and 'harmless' cartoon representations fueling the imposed mass stupor. This anesthetized sleepwalking is sold to us as the only option for living the 'good life', the replacing of authenticity with conformingly passive, servile groveling, and empty consumer desires that we are encouraged to accept and which become normalized from childhood straight through to senior citizenship.

Because the films are so predictable and standardized, the Toy Story franchise has been enormously profitable, which, of course, was the goal in the first place. But it is the characters of the Toy Story films that are especially 'meaningful' for its viewers. Popular movie stars such as Tom Hanks, Christina Hendricks, and Keanu Reeves voice characters that are either real toys like Mr Potato Head and Barbie, or toys based on their actual counterparts. There is a certain irony to using Hollywood personalities for these roles as these actors and actresses have already turned themselves into media products in accordance with the rules of celebrity and spectacle. Seeing things from our lives actually have lives of their own has a definite resonance for our consumerist society as we were personifying our possessions way before Toy Story was a gleam in an investment banker/lawyer/producer's eye. Many of us are encouraged to treat our belongings as if they were alive, engaging in relationships with inanimate objects that are far more passionate than with our fellow human beings. Look at the way some treat their cars, their iPhones, their Xboxes, their sneakers, etc. Some will kill another human being to possess these goods. Having supplants being and image is everything and nothing at the same time. The perceived value and actual costs of products have transformed not only how we interact with our possessions, but also how we interact with each other. The desire and attachment to toys is not a naïve child's folly, but the preparation for an adult's indoctrination into the world of commodities and consumerism. The Toy Story franchise is a key element of the training of submissive viewers and pliant consumers, 'a taste of the drill' as Walter Benjamin noted.[3] In this world, things are people and people are things; reality is representation and representation is reality. Everyone is exchangeable and can be bought and sold, just like our precious possessions. The films haven't adapted to their audience; the audience has adapted to the films.

It doesn't matter if it's Andy or Bonnie playing with the toys or being played by the toys, we are all the same, consumers and consumed. Play in Toy Story is presented as a passing, juvenile phase to be laughed at and ultimately rejected, just more capitalist pantomime and dead labor, emphasizing repressive production relations and the necessary negating of a liberatory imagination and genuine desires. The revolutionary potentials of play, amusement, non-competitive games, creativity, and knocking down the boundaries and barriers between 'playtime' and 'real life' are absent from the Toy Story franchise. Rather than suggesting that recreation and amusement are the ex-

3 Walter Benjamin, 'On Some Motifs in Baudelaire', *Illuminations* (New York: Random House, 2015).

pressions of radical utopian spontaneous pleasures, Toy Story packages childhood fun as the first stage of commodification and toys as the necessary appropriations to initiate indoctrination into a competitive stagnant false life. The Toy Story films are the media-saturated propaganda for this type of life, indoctrinating children and validated by infantilized adults as they happily eat their popcorn and drink their Cokes in the safe, acclimatized bubble of a movie theater, in a crowd yet isolated, separated from real life. This communal alienation is not limited to the movie theater, but is in homes, SUVs, schools, churches, anywhere one can access a cell phone or tablet and let the animated spectacle wash over us and our children. It is not so much the commercialized images of Toy Story, but, rather, the false relationships with others, with our surroundings, and with ourselves, which is continually modelled, imposed, and validated by those representations, that deceive us. Emotions, experiences, identities, and consciousness must be expressed and exchanged through things, commodities, totems, and facsimiles in all aspects of everyday life. Sometimes directness can be so direct that it obscures.

In his promotion for *Toy Story 4*, Tom Hanks claimed that the film would be the last in the series. *Toy Story*'s producer Mark Nielsen quickly responded to this finality by saying that Disney/Pixar had not decided yet if the lucrative franchise would continue.[4] My bet is that we will be seeing many more *Toy Story* films in the future, and if not actual *Toy Story* movies, movies that take the ethos of this franchise, the mollifying, uncritiqued nostalgia, the banal emotions, the total media saturation, the false representational life, the degradation of social relations, and the glorification of commodities, straight to the piggy bank.

4 The perfect antidote to *Toy Story*'s metastasizing global mesmerism that has engulfed parent and child alike would be a family viewing of Michael Haneke's horrific *Benny's Video*, which clinically presents the spectacle-saturated life of a teenage murderer and his enabling, selfish parents.

Ghost of an Idea

'I don't give a fuck what anybody says. If you don't have time to see it, don't. If you don't like it, don't. If it doesn't give you an answer, fuck you. I didn't make it for you anyway.'
—John Cassavetes

About the Author

ON THE DAY William Burns was born, crucial scenes for both *The Exorcist* and *The Wicker Man* were being filmed, forever marking him as a member of the Haunted Generation. The strange, the eerie, the unsettling, and the obscure have bedevilled him ever since. In search of lost futures, he has stumbled upon many forgotten ghosts and shadowy remembrances. *Ghost of an Idea: Hauntology, Folk Horror, and the Spectre of Nostalgia* is the culmination of a journey that began in the author's 2016 book, *The Thrill of Repulsion: Excursions into Horror Culture*.

Index